IMAGES
of Rail

NORFOLK SOUTHERN IN
HAMPTON ROADS

On the Cover: Pulled by engine No. 500, the Pocahontas, an overnight passenger train in the fleet of Norfolk Southern predecessor Norfolk & Western Railway, leaves the Norfolk Terminal Station bound for Cincinnati, Ohio, in August 1937. One of the railroad's named passenger trains, the *Pocahontas* ran from November 1926 until May 1971. Other Norfolk & Western named passenger trains included the Cavalier and the Powhatan Arrow. (Courtesy of Norfolk Southern.)

IMAGES
of Rail

NORFOLK SOUTHERN IN HAMPTON ROADS

Elizabeth Ownley Cooper

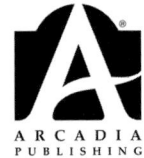

Copyright © 2021 by Elizabeth Ownley Cooper
ISBN 978-1-4671-0673-3

Published by Arcadia Publishing
Charleston, South Carolina

Printed in the United States of America

Library of Congress Control Number: 2021930015

For all general information, please contact Arcadia Publishing:
Telephone 843-853-2070
Fax 843-853-0044
E-mail sales@arcadiapublishing.com
For customer service and orders:
Toll-Free 1-888-313-2665

Visit us on the Internet at www.arcadiapublishing.com

Contents

Acknowledgments		6
Introduction		7
1.	The Norfolk & Western Railway	9
2.	Coal Comes to Norfolk	23
3.	Southern Railway and its Hampton Roads Lines	55
4.	Building a Resort at Virginia Beach	63
5.	The Virginian Railway	81
6.	The Railroad in Downtown Norfolk	97
7.	Berkley and Portlock	117

Acknowledgments

Untangling Norfolk Southern Railway's family tree as it weaves through southeastern Virginia is an interesting but complicated task. Many rail lines played significant roles in not only the formation of today's Norfolk Southern, but also in the growth of Hampton Roads. Thank you to those who shared photographs and knowledge about the railroad and its forebears, especially during the COVID-19 pandemic with its necessary social distancing.

Special thanks to Kurt Reisweber, author and rail historian, who provided many photographs and information about Norfolk Southern's Hampton Roads predecessors. Thank you also to my former colleagues at Norfolk Southern for their assistance in putting this book together: Stacey Mansfield, Jennifer McDaid, John Haworth, Susan Terpay, and Robin Chapman. I appreciate the time you spent sharing insights and memories and helping me find the right pictures.

The staff at the Meyera E. Oberndorf Central Library in Virginia Beach and the Sargeant Memorial Collection at the Norfolk Public Library also contributed photographs and information.

Finally, thanks always to my husband, Michael Cooper, for providing technical support and encouragement.

Introduction

With roots going back to the earliest days of American railroading, Norfolk Southern Railway and its nearly 400 predecessor lines have been vital components of the nation's transportation system for nearly two centuries, including more than 160 years in the Hampton Roads region of Virginia.

One of North America's largest Class 1 railroads, Norfolk Southern covers 19,500 route miles in 22 states and the District of Columbia, serves every major container port in the eastern United States, operates the most extensive intermodal network in the East, and carries a multitude of agriculture, construction, metals, and chemical products as well as coal, automobiles, and automotive parts. Norfolk Southern, along with CSX Transportation, is one of the largest rail operators based east of the Mississippi River.

In Virginia, Norfolk Southern operates approximately 1,900 miles of track, carving out routes from the mountains to the coast. Much of the foundation of Hampton Roads, both economic and cultural, can be traced to the Fortune 300 company and its predecessor railroads—including the first Norfolk Southern—that charted a transportation course through the region.

Today's Norfolk Southern was formed from the June 1982 merger between the Roanoke-based Norfolk & Western Railway and Washington, DC–based Southern Railway. The two railroads had been longtime competitors, but the consolidation that created an 18,000-route-mile system through 21 states transpired so smoothly that *U.S. News & World Report* called it "a model of its kind."

Both Norfolk & Western and Southern had historical ties to the Hampton Roads region through previous rail consolidations. The new joint holding company was named Norfolk Southern Corporation, reflecting the rich heritage of the two railroads. In addition, Norfolk Southern was the name of a small predecessor railroad organized in 1870 that initially ran between Norfolk and Elizabeth City, North Carolina.

Norfolk was chosen as the new company's headquarters, largely because both Norfolk & Western and Southern did substantial business in the port city. In 1988, the company completed construction of a 22-story office tower in downtown Norfolk's financial district. An unfortunate engraving error was discovered when the marble at the building's entrance was unveiled: Instead of Norfolk Southern Railway, it had been chiseled Norfork Southern Railway. The mistake was quickly corrected.

Now, after more than three decades headquartered in Norfolk, the railroad is pulling up its corporate stakes and moving to Atlanta in 2021. The December 2018 announcement of the impending move sent shock waves through the community, as political and business leaders lamented the loss of the corporate headquarters and about 400 of the nearly 1,000 Norfolk Southern employees working in Hampton Roads. However, while Norfolk Southern is moving its corporate functions to the Peach State, the railroad will still have a vital presence in Hampton Roads. Its trains continue to support the local economy by transporting a variety of intermodal, metal, construction, agricultural, chemical, paper, clay, and forest products in and out of local terminals.

In addition, Norfolk Southern's Lamberts Point Coal Terminal, a few miles from downtown Norfolk on the eastern point of the Elizabeth River, remains a critical cog in the nation's coal production. The terminal, which has an annual throughput capacity of 48 million tons, has been moving coal directly from railcars to export ships for more than 135 years. Norfolk & Western began construction on the facility in 1883 as its trains were hauling the first coal shipments to Norfolk from western Virginia and southern West Virginia. Today, the Lamberts Point Coal Terminal is known for its expertise in sourcing, blending, and moving the world's highest-quality steam and metallurgical coal.

Lamberts Point's 425 acres are home to Coal Pier 6, the largest and fastest coal-loading facility in the northern hemisphere, as well as the Norfolk Southern 38th Street Car Shop, one of the mechanical shops where railcars are maintained. Coal operations cover 400 acres of Lamberts Point, with the entire facility able to hold 6,500 railcars on 150 miles of track.

Along with Lamberts Point, the railroad operates the Portlock Yard, an intermodal facility in the South Norfolk section of Chesapeake. Portlock also offers rail interchanges for short line railroads in Hampton Roads. In addition, Virginia International Gateway, a marine container terminal on the Elizabeth River in Portsmouth leased to the Virginia Port Authority, and Norfolk International Terminals, the port authority's largest terminal, have direct on-dock rail access to Norfolk Southern trains providing double-stack service to the Midwestern markets via the railroad's Heartland Corridor.

One
The Norfolk & Western Railway

Norfolk & Western Railway traces its lineage to 1837 when the nine-mile City Point Railroad was built from Petersburg to City Point, Virginia. With the new railroad intensifying the rivalry between Petersburg and Norfolk for maritime trade, Norfolk leaders lobbied the Virginia General Assembly for a railroad to connect the city's deepwater port with interior Virginia. Legislators agreed and chartered the Norfolk & Petersburg Railroad in 1851. Construction began in 1854.

Twenty-six-year-old William Mahone, a Southampton County native and Virginia Military Institute civil engineering graduate, became the railroad's chief engineer, charged with building a direct rail line from Norfolk to Petersburg. He soon earned his $2,500 annual salary by designing an innovative corduroy roadbed using a log foundation across the Great Dismal Swamp between Norfolk and Suffolk. Builders cut a 100-foot path through the swamp, felled and trimmed trees, and laid them at right angles beneath the swamp's surface. The logs sank into the marsh where they were preserved and remain in use today. The railroad also employed a straight track for about 52 of its 81 miles. At the time, it was the world's longest tangent track.

At $75,000 per mile of right-of-way, the Norfolk & Petersburg was one of the most expensive railroads built during that era. The first train ran between its namesake cities in August 1858. However, during the Civil War, the Union army destroyed 10 miles of the railroad near its Petersburg terminus. In 1870, Mahone, by then the Norfolk & Petersburg's president, led a drive to consolidate the railroad with the South Side and Virginia & Tennessee Railroads to form the Atlantic, Mississippi & Ohio (AM&O) Railroad. The AM&O extended from Norfolk to Bristol but went bankrupt by 1876. Philadelphia financial firm E.W. Clark & Company purchased the railroad in 1881 and renamed it the Norfolk & Western Railroad with Norfolk as the eastern terminus.

Two years later, a Norfolk & Western train hauled the first of many shipments of coal to southeastern Virginia from the newly opened Pocahontas mining fields in western Virginia and southern West Virginia. By 1900, Norfolk was the leading coal exporter on the East Coast, cementing Norfolk & Western's presence in Hampton Roads.

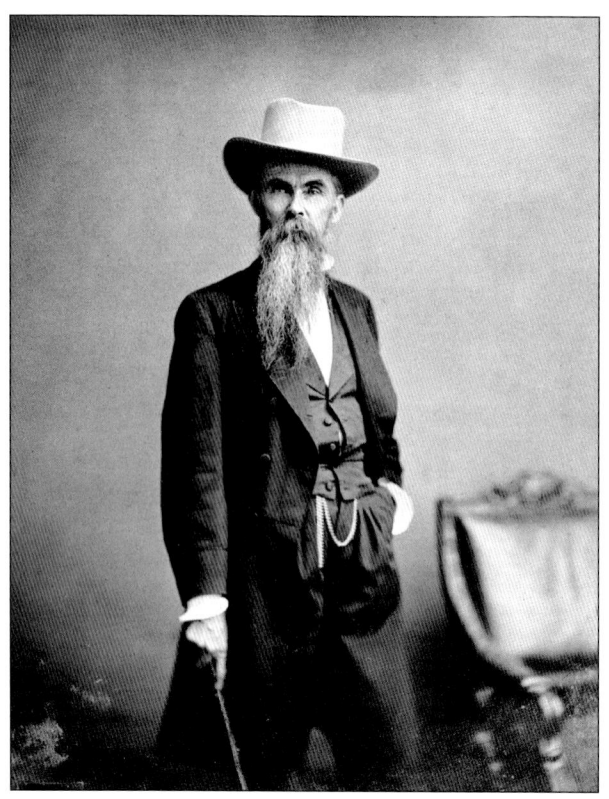

As the chief engineer of the Norfolk & Petersburg Railroad, William Mahone (1826–1895) refused to listen to naysayers who told him it was madness to put rails through the Great Dismal Swamp. His innovative corduroy roadbed provided a direct route through the swamp and is still used today. Mahone also believed the railroad would eventually require a double track, so he laid the first track off to the side to make room for a second in the future. That decision paid off decades later when the line became a major route for transporting coal. (Courtesy of Norfolk Southern.)

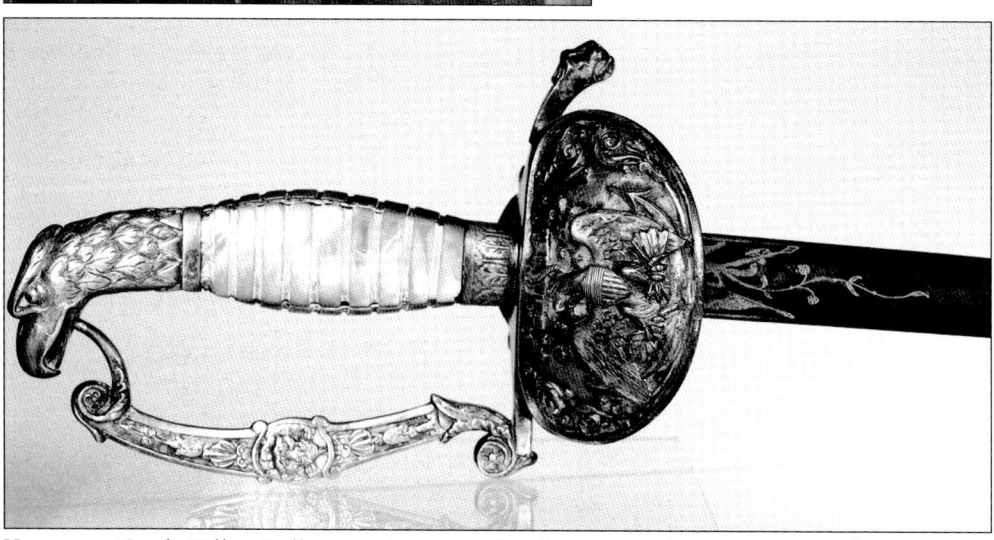

Known as "Little Billy," William Mahone was five feet, five inches tall and weighed only 100 pounds, but his small stature did not limit him. A Confederate general in the Civil War, Mahone led a counterattack against the Union army on July 30, 1864, in the Battle of the Crater during the Siege of Petersburg. After the war, Mahone unsuccessfully ran for Virginia governor. He also represented Virginia in the US Senate from 1881 to 1887 as a member of the Readjuster Party, a coalition of Democrats, Republicans, and African Americans seeking to reduce the state's prewar debts, improve public education, and ensure blacks and poor whites were able to vote. Norfolk Southern later acquired Mahone's sword, pictured here. (Courtesy of Norfolk Southern.)

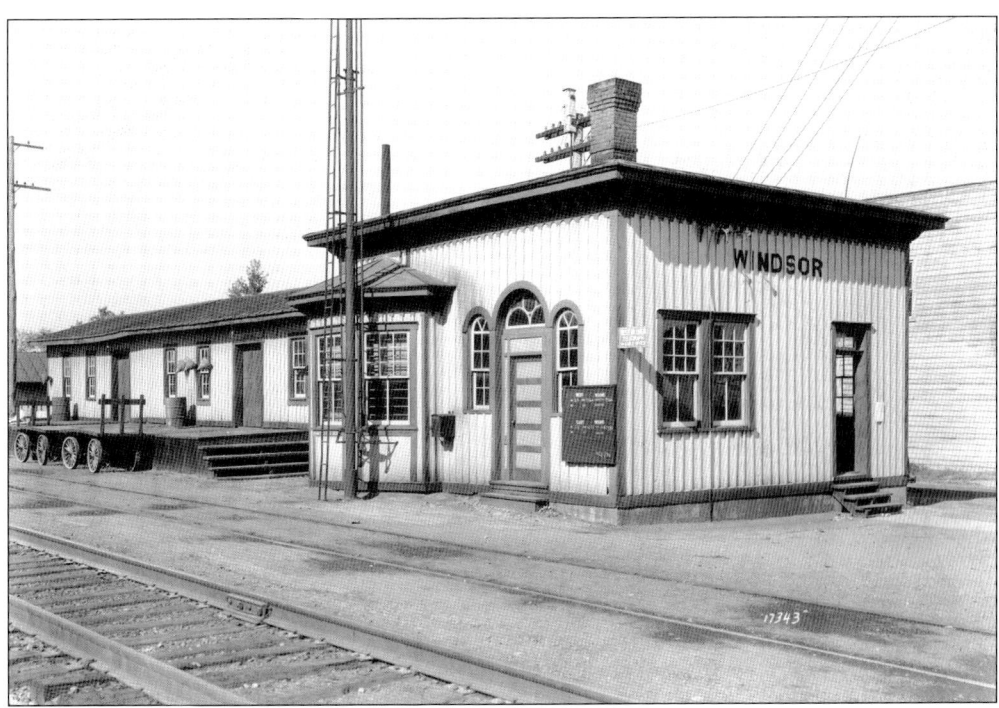

William Mahone and his wife, Smithfield native Otelia Butler Mahone, traveled along the newly completed Norfolk & Petersburg route to determine where to locate depots between Suffolk and Petersburg. A fan of Scottish novelist Sir Water Scott, Otelia Mahone wanted to name the stations after characters or places found in Scott's books. Windsor was in Scott's novel *Ivanhoe* and is also the region where Scott was born. Built in 1866, the Windsor depot was closed in 1974 and razed in the mid-1980s. During its early years, young men were said to have drilled holes in the depot's storage area floor and into whiskey kegs. The kegs were empty when the owners came to collect them. (Courtesy of Norfolk Southern.)

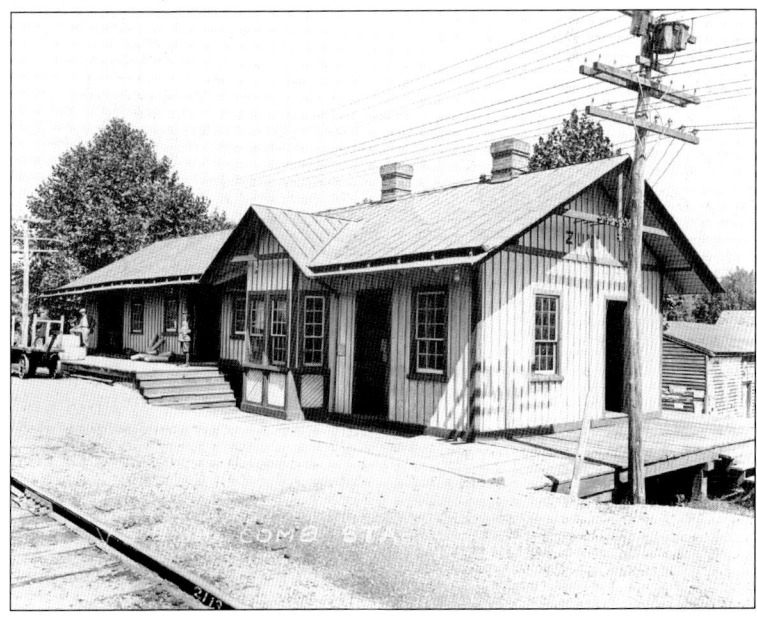

The Zuni station is pictured during its service as a Norfolk & Western depot. During the Civil War, the Union army controlled the portion of the Norfolk & Petersburg Railroad east of the Blackwater River at Zuni. (Courtesy of Norfolk Southern.)

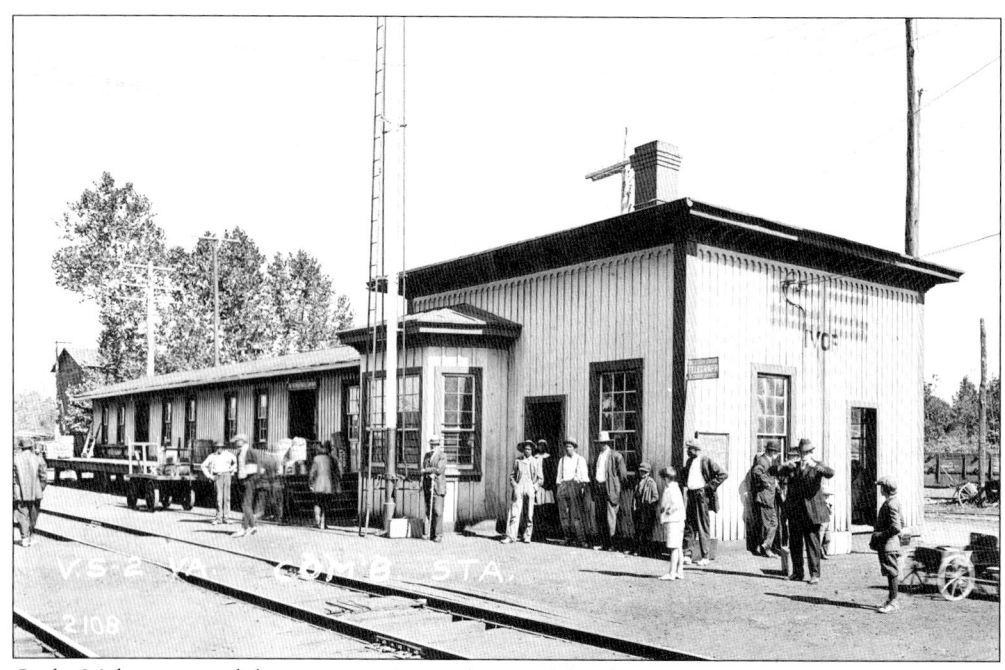

Otelia Mahone named this train stop Ivor in honor of the characters Fergus MacIvor and his sister Flora in Sir Walter Scott's novel *Waverly*. In the early 20th century, Norfolk & Western developed a 200-acre farm near the station to support the area's agricultural industry. This photograph was taken in 1917 when the depot also housed the Southern Express Company and Western Union telegraph office. (Courtesy of Norfolk Southern.)

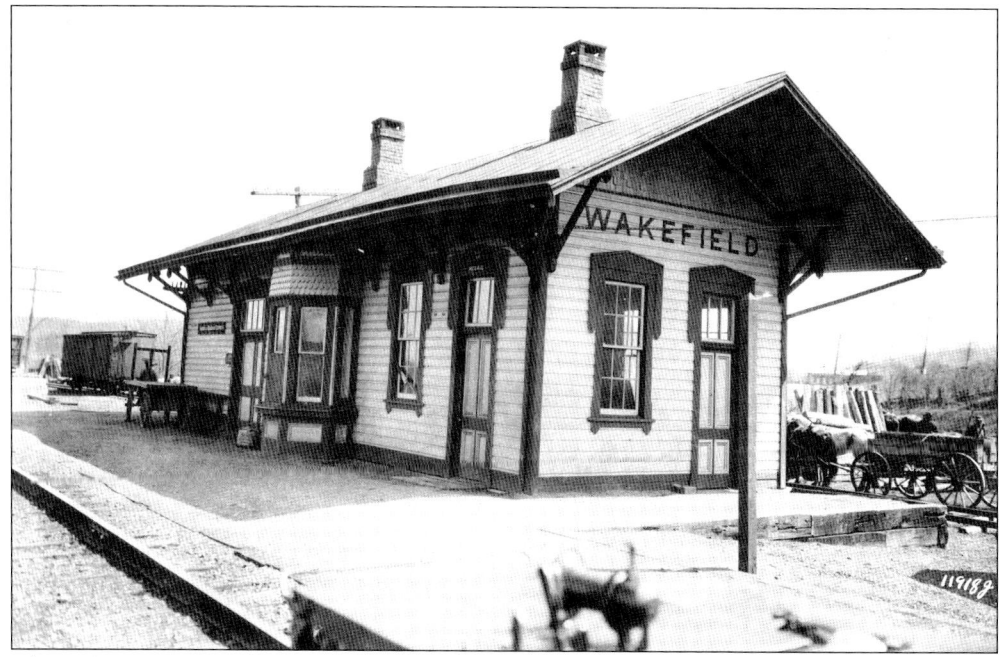

The Mahones named this station Wakefield, ostensibly for one of Sir Walter Scott's favorite novels, *Vicar of Wakefield* by Oliver Goldsmith. There was also a character named Harry Wakefield in Scott's short story *The Two Drovers*. (Courtesy of Norfolk Southern.)

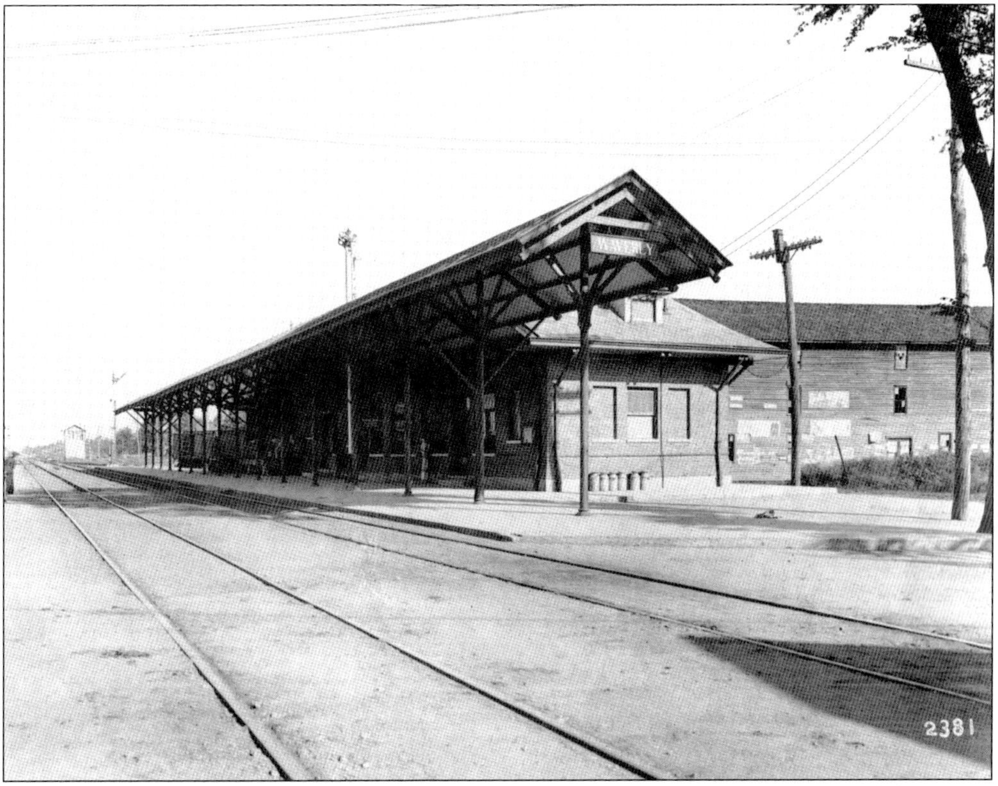

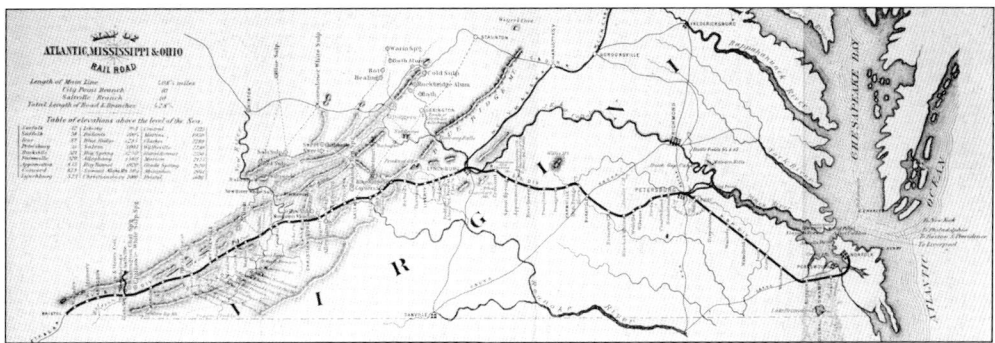

William and Otelia Mahone named the Waverly passenger station in honor of Sir Walter Scott's first novel, *Waverly*, and its title character, Edward Waverly. Waverly holds the distinction of sending the most senators and delegates to the Virginia General Assembly of any Virginia town with a population under 3,000. (Courtesy of Norfolk Southern.)

In 1867, the Virginia General Assembly authorized the consolidation of the Norfolk & Petersburg, the South Side, and Virginia & Tennessee Railroads to form the Atlantic, Mississippi & Ohio Railroad. After overcoming financial issues, the merger was completed in 1870, with William Mahone as the new railroad's president and headquarters in Lynchburg, Virginia. This 1878 map highlights the railroad's 408-mile main line from Bristol to Norfolk. (Courtesy of Norfolk Southern.)

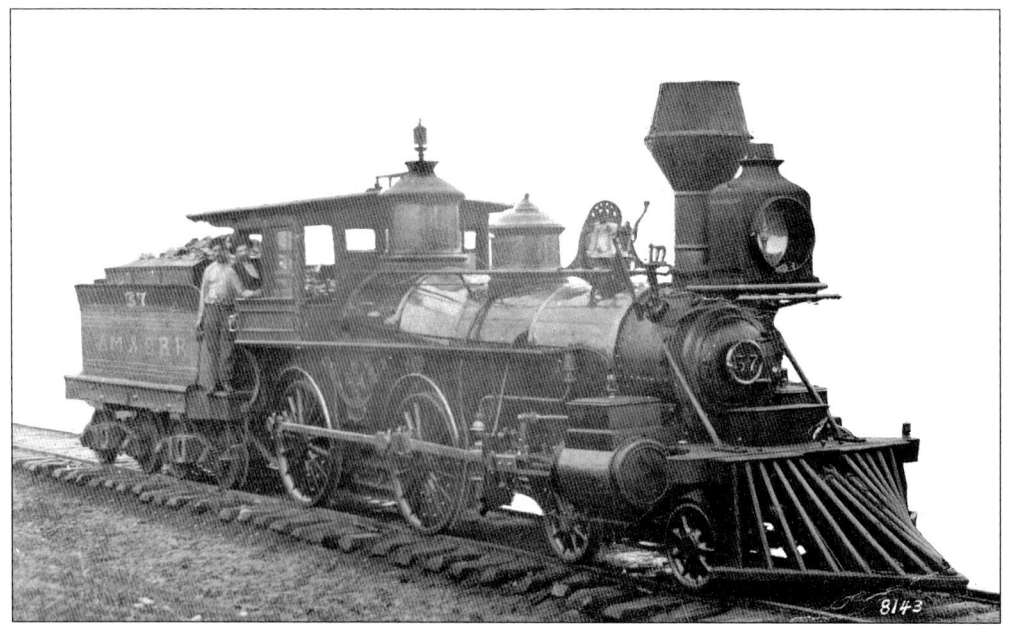

This 1880 photograph shows Atlantic, Mississippi & Ohio locomotive No. 37 and its crew. Formerly the Virginia & Tennessee Railroad's locomotive, the engine was used on the new Atlantic, Mississippi & Ohio Railroad. Critics of AM&O president William Mahone claimed the railroad's initials stood for "All Mine and Otelia's." The railroad was bankrupt by 1876. (Courtesy of Norfolk Southern.)

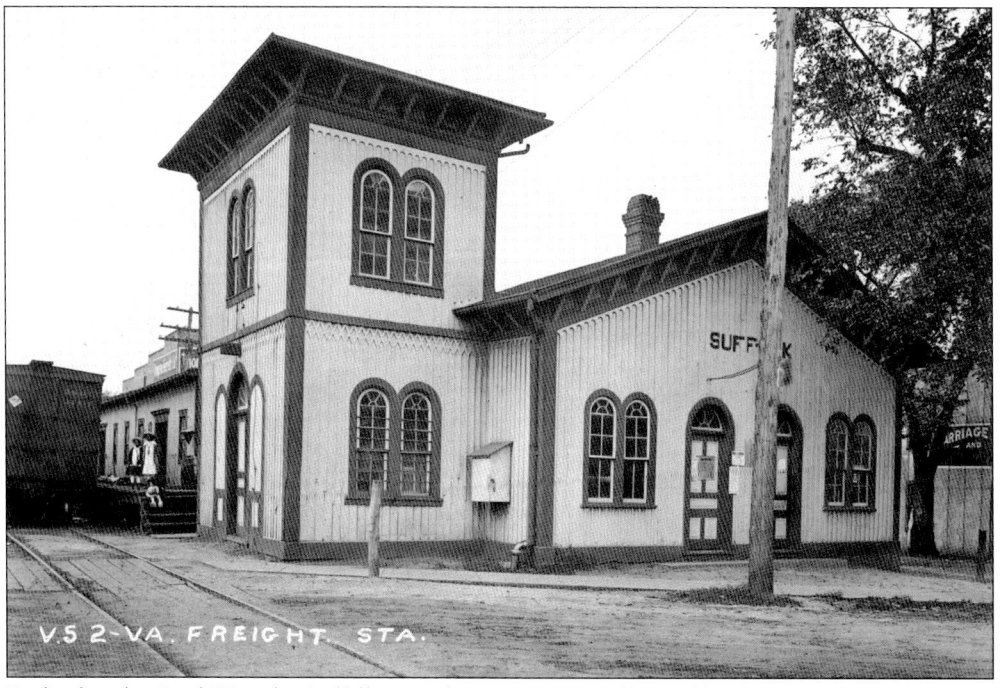

Built after the Civil War, the Suffolk train depot was originally used by the Norfolk & Petersburg Railroad. The large Italianate station became a Norfolk & Western freight depot when a new passenger depot was built in 1910. (Courtesy of Norfolk Southern.)

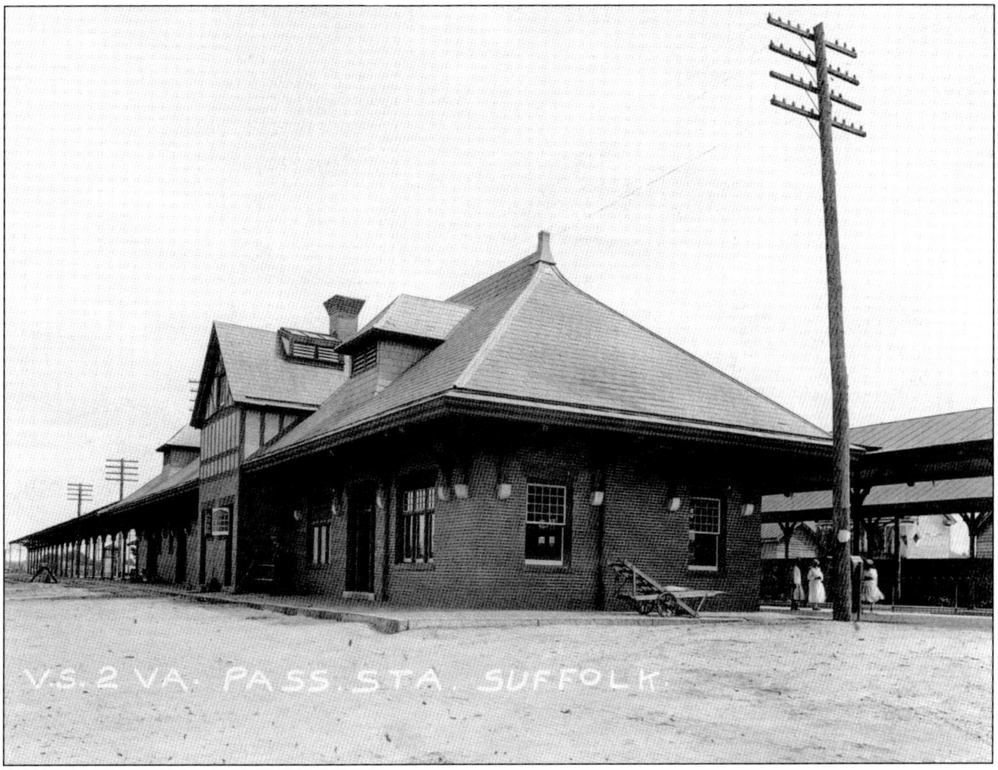

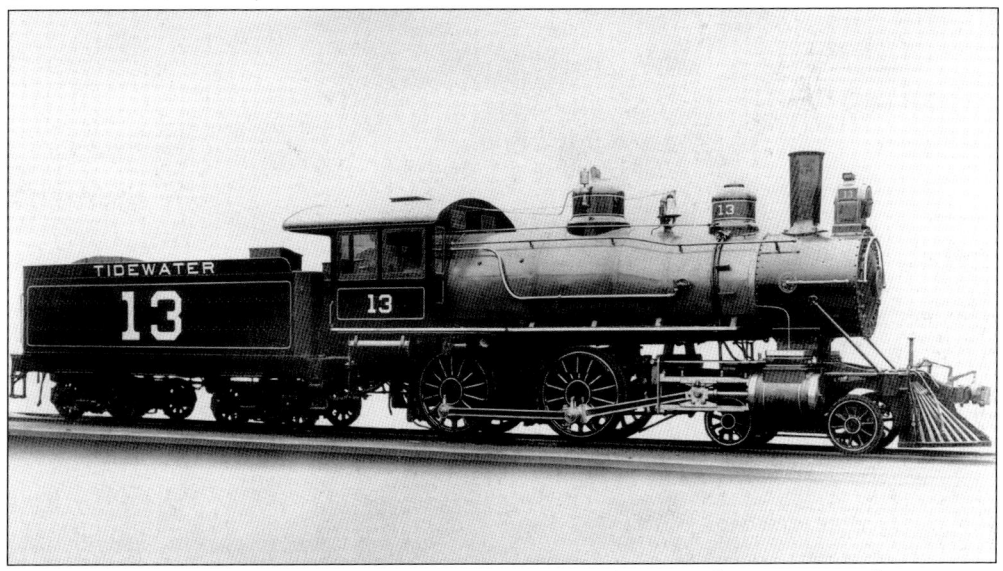

Norfolk & Western's Union Station passenger depot was at the corner of Holladay Street and Norfolk and Western Avenue in Suffolk. It was designed by architect Charles S. Churchill, who also designed the railroad's general office building in Roanoke in 1896. This photograph was taken in 1927. (Courtesy of Norfolk Southern.)

Locomotive No. 13, known as the *Tidewater*, was one of the more than 150 steam locomotives produced for Norfolk & Western at the Roanoke Machine Shops between 1884 and 1893. Norfolk & Western acquired the shops in 1883. (Courtesy of Norfolk Southern.)

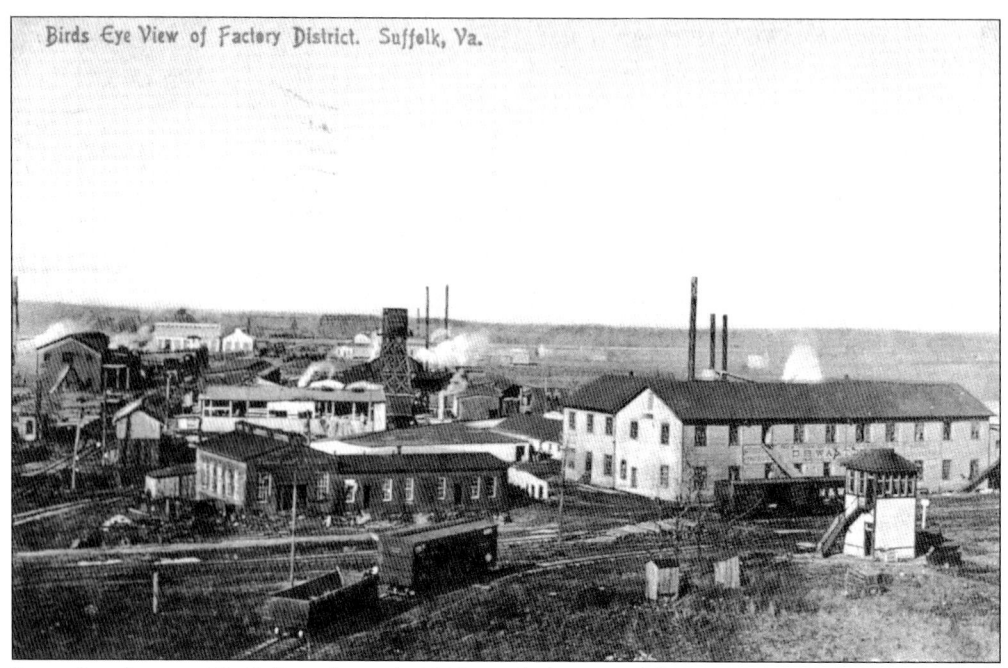

Six railroads served Suffolk in the early 1900s, including Norfolk & Western, Seaboard Air Line, the Virginian Railway, Atlantic Coastline, Atlantic & Danville, and Norfolk Southern's Suffolk & Carolina Branch. Norfolk & Western railcars are seen in this bird's-eye view of Suffolk's busy factory district in the early 20th century. (Courtesy of Norfolk Southern.)

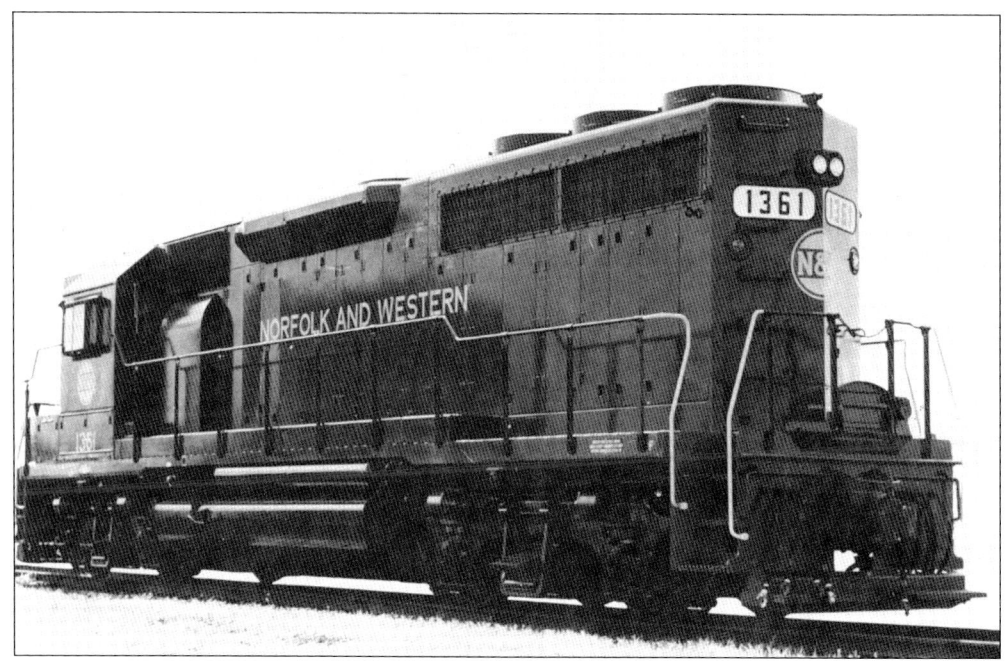

Norfolk & Western's locomotive No. 1361 was one of 175 diesel locomotives built by Alco-Richmond and Baldwin Locomotive Works between 1912 and 1918. The engines were used until the late 1950s. (Courtesy of Norfolk Southern.)

This advertisement, published in an October 1956 issue of the *Suffolk News-Herald*, reminded readers of the role Norfolk & Western and its forebear, the Norfolk & Petersburg, played in transporting peanuts, the city's major export. Amedeo Obici, founder of Planters Nut and Chocolate Company (now Planters Peanuts), moved his business from Wilkes-Barre, Pennsylvania, to Suffolk, the peanut capital of the world, in 1913. Obici built his Suffolk processing plant over Norfolk & Western tracks, allowing workers to load peanuts out of the rain and trains to then deliver the best-quality goods. (Courtesy of Norfolk Southern.)

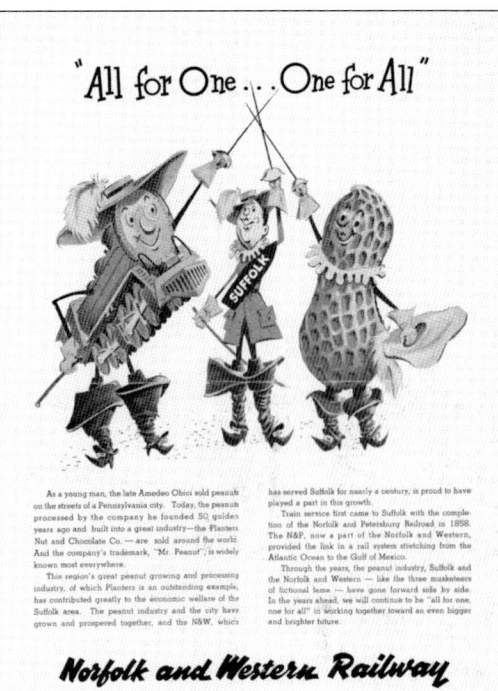

Aimed at commercial shippers, this 1962 Norfolk & Western advertisement notes that the world's largest naval base was established in Norfolk because of the city's central location on the East Coast and large ice-free natural harbor. Those reasons, along with efficient railroad cargo piers and a direct rail link to the industrial Midwest, also encouraged shippers to choose Norfolk & Western to transport their freight. (Courtesy of Norfolk Southern.)

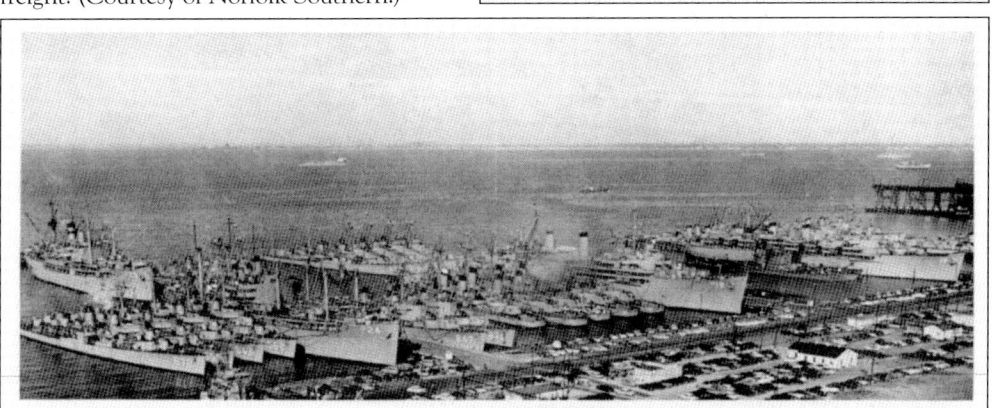

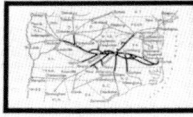

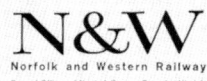

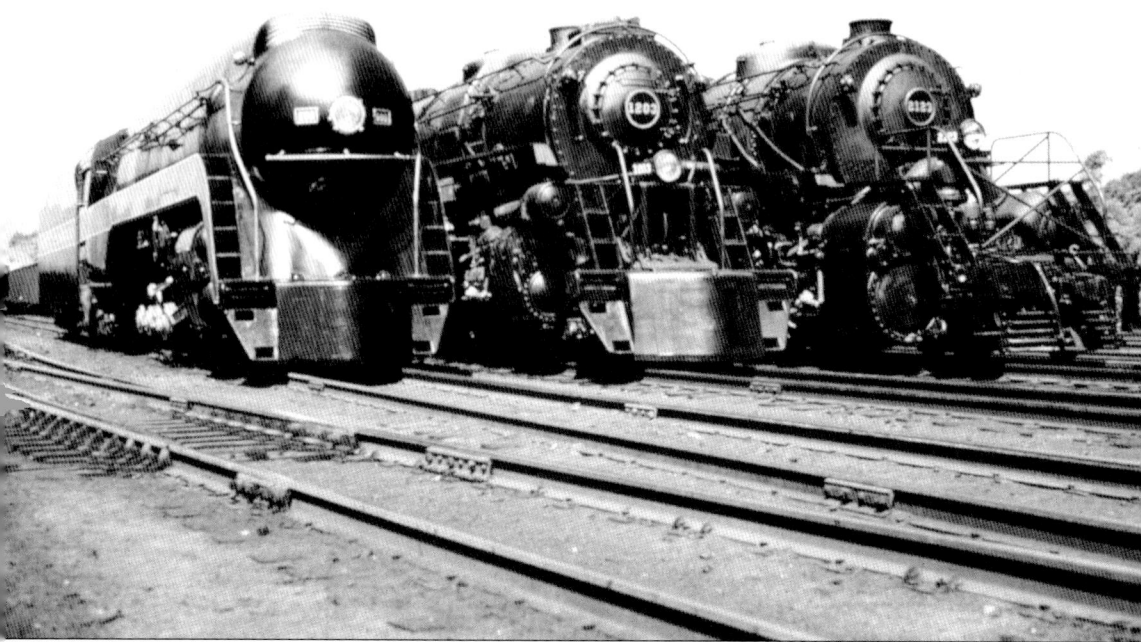

Known as the "Magnificent Three," Norfolk & Western's three top coal-burning steam locomotives were the J, the A, and the Y. Built at the railroad's Roanoke Shops, the locomotives represented the best in steam engine design—low initial investment, high usage, low-cost operation and maintenance, and dependable performance. Many were built during World War II and were designed to transport coal, merchandise, and passengers between Norfolk and Cincinnati, Ohio. Norfolk & Western used steam engines until 1960. (Courtesy of Norfolk Southern.)

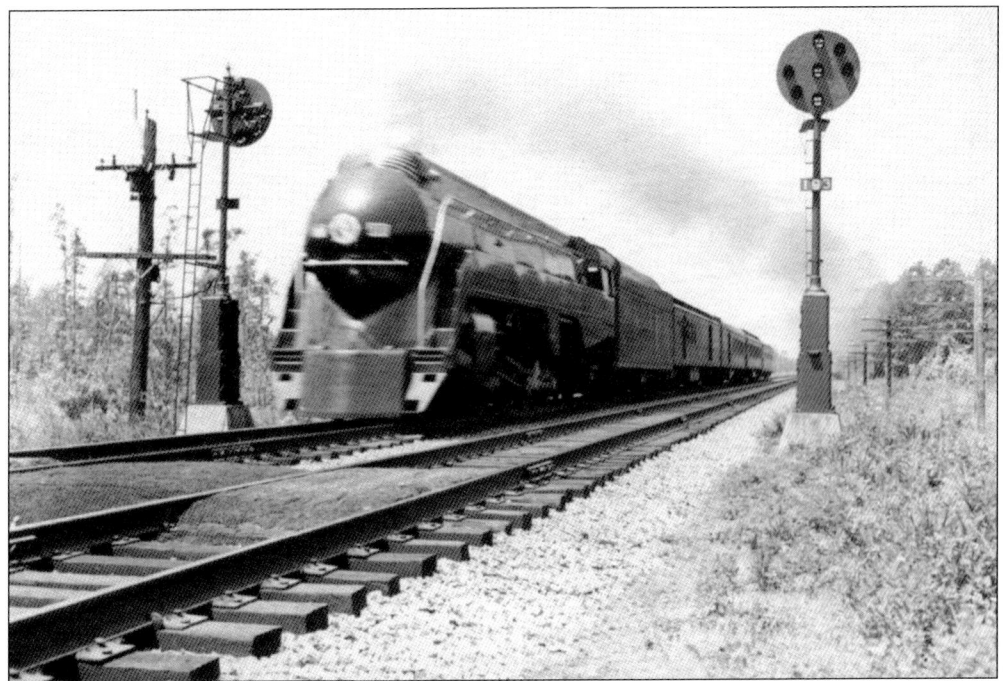

Norfolk & Western's passenger train, the Cannonball, which operated between Norfolk and Richmond, is traveling east of Suffolk in this June 1949 photograph. The Cannonball was retired in 1967 after becoming a sleeper train from New York to Norfolk. (Courtesy of Norfolk Southern.)

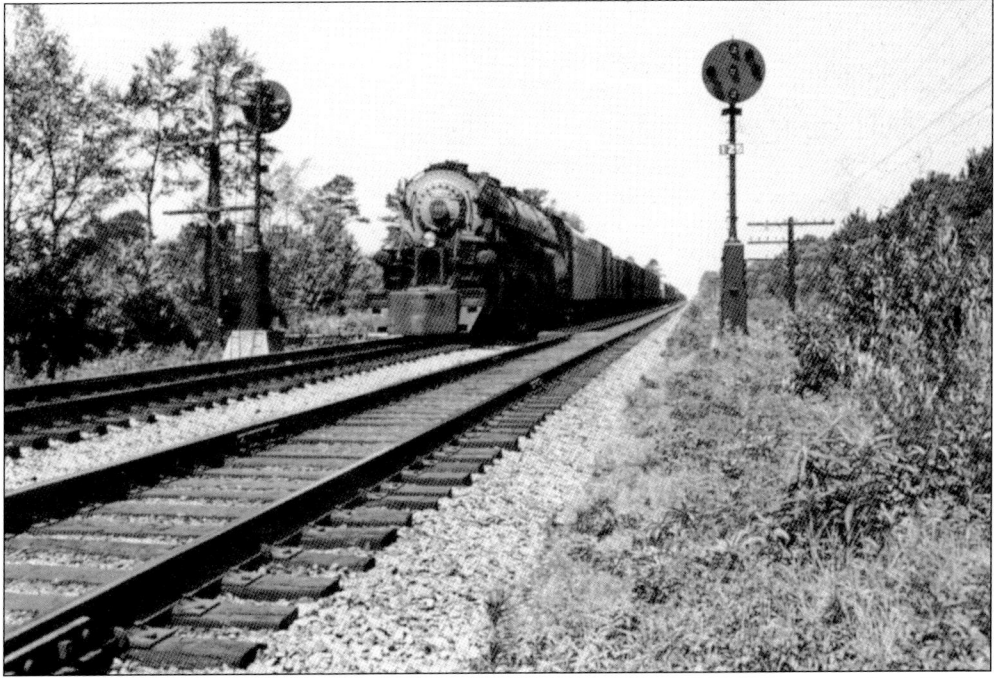

This 1949 photograph shows a Norfolk & Western freight train at milepost 13, near Norfolk. The railroad's original network encompassed just over 2,000 route miles, connecting Norfolk with Cincinnati and Columbus. (Courtesy of Norfolk Southern.)

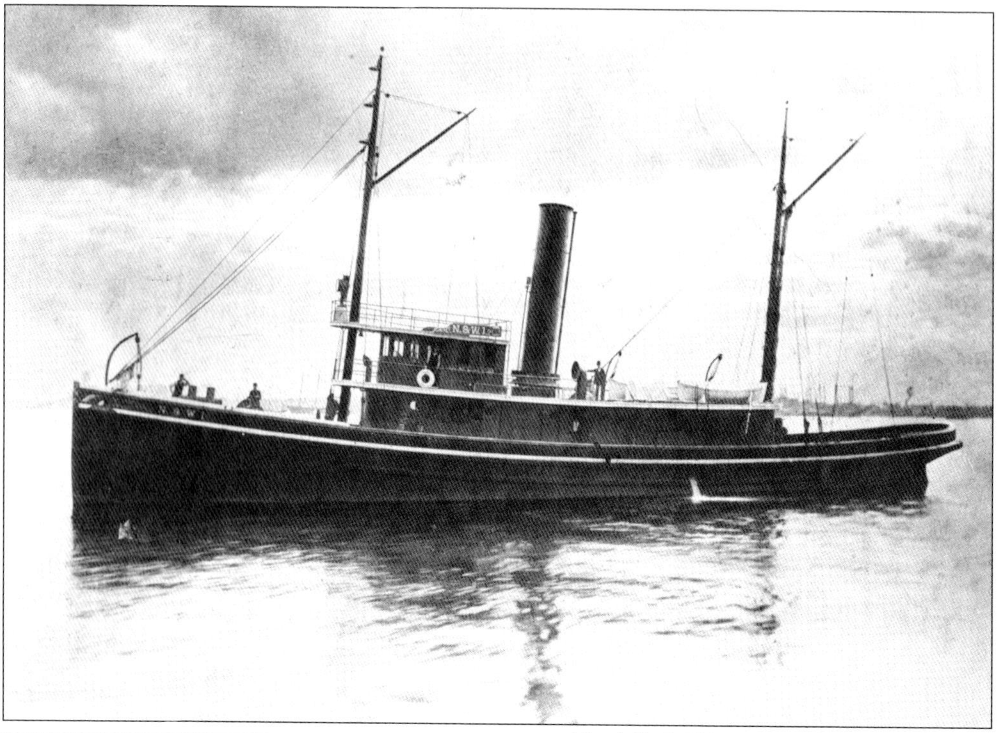

Norfolk & Western tugboat No. 1 is seen on the Elizabeth River in this 1931 photograph. The steam-powered tug was built in 1890. (Courtesy of Norfolk Southern.)

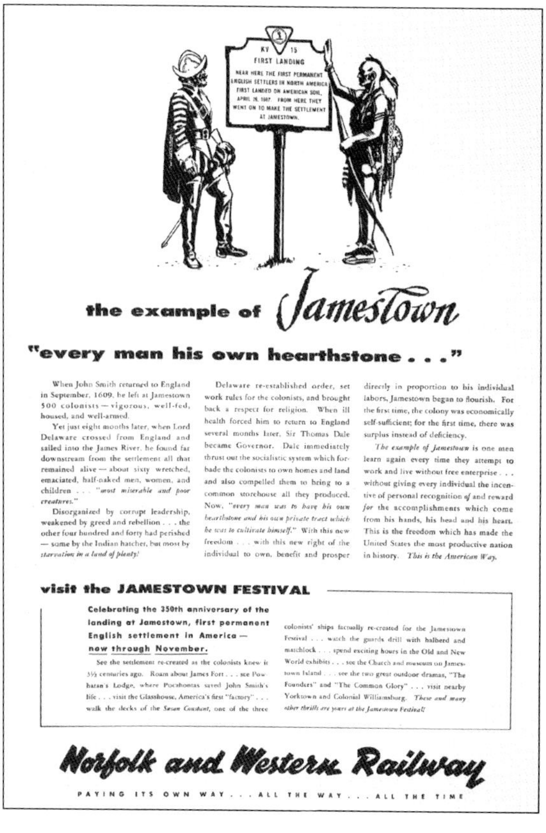

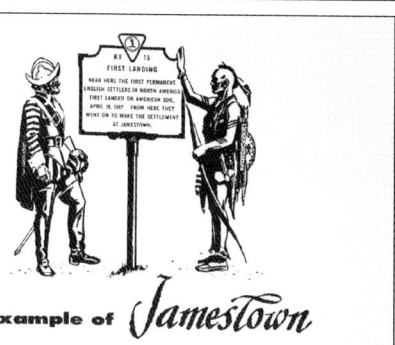

In 1957, Norfolk & Western celebrated the 350th anniversary of the Jamestown settlement with this advertisement that encouraged travelers to visit the re-created settlement commemorating the first permanent English colony in North America. Known as the Jamestown Festival, the eight-month-long celebration attracted more than one million visitors to the region, including Queen Elizabeth II of England and Vice Pres. Richard M. Nixon. (Courtesy of Norfolk Southern.)

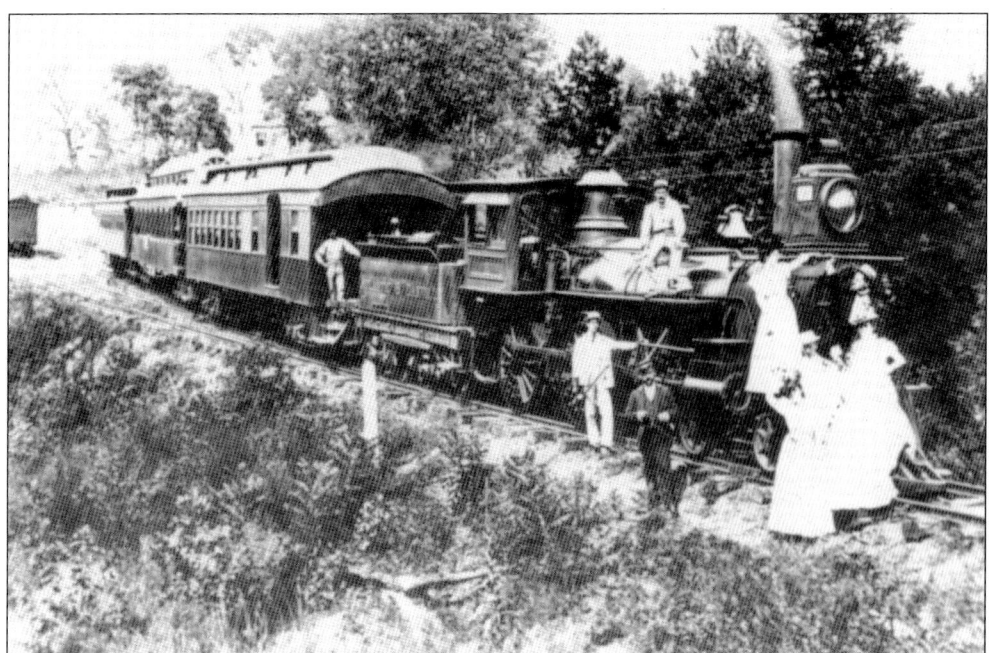

Organized in 1882, the Atlantic & Danville Railroad opened a main line between Portsmouth and Danville in 1890. Southern Railway leased the railroad from 1899 to 1949. The Atlantic & Danville then operated as an independent company until filing for bankruptcy in 1960. (Courtesy of Norfolk Southern.)

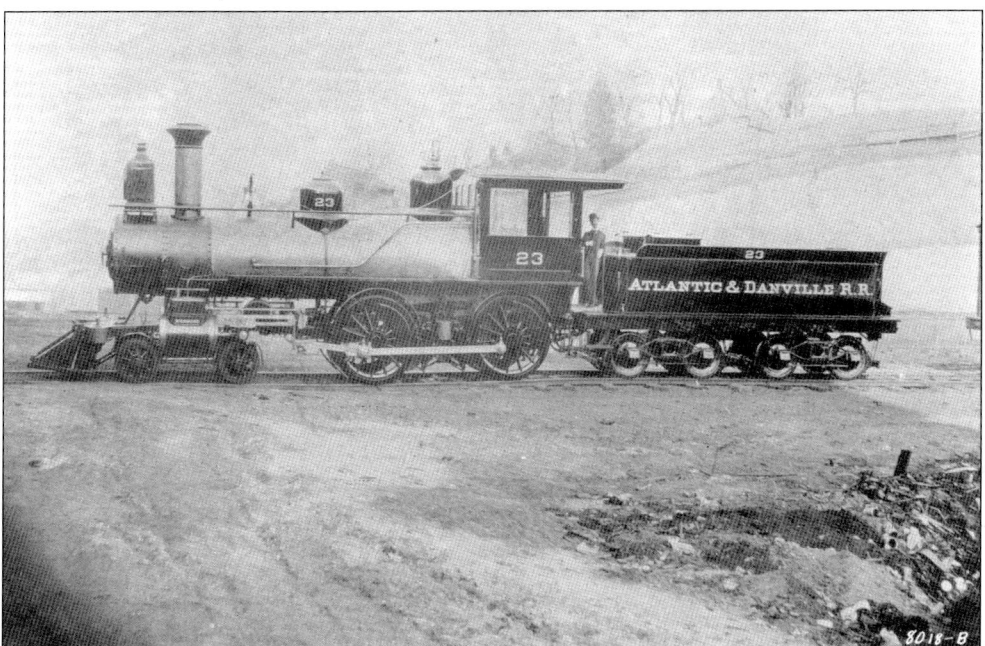

Norfolk & Western was the only bidder at a 1962 auction for the bankrupt 213-mile Atlantic & Danville Railroad. The railroad purchased the Atlantic & Danville for $1.5 million and reorganized it as the Norfolk, Franklin & Danville. It was dissolved after the formation of Norfolk Southern in 1982. (Courtesy of Norfolk Southern.)

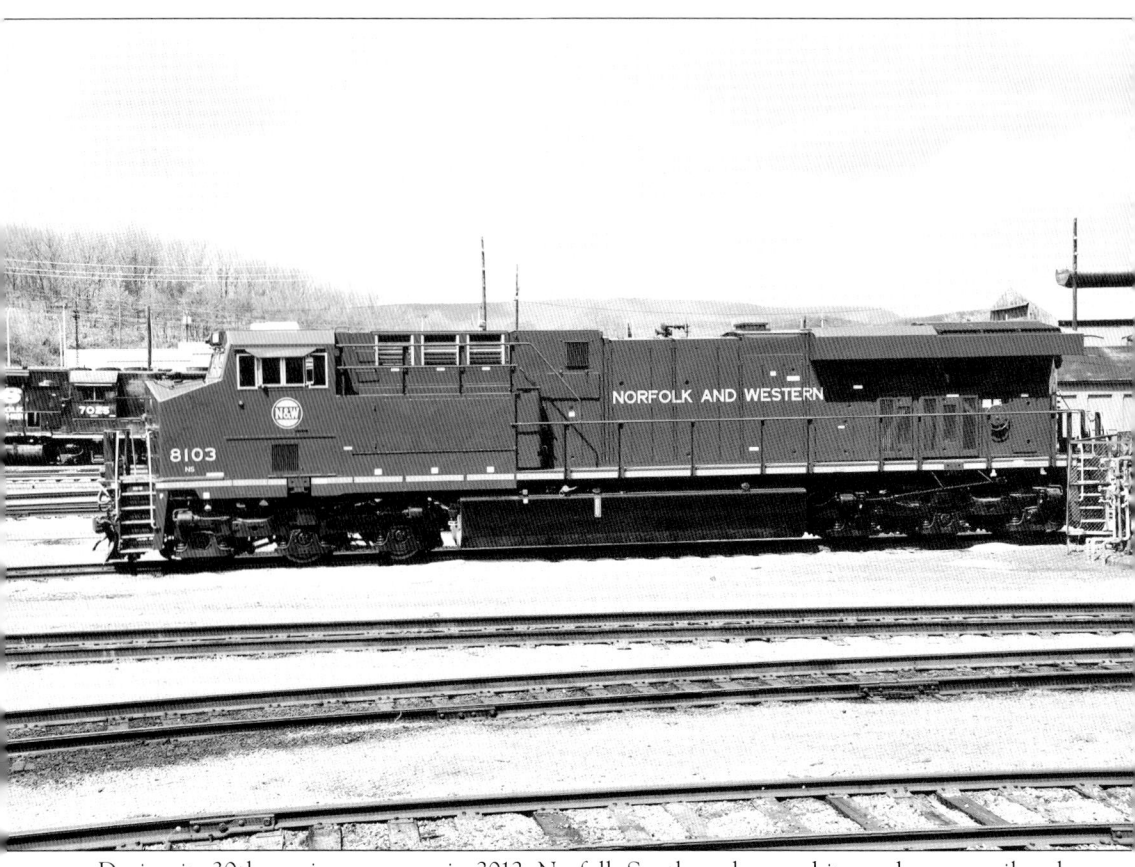

During its 30th anniversary year in 2012, Norfolk Southern honored its predecessor railroads, including Norfolk & Western, by painting 20 new locomotives in commemorative schemes displaying the railroad's heritage. Each paint scheme was modified to fit contemporary locomotives while remaining as true as possible to the original designs. The heritage locomotives were put to work hauling freight across the Norfolk Southern network. (Courtesy of Norfolk Southern.)

Two

Coal Comes to Norfolk

A festive atmosphere awaited the first railcar filled with coal from western Virginia's Pocahontas coalfields when it arrived in Norfolk in March 1883, setting the city on a path to become the top East Coast exporter of the valuable commodity.

Norfolk & Western president Frederick Kimball presented the carload bearing 40,000 pounds of coal to Norfolk mayor William Lamb, as the Norfolk Light Artillery Blues, a state militia unit, provided a salute. The 20-ton gondola transporting the black gold was detached from the train, and Mayor Lamb and Norfolk policemen joined railroad officials and clerks aboard the engine and car for what the *Norfolk Virginian* called "an ovation tour" to Norfolk & Western's downtown piers.

Cheering spectators who lined the streets leading to the piers tried to grab souvenir chunks of coal. "As the car moved slowly along, many a head that appeared at a window to catch a glimpse of the sight caught something else in the shape of a small memento of our natural resources, skillfully hurled by the muscular arm of some gay and festive Norfolk & Western clerk," the *Norfolk Virginian* reported.

Lamb, Norfolk's mayor from 1880 to 1886, described the carload of coal as "the precursor of a trade which is destined to make our port the most important coaling station of the Atlantic coast." His prediction proved accurate. By 1900, Norfolk was the leading coal exporting port on the East Coast.

Norfolk & Western soon discovered its downtown piers would not be adequate to handle the burgeoning coal trade, leading the railroad to purchase approximately 325 acres of waterfront farmland north of the city where it began construction on the Lamberts Point Coal Terminal. The 984-foot Coal Pier 1 was still under construction when it dumped its first load of coal onto the *Samuel B. Vrooman* in March 1885.

As the coal business grew, the railroad expanded operations at Lamberts Point and built additional piers, culminating with Coal Pier 6, a 1,850-foot pier with three berths and two shiploaders that can handle up to 8,000 tons of coal per hour.

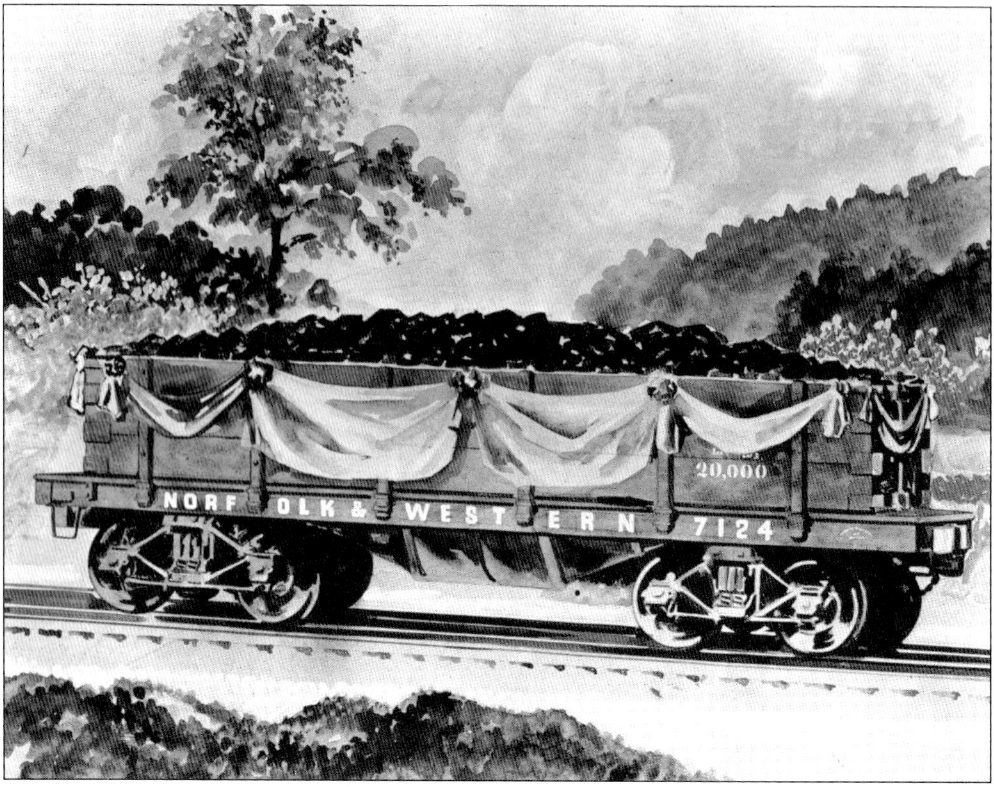

Decorated with bunting, the 20-ton gondola filled with the first coal from the Pocahontas coalfields displayed the inscription, "From Pocahontas to Norfolk. For Mayor Lamb." Opened in 1882, the Pocahontas coalfields' first mine, Pocahontas Mine No. 1, is listed in the National Register of Historic Places. (Courtesy of Norfolk Southern.)

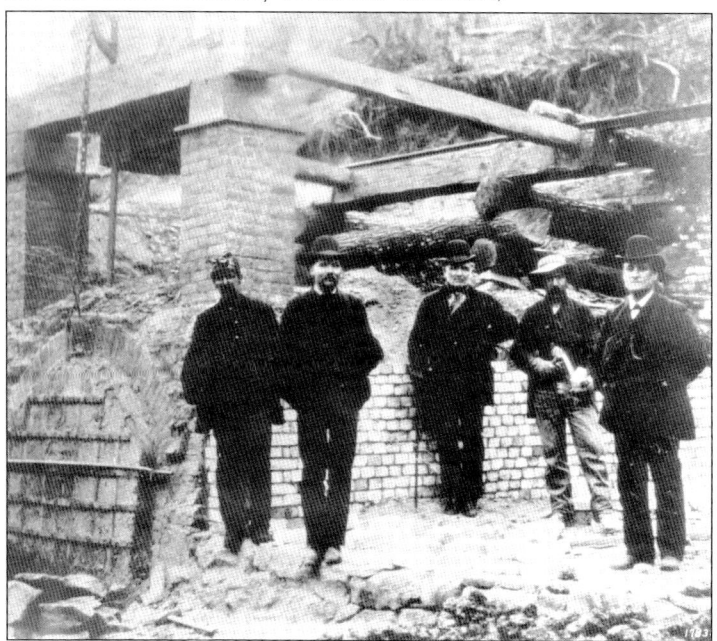

John Cooper, a native of England, made his fortune in the southern West Virginia coal mines in the late 1800s. His mine in Bramwell, West Virginia, shipped its first coal from the Pocahontas coalfields on Norfolk & Western in November 1884. Cooper (far right) stands with several unidentified men in front of an experimental coke oven in the Pocahontas coalfields between 1884 and 1894. (Courtesy of Norfolk Southern.)

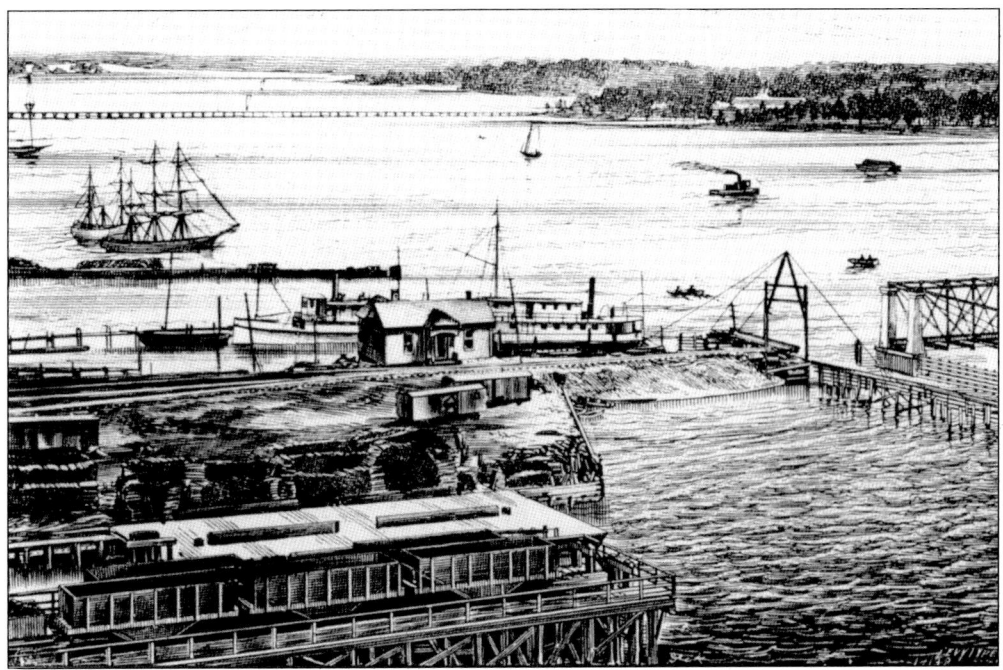
Norfolk & Western's first coal pier on the downtown Norfolk waterfront is depicted in this late-19th-century drawing. A railroad bridge is in the background. The railroad soon determined that its downtown property would not be adequate to accommodate a thriving coal business and began construction on the Lamberts Point Coal Terminal. (Courtesy of Norfolk Southern.)

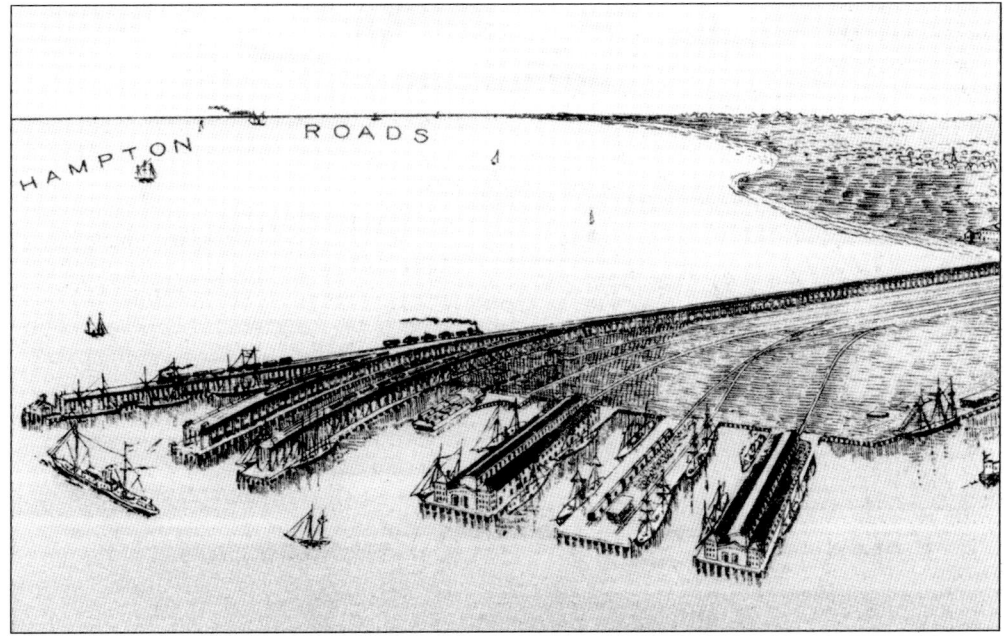
This architectural rendering of the Lamberts Point terminal from the 1890s shows plans for three coal piers alongside merchandise piers, which were in operation by the early 1900s. Norfolk & Western tracks were extended to Lamberts Point in the mid-1880s. The railroad's property at Lamberts Point encompassed nearly two miles of waterfront. (Courtesy of Kurt Reisweber.)

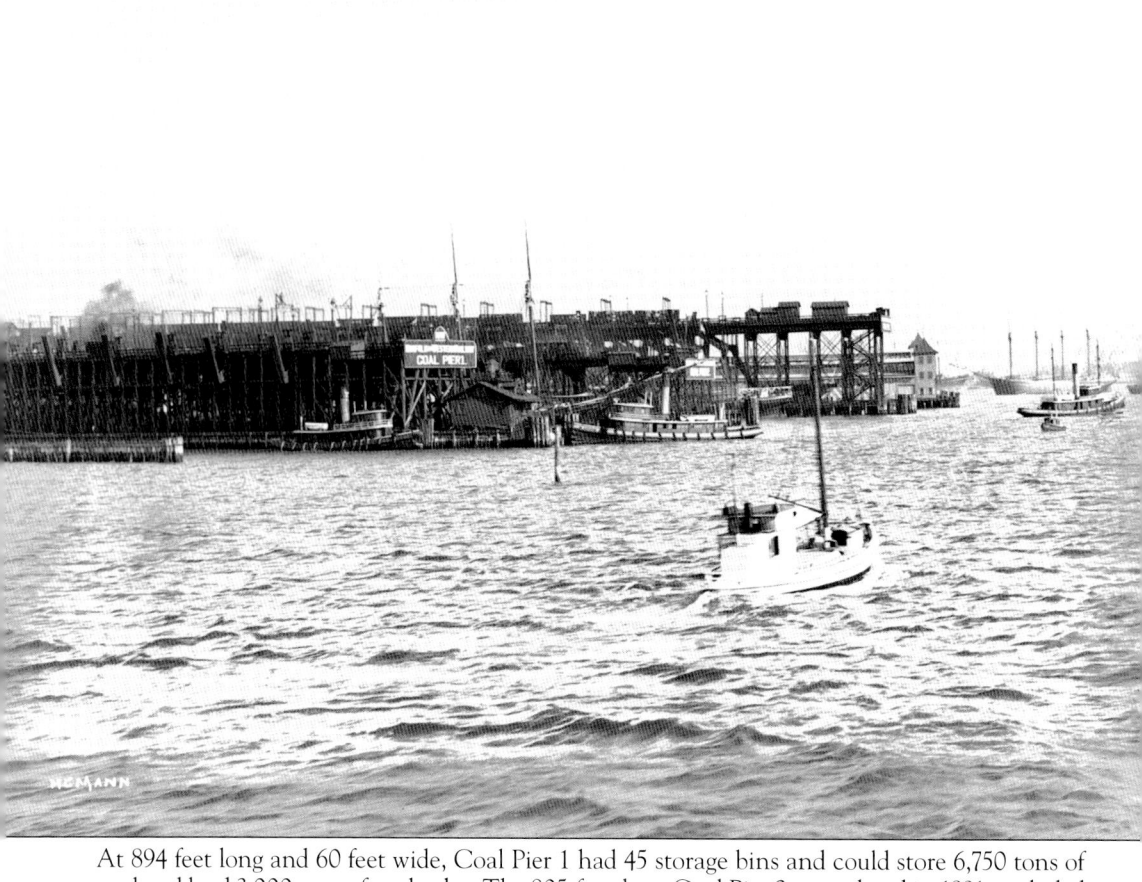

At 894 feet long and 60 feet wide, Coal Pier 1 had 45 storage bins and could store 6,750 tons of coal and load 3,000 tons of coal a day. The 805-foot-long Coal Pier 2, completed in 1891, included 22 gravity-loading chutes. In the 1890s, the railroad built an electric plant to operate its growing pier complex and increase international trade through Norfolk. (Courtesy of Norfolk Southern.)

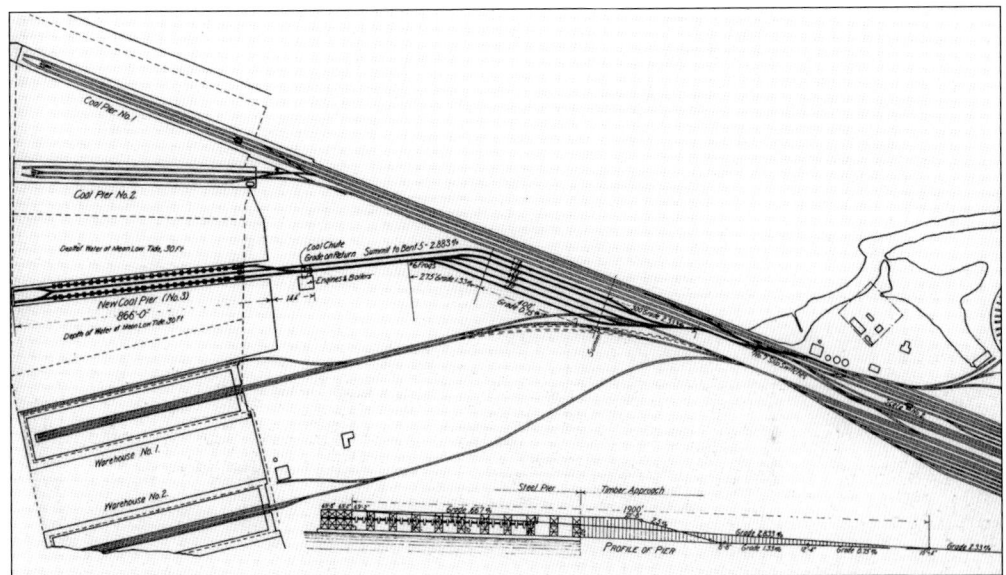

This c. 1900 drawing shows designs for the new Coal Pier 3, including plans for dumping coal directly from hopper cars into chutes atop the pier. With the addition of Coal Pier 3 in 1901, Norfolk & Western was becoming one of the East Coast's predominant shippers of coal. The railroad shipped a record 8.18 million tons of coal in 1905, and 26 million tons by 1920. (Courtesy of Kurt Reisweber.)

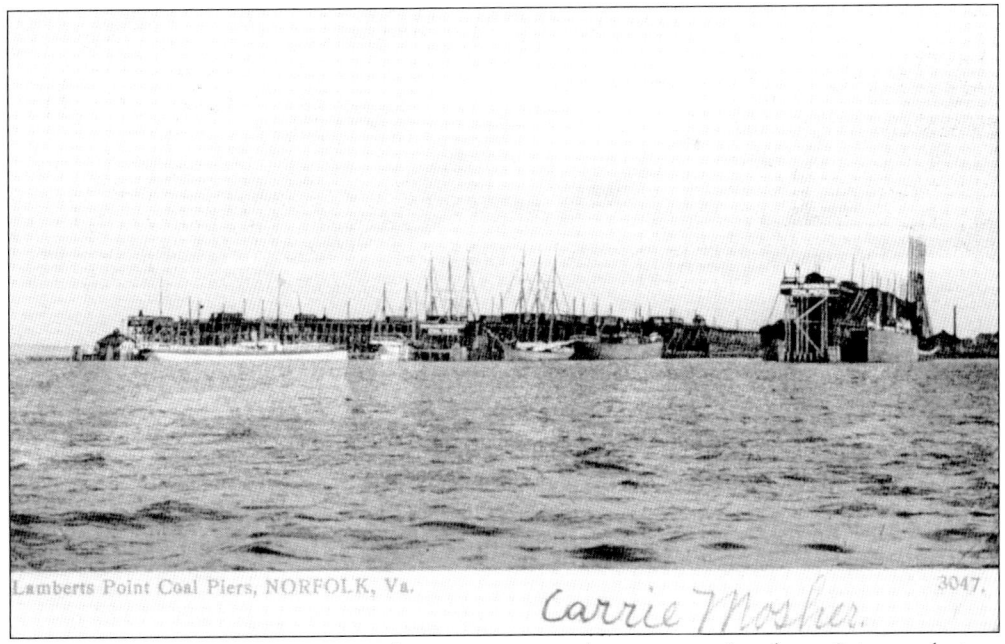

This 1907 postcard paints a scene of oceangoing vessels arriving at Lamberts Point coal piers, including the new Coal Pier 3. Lamberts Point was named for Thomas Lambert, who was awarded a 100-acre tract of land from the English crown in 1635. The grant included the area where the Lamberts Point Coal Terminal now stands as well as the Lamberts Point neighborhood. (Author's collection.)

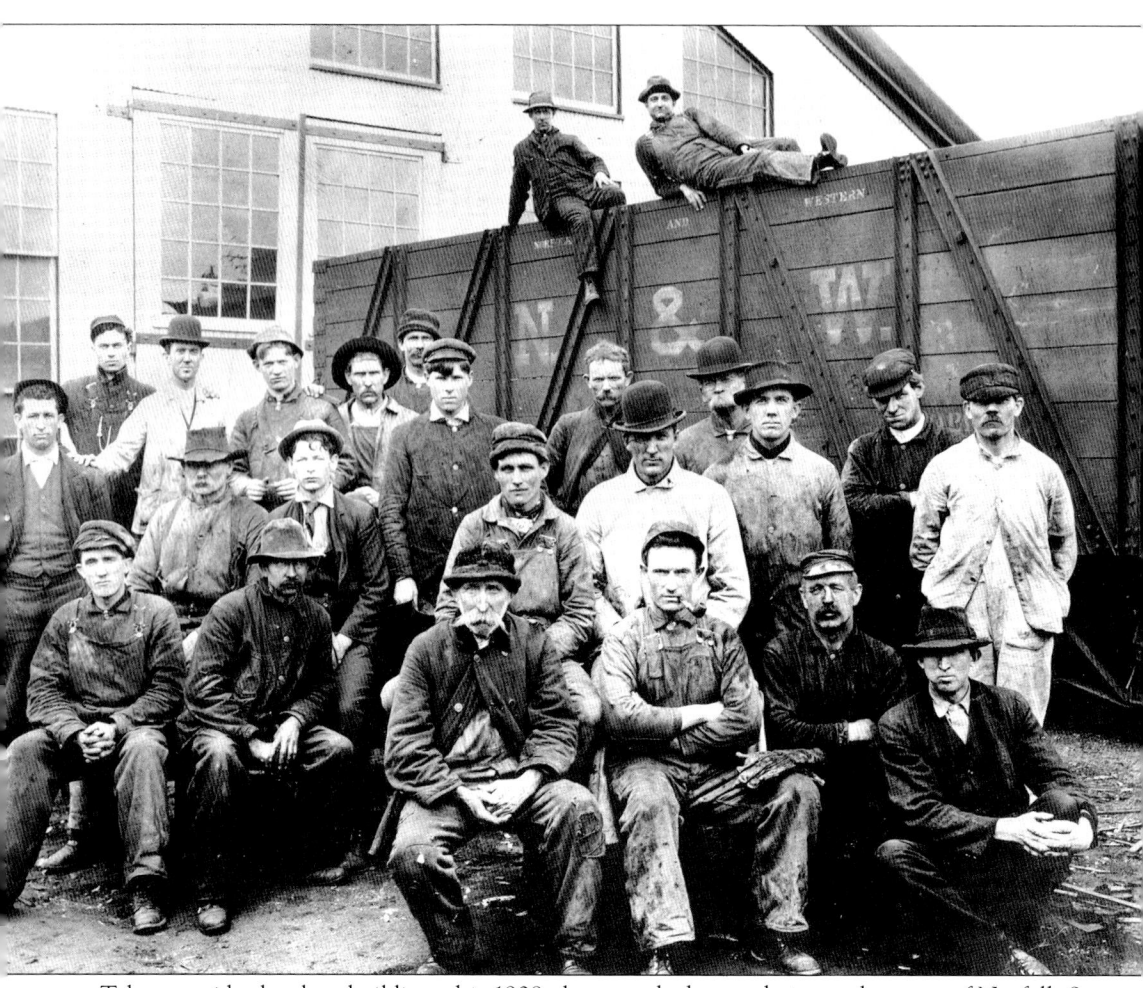

Taken outside the shop building, this 1908 photograph shows what was then one of Norfolk & Western's largest hopper coal cars built of wood. From left to right are (first row) J.O. Franklin, car repairer; A.W. Weltzel, air brake repairer; James Hall, car repairer; and General Bryant, car repairer; (second row) Dan Terry, car repairer; A.L. Hall, inspector and later assistant car foreman; J.L. Pritchart, car repairer; ? Lewis, section laborer; C.B. Heath, car repairer; W.J. Ellis, gang foreman; and J.B. Wright, car repairer; (third row) L.W. Taylor, car repairer; A.E. Bradshaw, wheel lathe man, later fireman; R.H. Carper, air braker repairer, later gang foreman; P.B. Tyson, painter; C.B. Bowles, car repairer; and W.H. Smelser, car repairer; (fourth row) John Alford, car repairer; W.R. Etheridge, car repairer; Samuel Orgain, car repairer; Samuel Orgain II, bolt threader, and unidentified; (on top of car) Clark and Joel Powell, car repairers. (Courtesy of Norfolk Southern.)

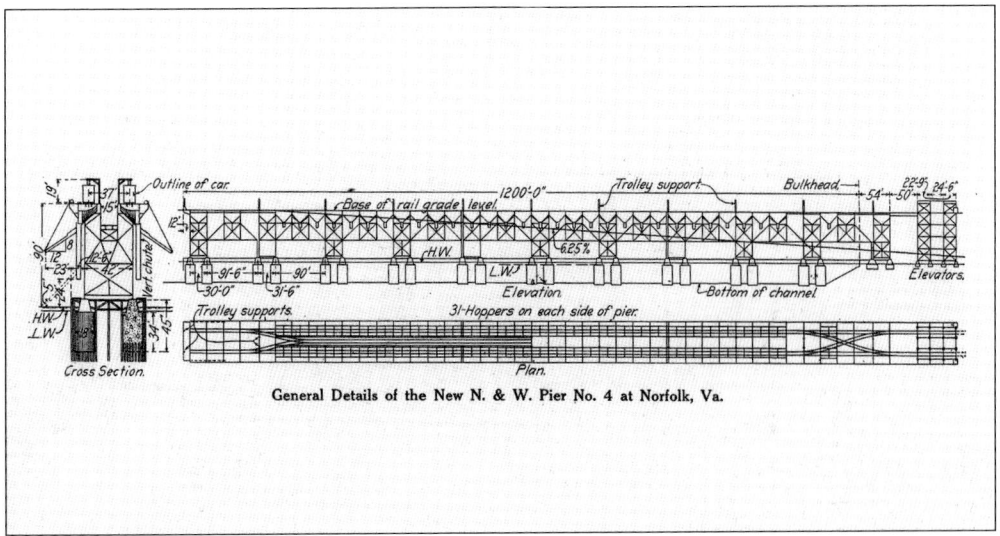

This architectural drawing provides general details of Norfolk & Western's Coal Pier 4. Construction on Coal Pier 4 began in 1913, two years after Lamberts Point was annexed by the City of Norfolk. (Courtesy of Kurt Reisweber.)

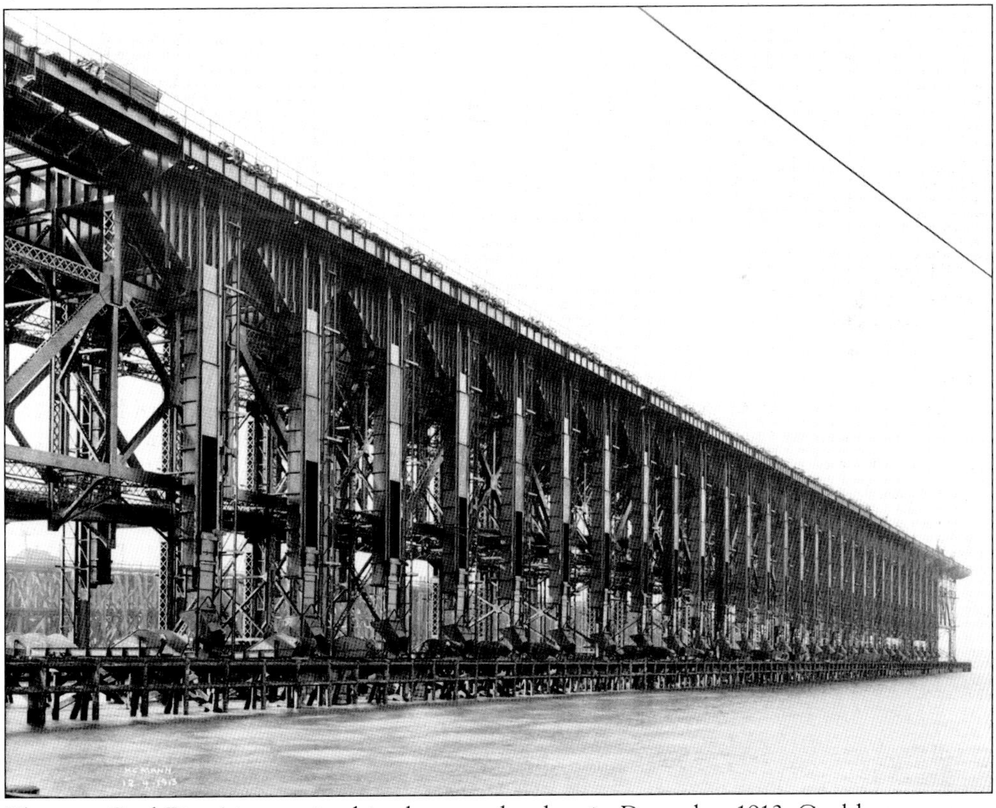

The new Coal Pier 4 is seen in this photograph taken in December 1913. Coal hoppers were dumped into electric pier cars. An elevator then carried the car to the top of the pier, where the coal was discharged into loading chutes. Six hundred coal cars could be emptied per day. (Courtesy of Norfolk Southern.)

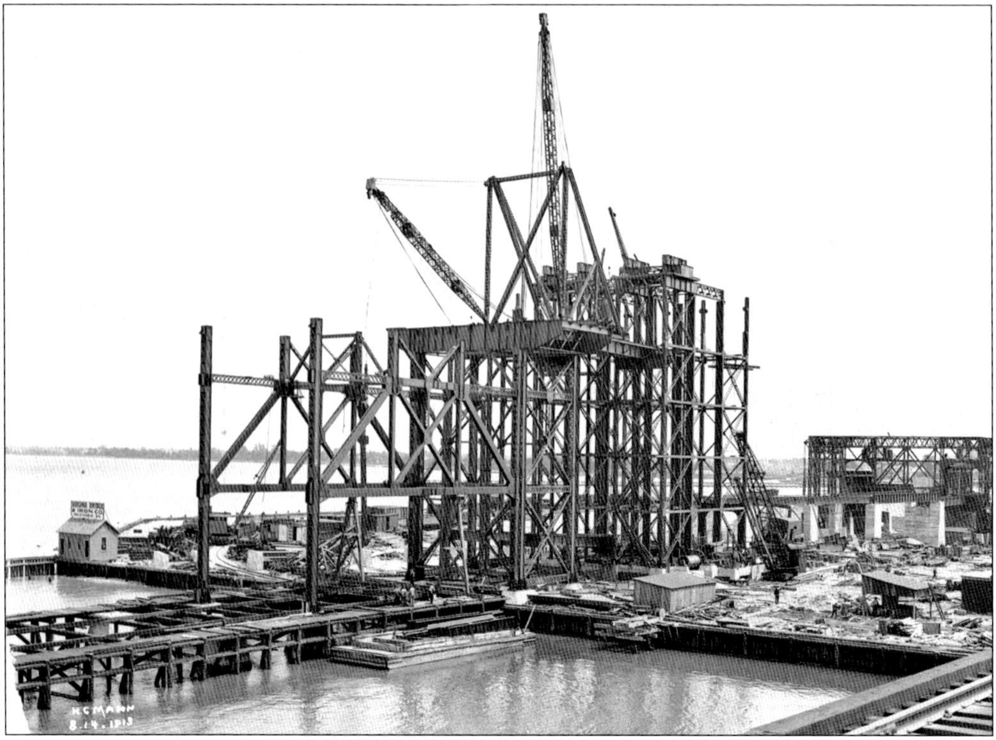

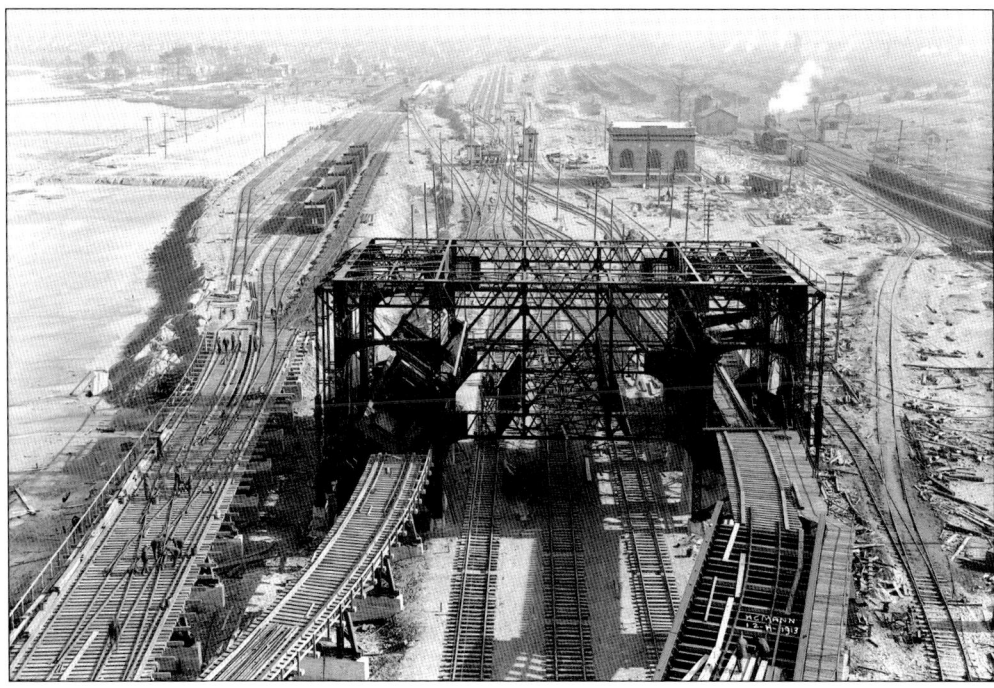

Norfolk & Western built Coal Pier 4 in response to the Virginian Railway's technologically advanced Coal Pier 1, which opened at Sewells Point in 1909. Described as being dramatically different from the first three piers built at Lamberts Point, Coal Pier 4 was 1,200 feet long, 70 feet wide, and 90 feet above water. (Both, courtesy of Norfolk Southern.)

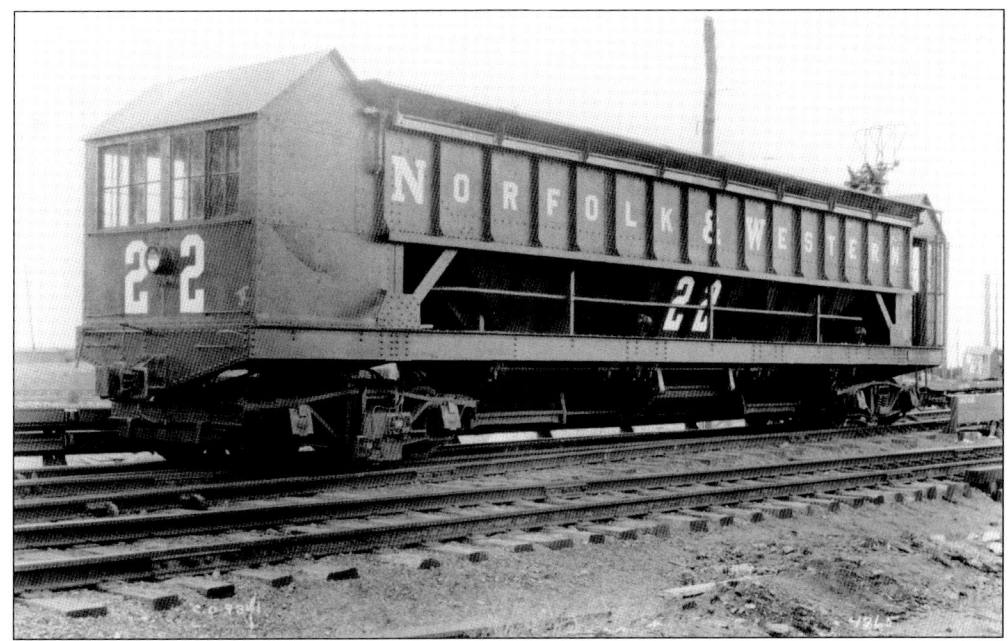

An electric pier car used on Coal Pier 4 is seen here. Coal was dumped from hoppers into the large electric cars, which were then carried by elevator to the top of the pier. From there, the cars ran along a platform on an electric trolley line, dumping coal into ships through chutes. Later, a more modern dumper-conveyor system replaced the pier cars. (Courtesy of Kurt Reisweber.)

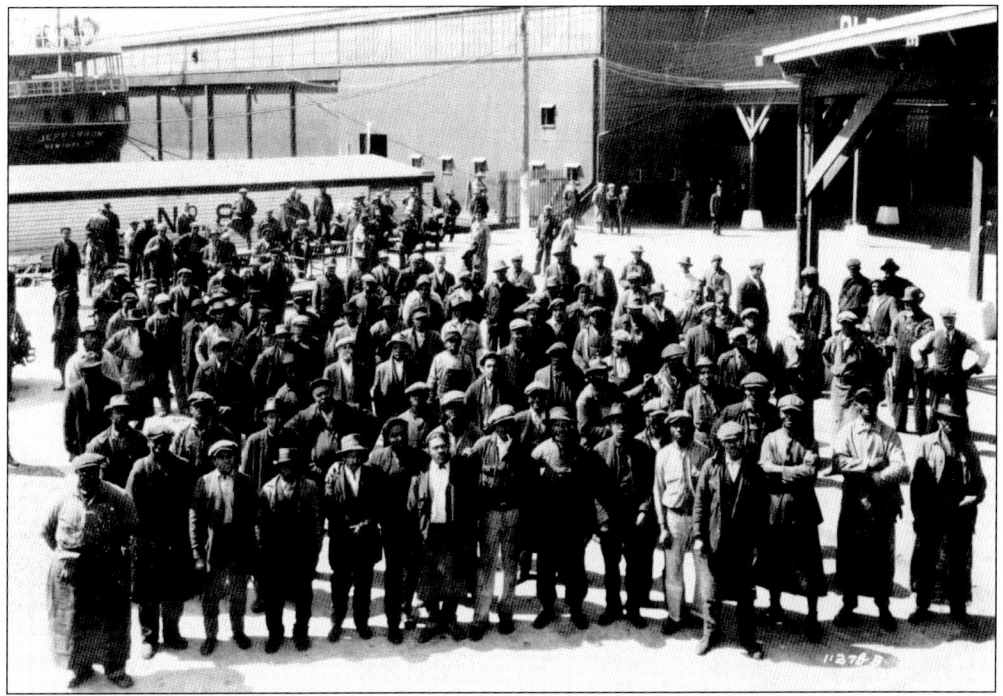

In this early 1900s photograph, African American workers stand in front of a warehouse at Lamberts Point. Many workers lived in the adjacent Lamberts Point neighborhood, which was developed as housing for railroad employees. (Courtesy of Norfolk Southern.)

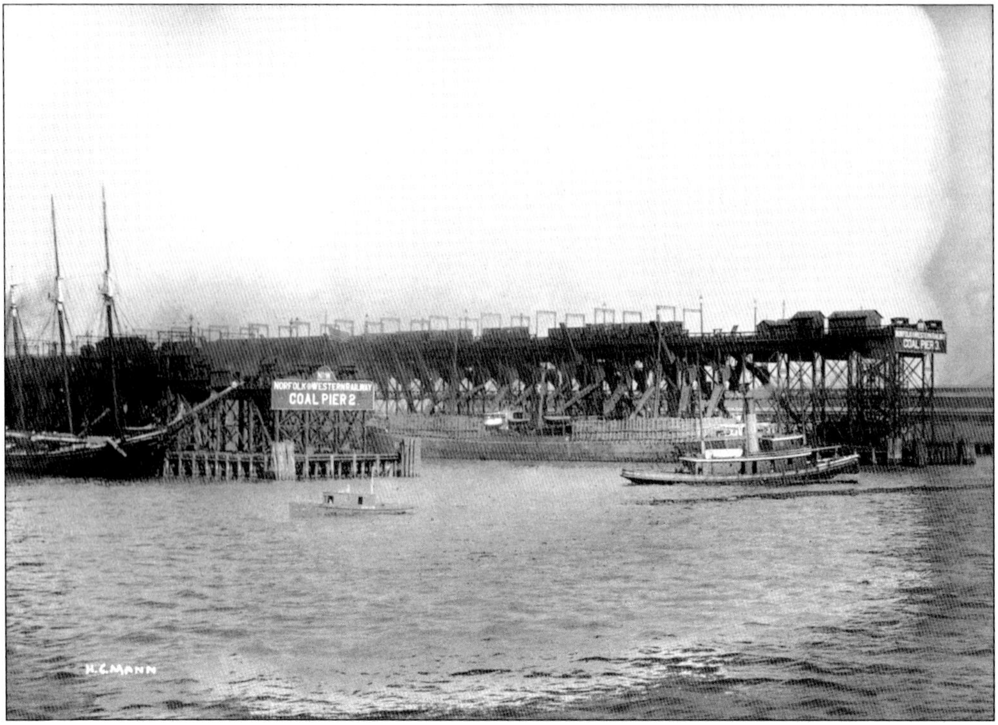

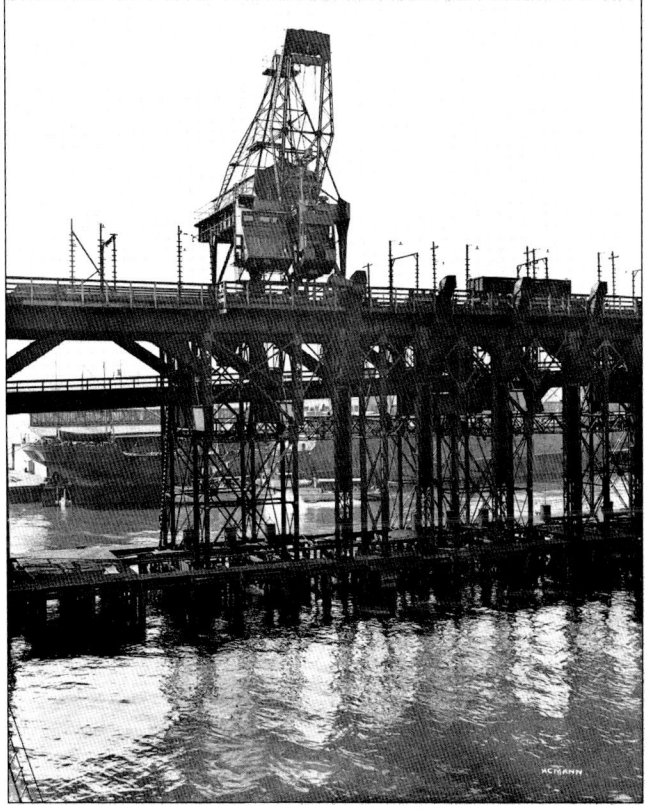

In 1923, Norfolk & Western installed a system of electric-powered dump cars at Coal Piers 2 and 3. Coal in open railcars was dumped into transfer cars and then moved onto the piers to unload the coal into ships. (Courtesy of Norfolk Southern.)

Coal Pier 4 is shown in 1920. Upgraded in 1953, Coal Pier 4 could empty 600 coal cars during a 10-hour workday. When it was retired a decade later, the pier had loaded more than 200 million tons of coal since its completion in 1914. (Courtesy of Norfolk Southern.)

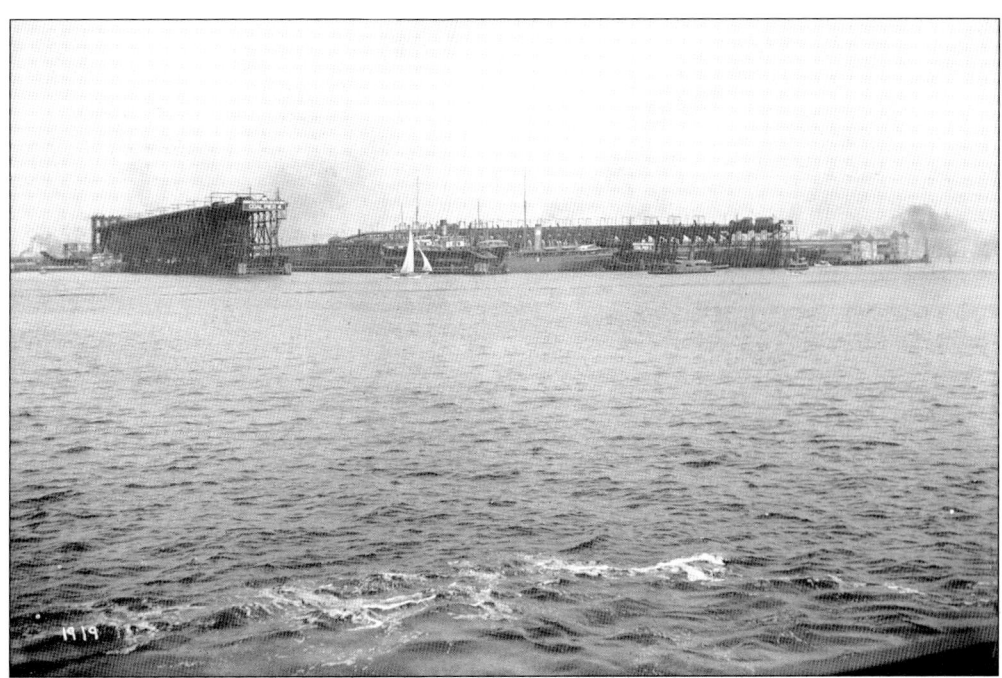

Coal Piers 2, 3, and 4 are shown in this c. 1920s photograph. Norfolk & Western became more prosperous as coal traffic increased on the railroad in the early 20th century and was soon nicknamed "King Coal." The valuable commodity fueled half of the world's navies, and in the 21st century powers steel mills and power plants throughout the world. (Courtesy of Norfolk Southern.)

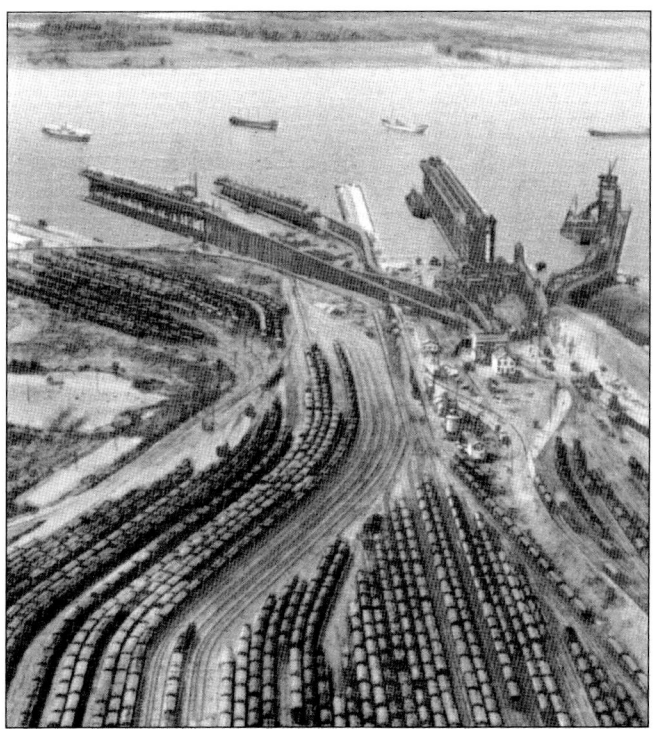

Five piers and a portion of the storage yard are seen on this 1930s postcard of Lamberts Point. At center, the superstructure of Coal Pier 1 had been removed in 1915, and the pier was overhauled to handle pig iron and lumber. It was razed to water level by 1935. Coal Pier 2 was retired in 1937, along with Coal Pier 3, which had opened in 1901. The yard was originally laid out so that everything funneled straight onto Coal Pier 1. (Courtesy of Kurt Reisweber.)

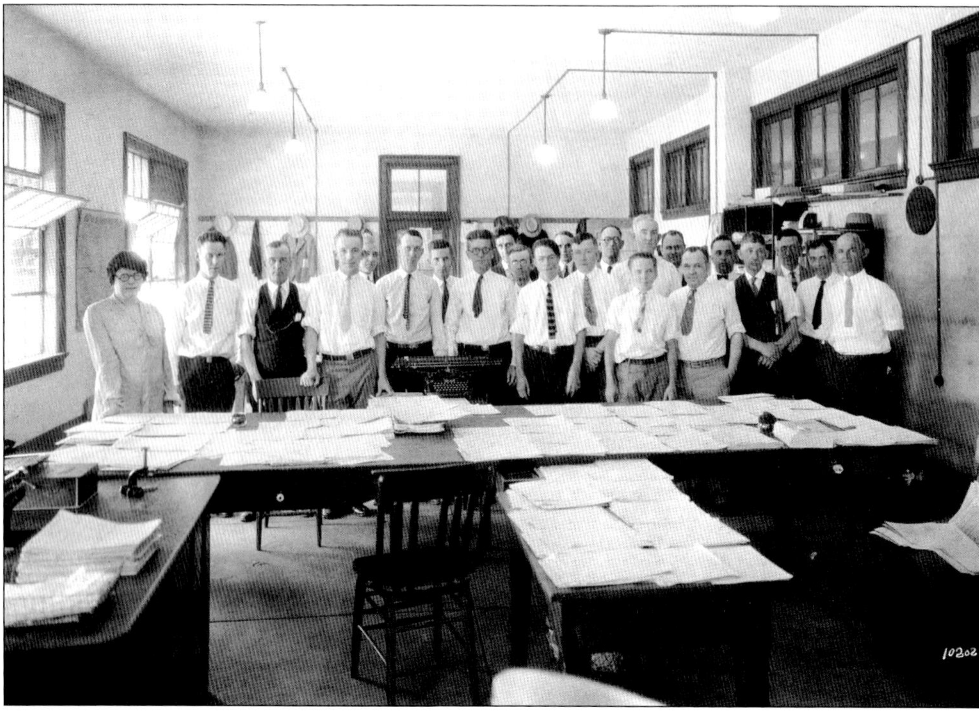

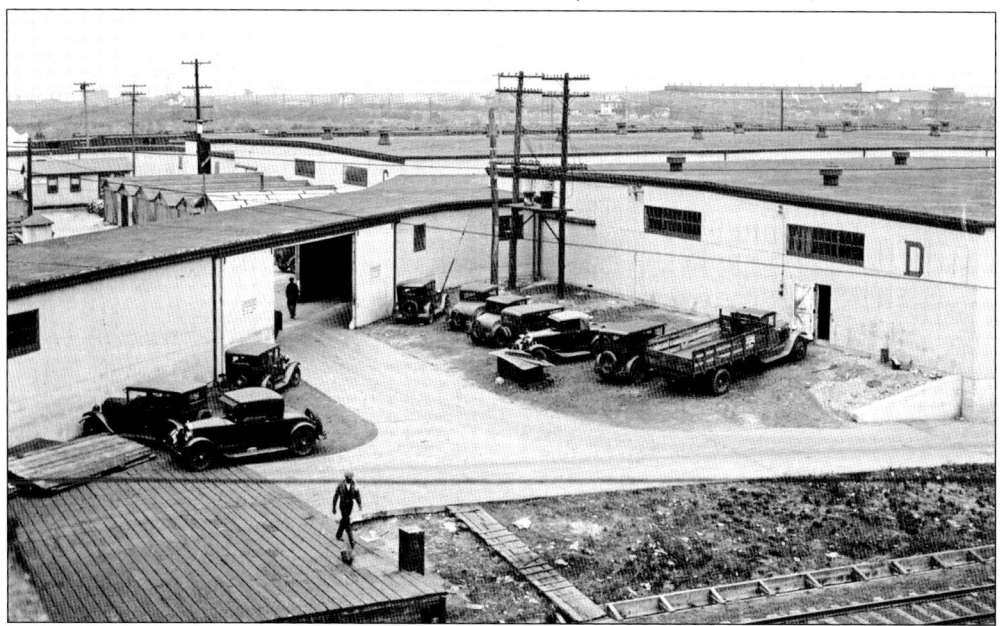

Norfolk & Western forwarding agents are seen in their office at Lamberts Point in this c. 1930s photograph. Forwarding agents were responsible for ensuring that shipments were loaded onto the trains and delivered to their destinations. (Courtesy of Norfolk Southern.)

Norfolk & Western's rail yard at Lamberts Point looks fairly tranquil in this December 1931 photograph. Today, Norfolk Southern employees at Lamberts Point perform a variety of jobs that keep the facility and its vast array of tracks, railcars, and other equipment running smoothly. (Courtesy of Sargeant Memorial Collection, Norfolk Public Library.)

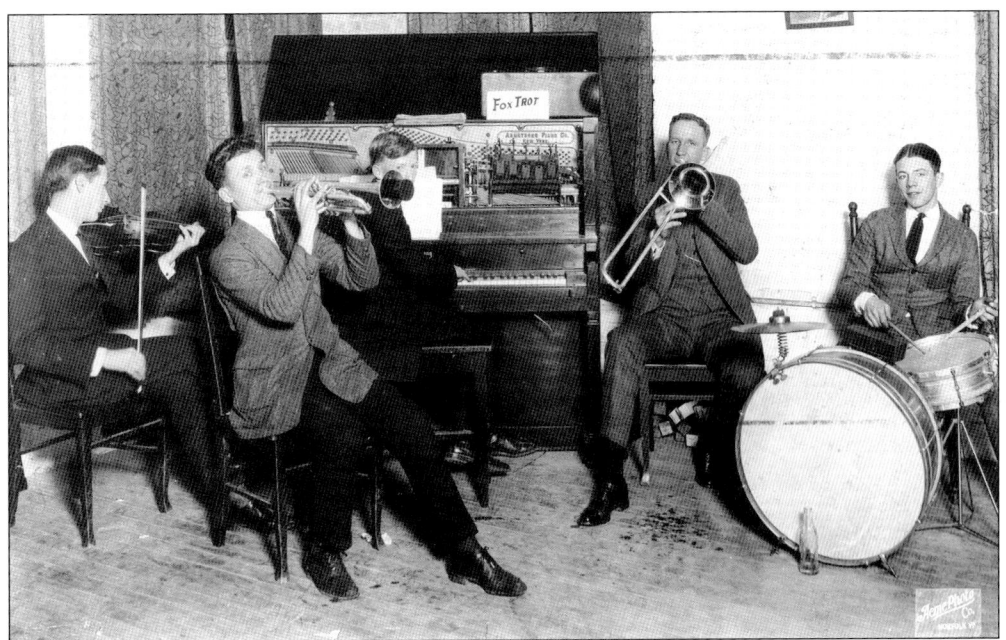

Before Norfolk Southern's official band The Lawmen formed in the 1950s, the Lamberts Point Shop Orchestra entertained their fellow railroaders. This photograph, taken around the 1930s, shows some of these musical employees. (Courtesy of Norfolk Southern.)

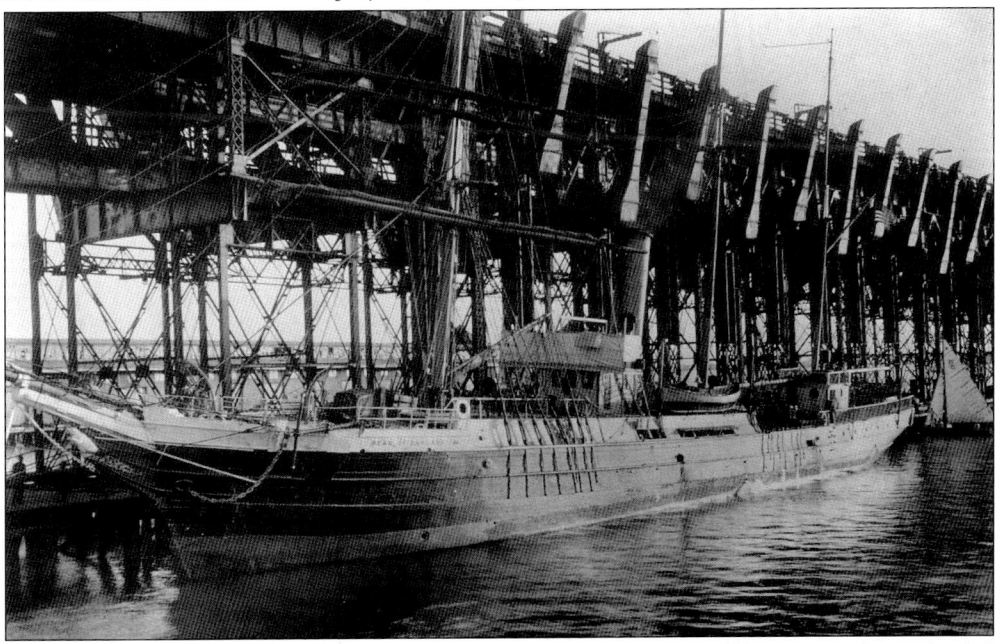

The *Bear of Oakland* was photographed at Coal Pier 4 in October 1933 as it was being loaded with coal in preparation for Adm. Richard E. Byrd's South Pole expedition. Also known as the SS *Bear*, the wooden-hulled, dual-powered steam schooner was built in Scotland and served the US Revenue Cutter Service, the US Coast Guard, and the US Navy before being transferred to the City of Oakland to be used as a museum ship. In 1932, Byrd purchased the vessel for his expedition to Antarctica and renamed it. (Courtesy of Norfolk Southern.)

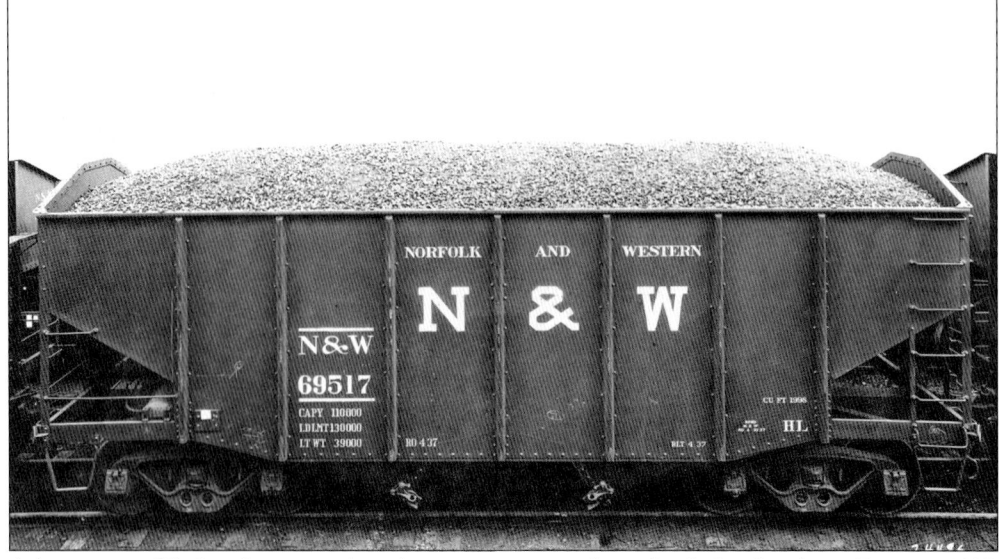

A hopper car filled with pea-sized coal awaits its turn to be unloaded at Lamberts Point in 1937. Today, coal arriving at Lamberts Point originates from mines in Virginia, West Virginia, Ohio, and Pennsylvania. Largely low-sulfur and low-ash metallurgical coal, the commodity goes to steel manufacturers in nearly three dozen countries, mainly in Europe, South America, and Asia. (Courtesy of Norfolk Southern.)

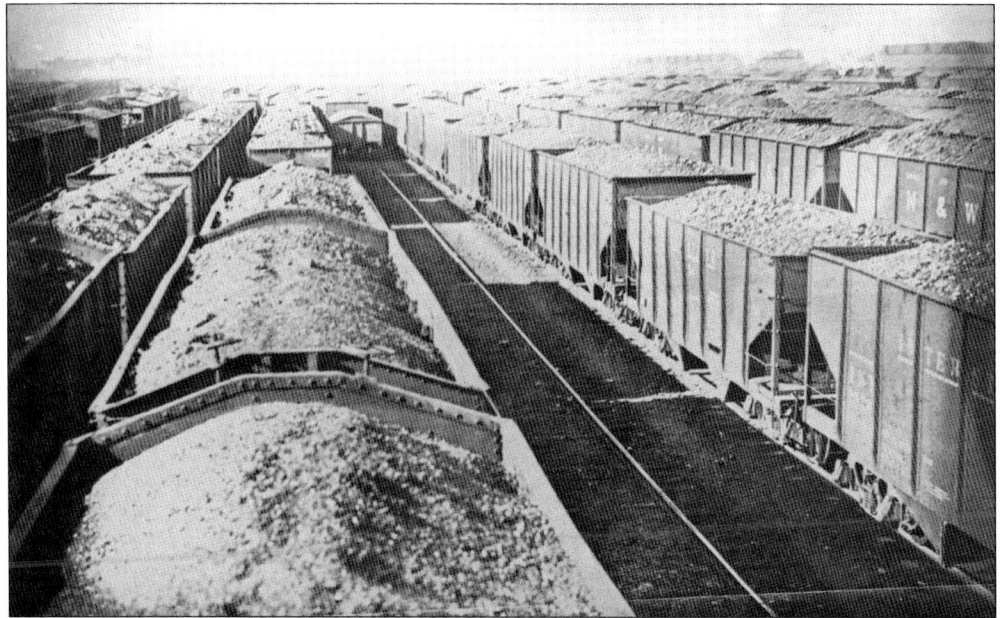

Trains are loaded with coal as far as the eye can see in this December 1926 photograph of the Lamberts Point rail yard. Coal is stored in railcars until transferred to ships. In the modern era, Norfolk Southern controls coal dust at Lamberts Point by spraying loaded coal cars with water and a dust suppression agent as they are overturned in the dumpers to transfer the coal to conveyor belts shielded by hoods and wind guards. Sprinklers hold down dust at transfer points along the conveyor belts, and vacuum trucks sweep coal from the deck of Coal Pier 6. (Courtesy of Sargeant Memorial Collection, Norfolk Public Library.)

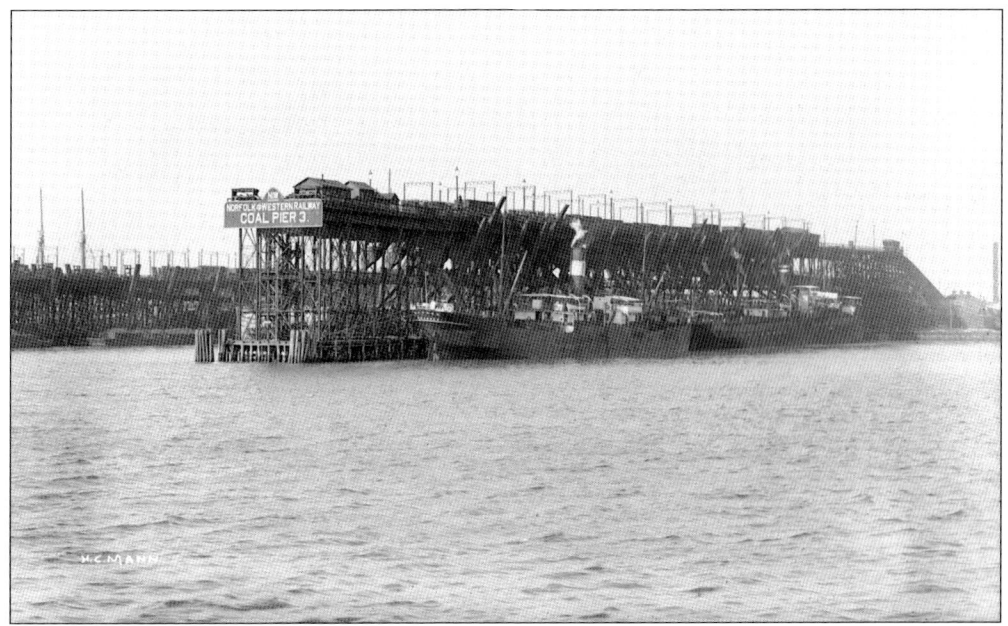

Ships from all over the world regularly dock at Lamberts Point, including this vessel from Norway loading coal at Coal Pier 3 in the early 1930s. Today, ship loaders at Coal Pier 6 can accommodate vessels with a beam of 175 feet and a draft of 74 feet. (Courtesy of Norfolk Southern.)

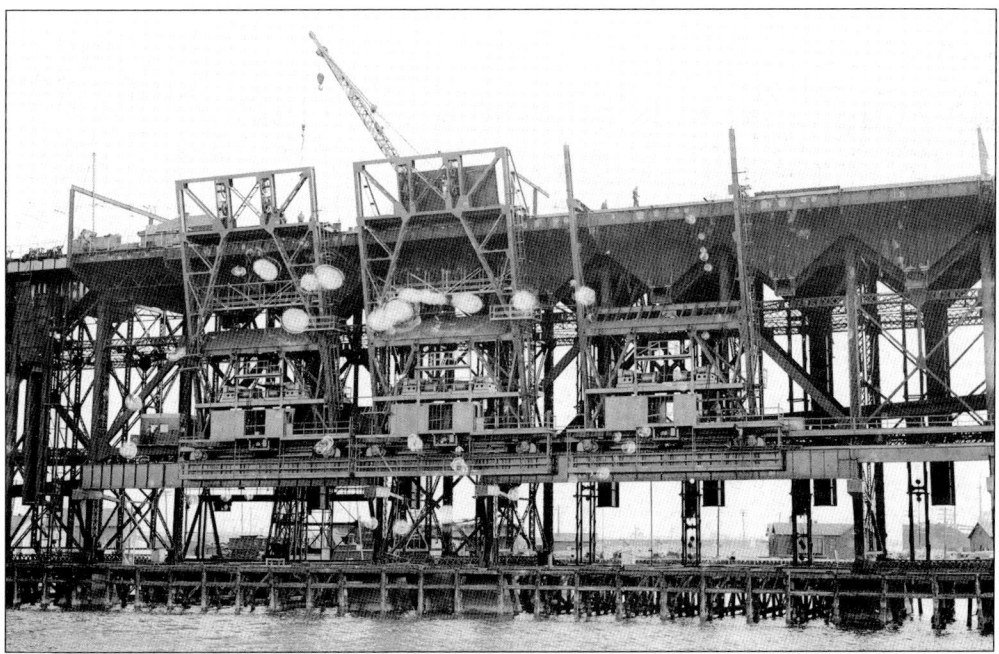

This September 1938 photograph shows Norfolk & Western's new sidewall coal loaders at Coal Pier 4. With the three sidewall loaders, the railroad could dump 100 tons of coal at a time into three holds of a ship. The loaders could be spaced to any length, extended or joined, and the electrically controlled dumpers shoveled the coal to one side or the other. The loaders and electrical machinery represented a nearly $700,000 investment by the railroad. (Courtesy of Sargeant Memorial Collection, Norfolk Public Library.)

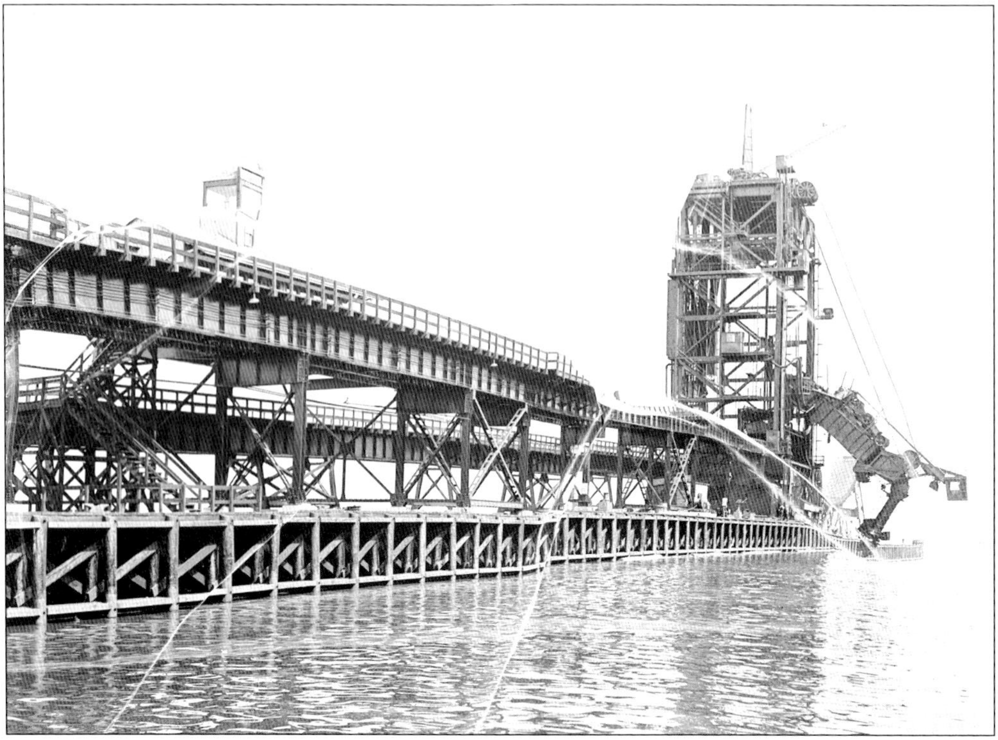

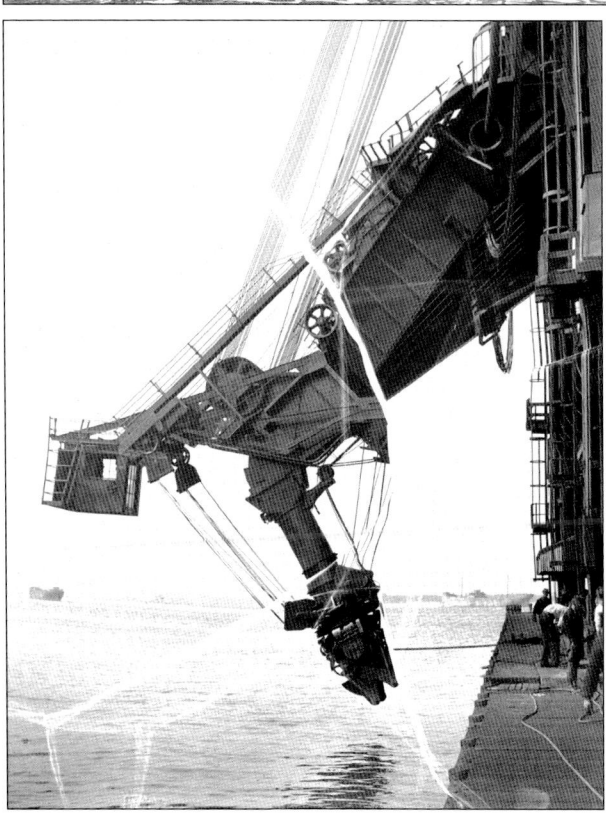

Lamberts Point's new Coal Pier 5, designed and built by Heyl and Patterson of Pittsburgh, Pennsylvania, is shown in these 1936 photographs. Construction on the $1.4 million pier began in 1935 and was completed in 1937. Coal Pier 5 was known as a lake type pier because structures of that sort were first widely used on the Great Lakes. The 1,000-foot-long pier had a capacity of about 50 seventy-ton hopper cars per hour. (Both, courtesy of Sargeant Memorial Collection, Norfolk Public Library.)

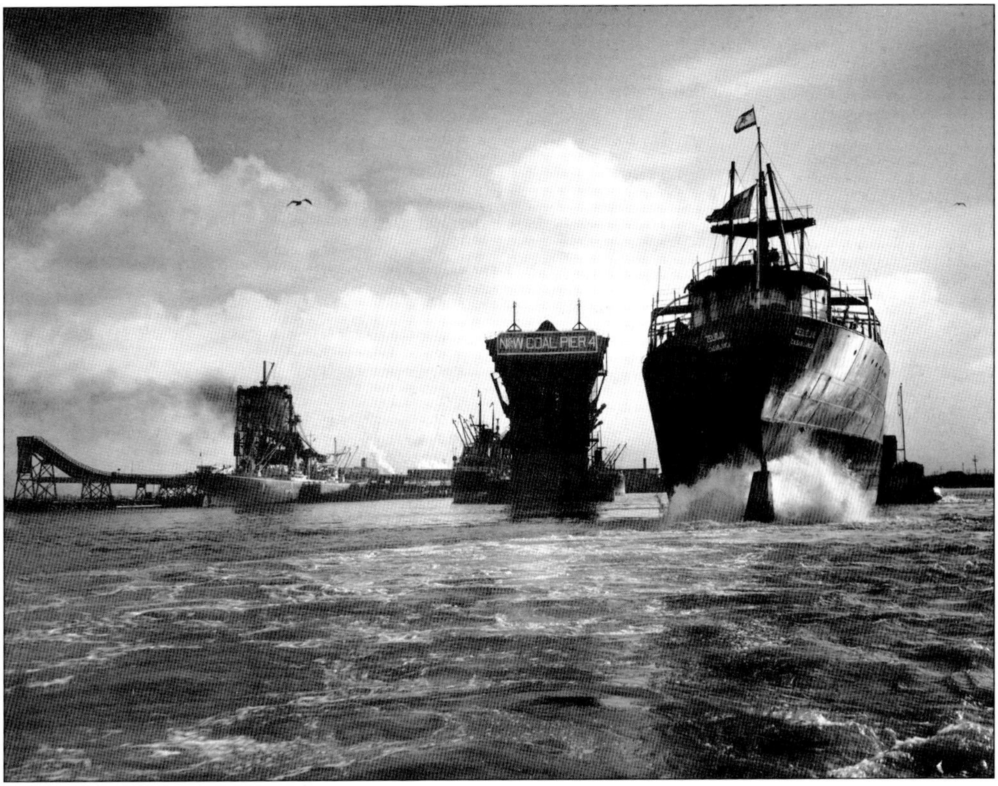

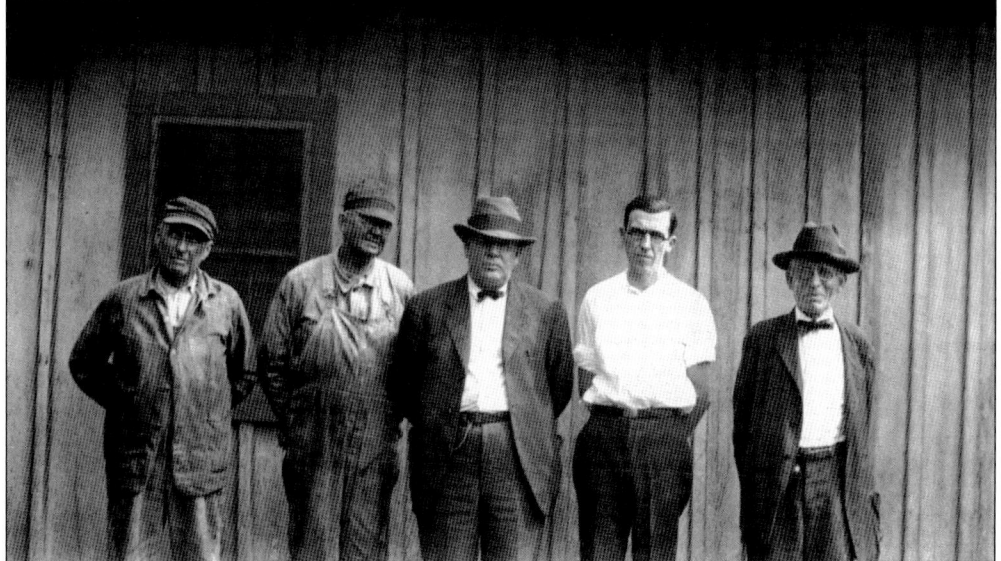

The vessel *Zelidja* from Casablanca is shown leaving Coal Pier 4 in this early-1950s photograph. Coal Pier 5 is in the background. Domestic and international coal shipments have declined on Norfolk Southern in recent years, but the commodity remains an important market for the railroad. (Courtesy of Norfolk Southern.)

Unidentified Lamberts Point employees are seen in this c. 1930s photograph. Today, about 400 people are employed at the Lamberts Point Coal Terminal. (Courtesy of Norfolk Southern.)

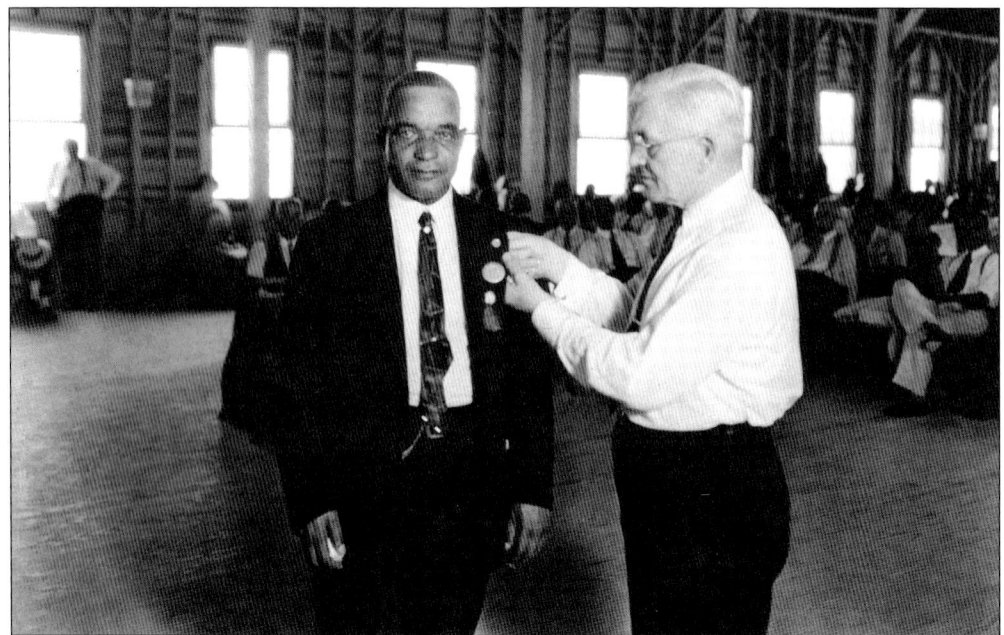

Lewis Wesley White (1865–1953) received his 50-year diamond service pin from W.H. Johnson, general agent and pier superintendent of terminals in Norfolk, during a July 1934 meeting of 250 African American railroad veterans at Ocean Breeze, a Chesapeake Bay resort in what is now the Baylake Pines section of Virginia Beach. White, who joined Norfolk & Western in 1885, had been a pier brakeman at Lamberts Point since 1891. When Johnson presented the 50-year pin to White, he noted, "This is a record which is attained by few, and I assure you that your long, faithful and loyal service is appreciated." White retired in 1935. (Courtesy of Norfolk Southern.)

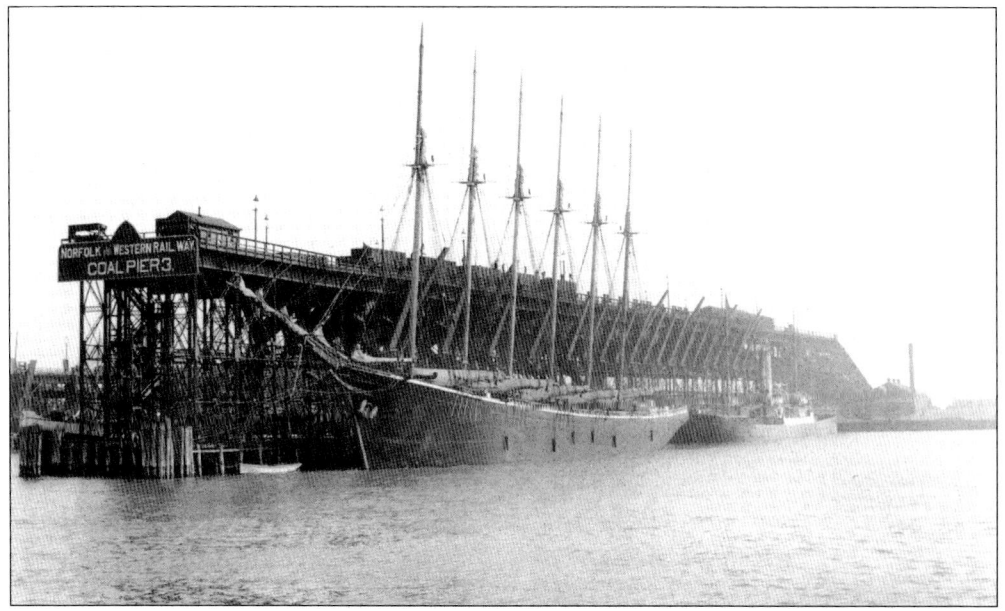

This 1930s photograph shows the busy Coal Pier 3 at Lamberts Point. The piers were advertised as a short trolley ride from the central part of Norfolk and visible from the docks of various steamships entering the city. (Courtesy of Norfolk Southern.)

A Norfolk & Western train makes its way into the Lamberts Point Coal Terminal in this 1950s photograph. The Lamberts Point facility can hold up to 6,500 coal cars on 150 miles of track. (Courtesy of Norfolk Southern.)

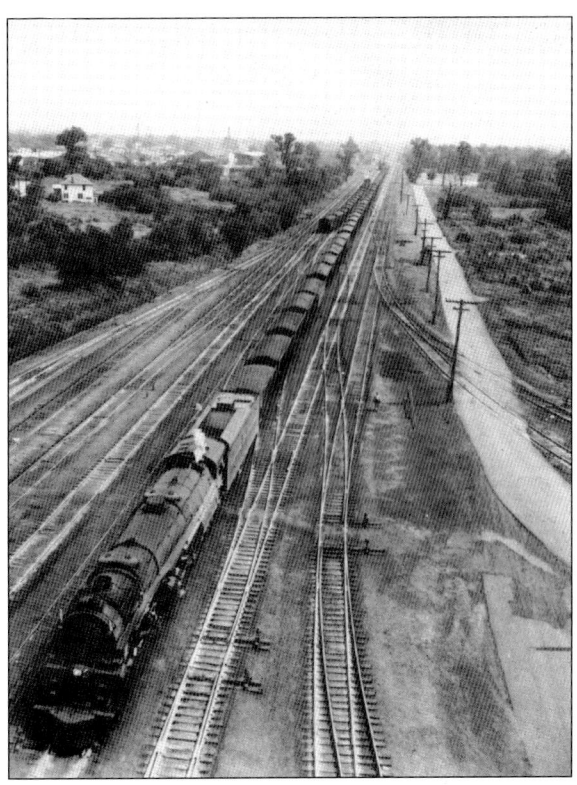

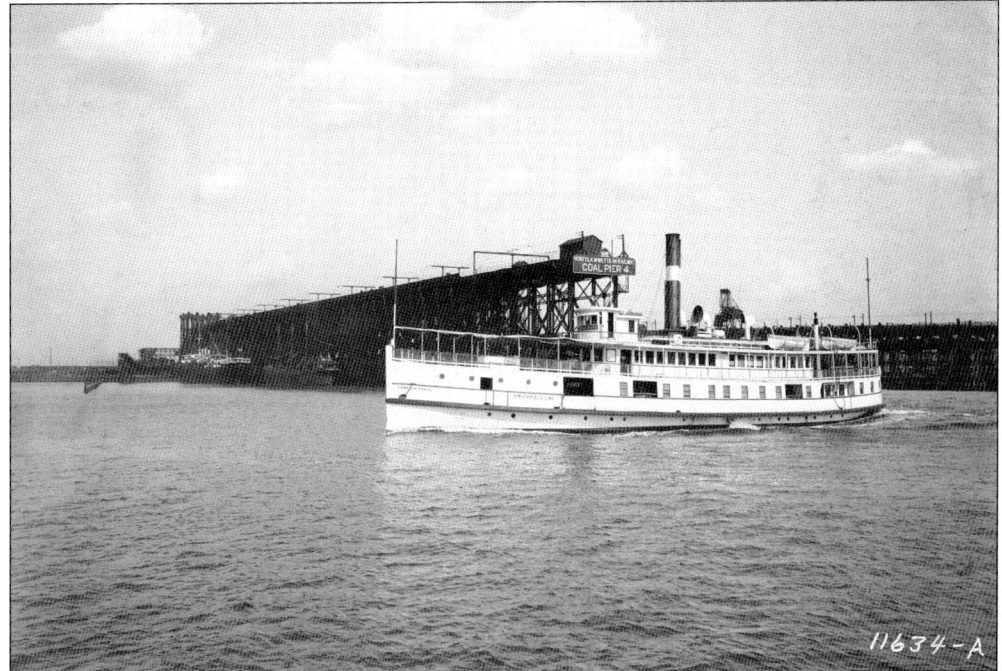

The Smithfield Line ferry *Hampton Roads* cruises past Coal Pier 4 in this mid-20th-century photograph. Before the opening of the Downtown Tunnel in 1952, ferries transported passengers and vehicles from Norfolk to Portsmouth on the Elizabeth River. (Courtesy of Norfolk Southern.)

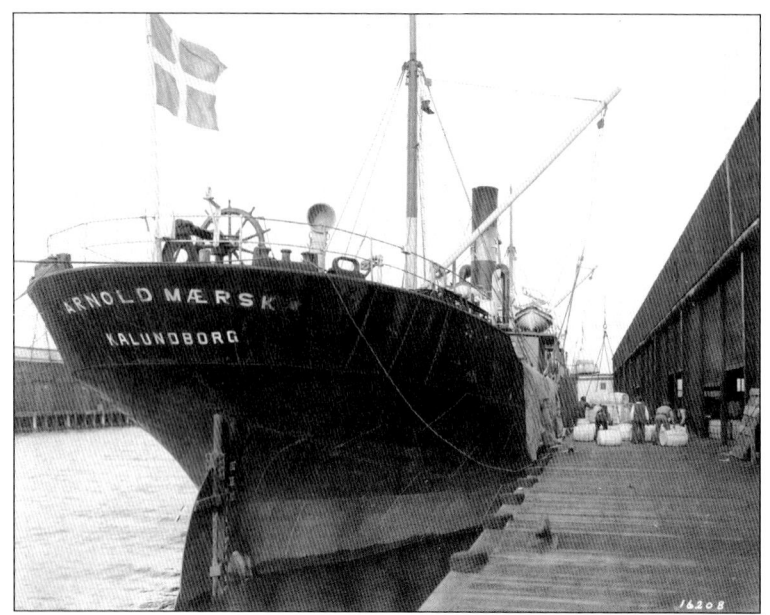

In this 1931 photograph, barrels of apples are loaded onto the vessel *Arnold Maersk* docked at Pier L. Pier L is part of Lambert's Point Docks, a Norfolk Southern subsidiary that has served shippers, manufacturers, and brokers for more than 65 years. (Courtesy of Norfolk Southern.)

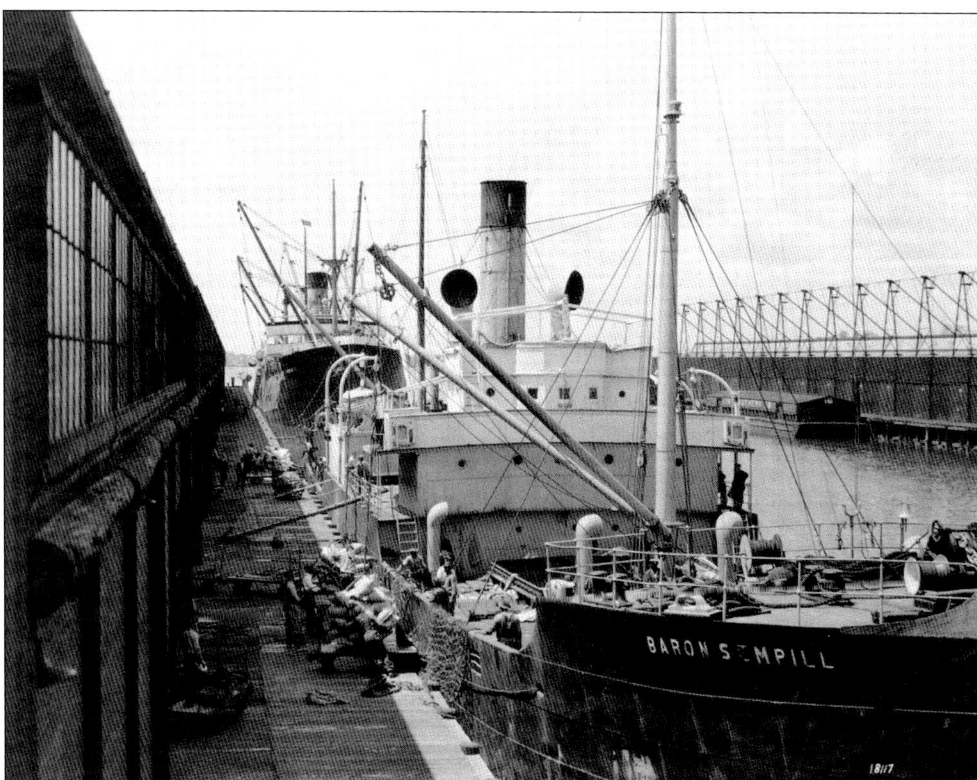

Sugar and tobacco are unloaded at Pier L on Lambert's Point Docks in this May 1933 photograph. Norfolk & Western cut a 70-foot-wide, 21-foot-deep channel in the Elizabeth River in 1884, which allowed larger vessels to navigate the river. (Courtesy of Norfolk Southern.)

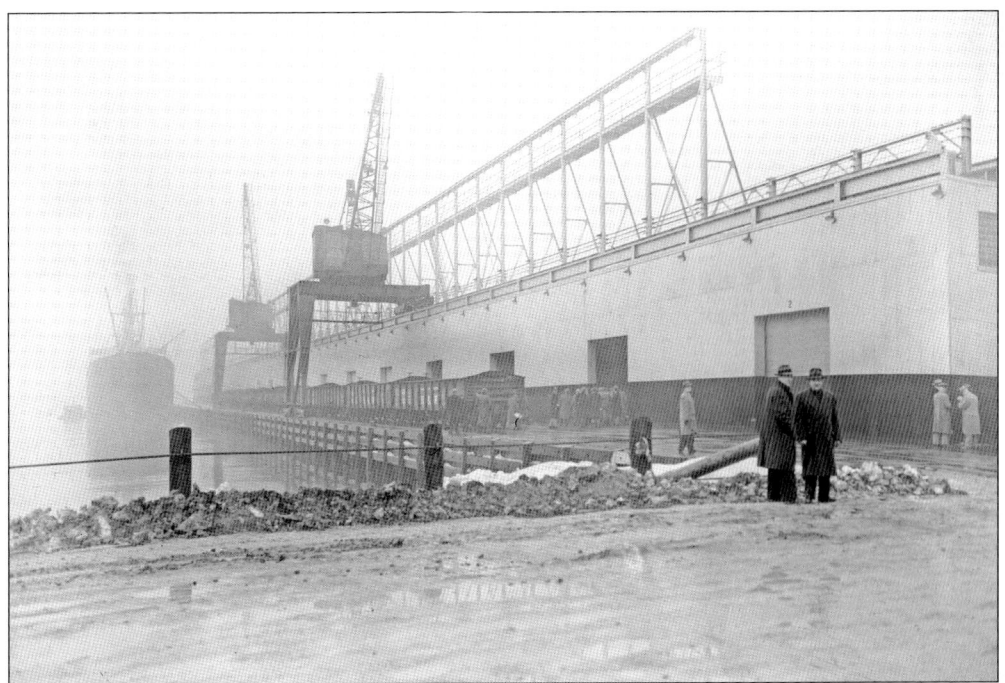

Norfolk & Western called Pier N the king of its five merchandise piers at Lambert's Point Docks. The $6 million, 1,000-foot pier opened in early 1948 and was the longest single-deck freight pier on the Atlantic seaboard. (Courtesy of Sargeant Memorial Collection, Norfolk Public Library.)

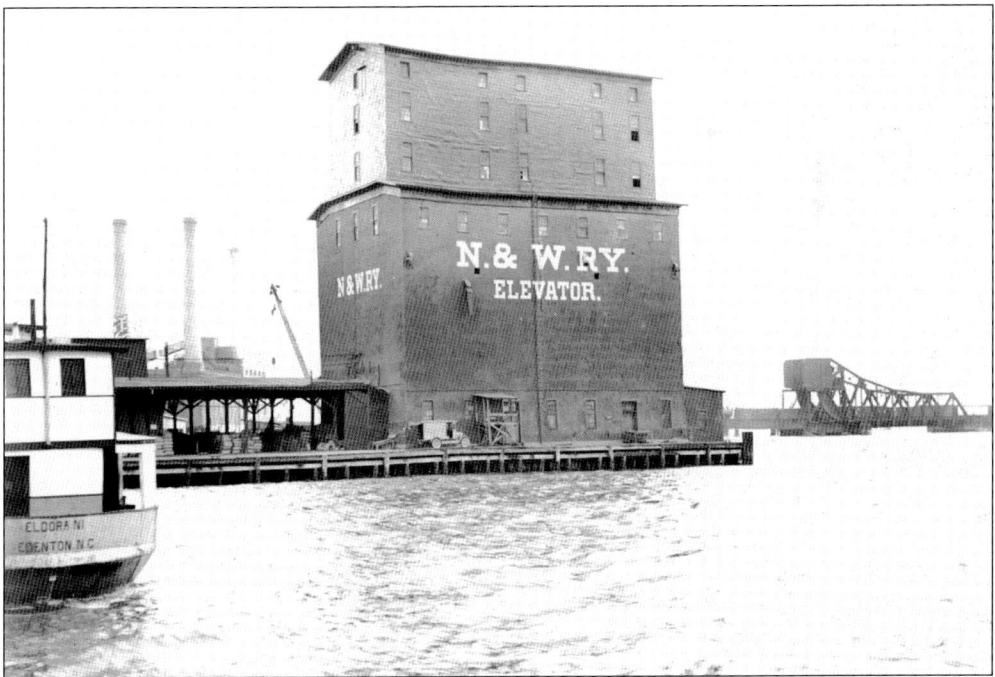

Norfolk & Western's grain elevator at Lamberts Point is highlighted in this March 1935 photograph. At left is the cargo ship *Eldora Ni* of Edenton, North Carolina. (Courtesy of Sargeant Memorial Collection, Norfolk Public Library.)

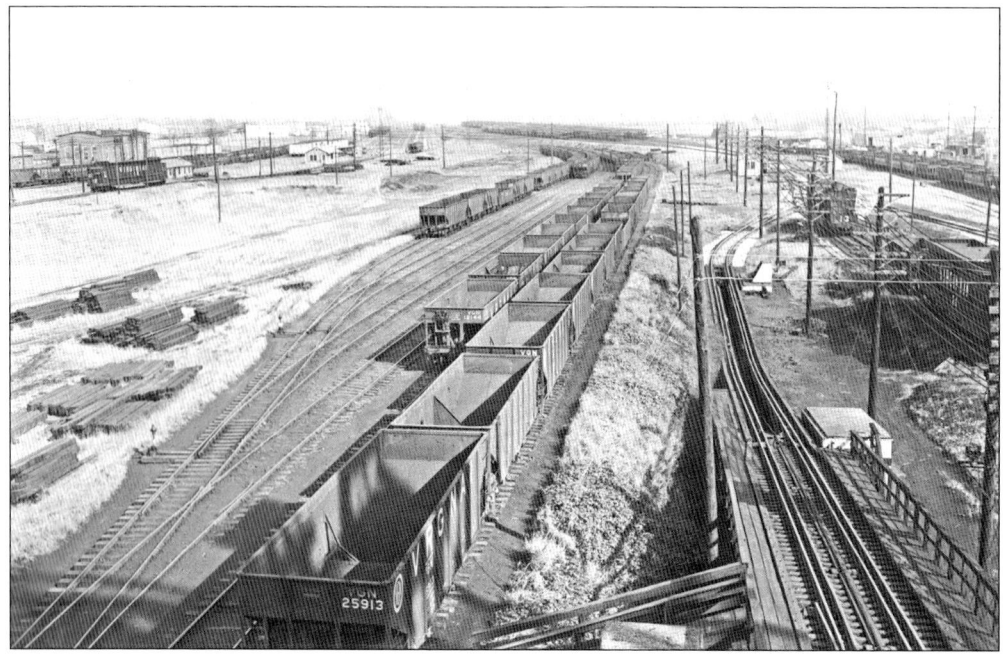

Empty coal hoppers are shown in this February 1950 photograph of the rail yard at Lamberts Point. The growth in US coal exports, along with the acquisition of the Virginian Railway in 1959, began to strain Norfolk & Western's piers and rail yard, leading the railroad to develop plans for a new coal pier. (Courtesy of Sargeant Memorial Collection, Norfolk Public Library.)

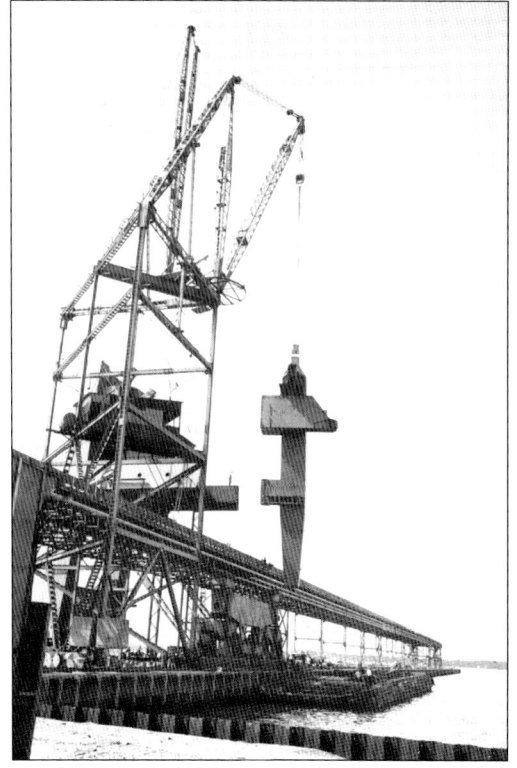

Construction on Norfolk & Western's $25 million Coal Pier 6 began in 1961. Initially 1,600 feet long and 82 feet wide, the pier was built to meet demands associated with the growing increase in US coal exports. The high-capacity pier can blend various types of coal to precise mixtures as loaded. (Courtesy of Norfolk Southern.)

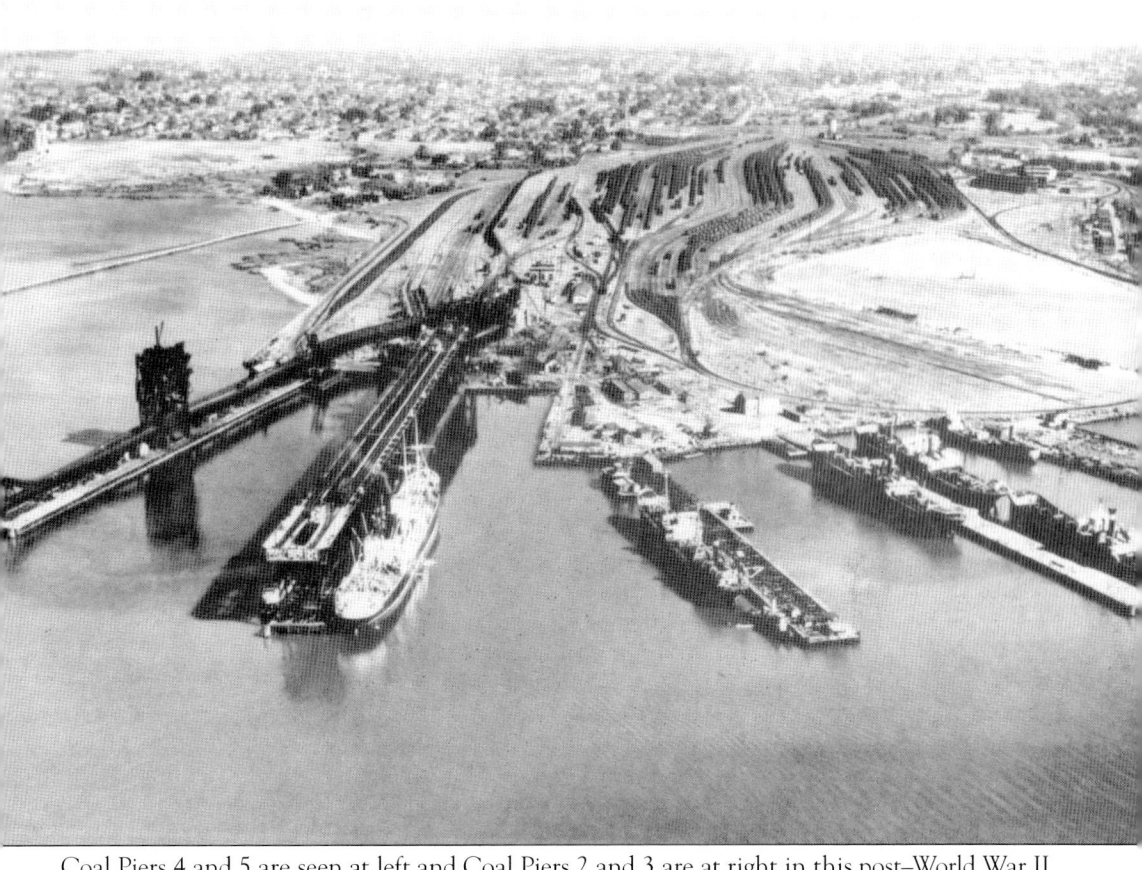
Coal Piers 4 and 5 are seen at left and Coal Piers 2 and 3 are at right in this post–World War II photograph. Coal Pier 1 had been demolished by that time. (Courtesy of Kurt Reisweber.)

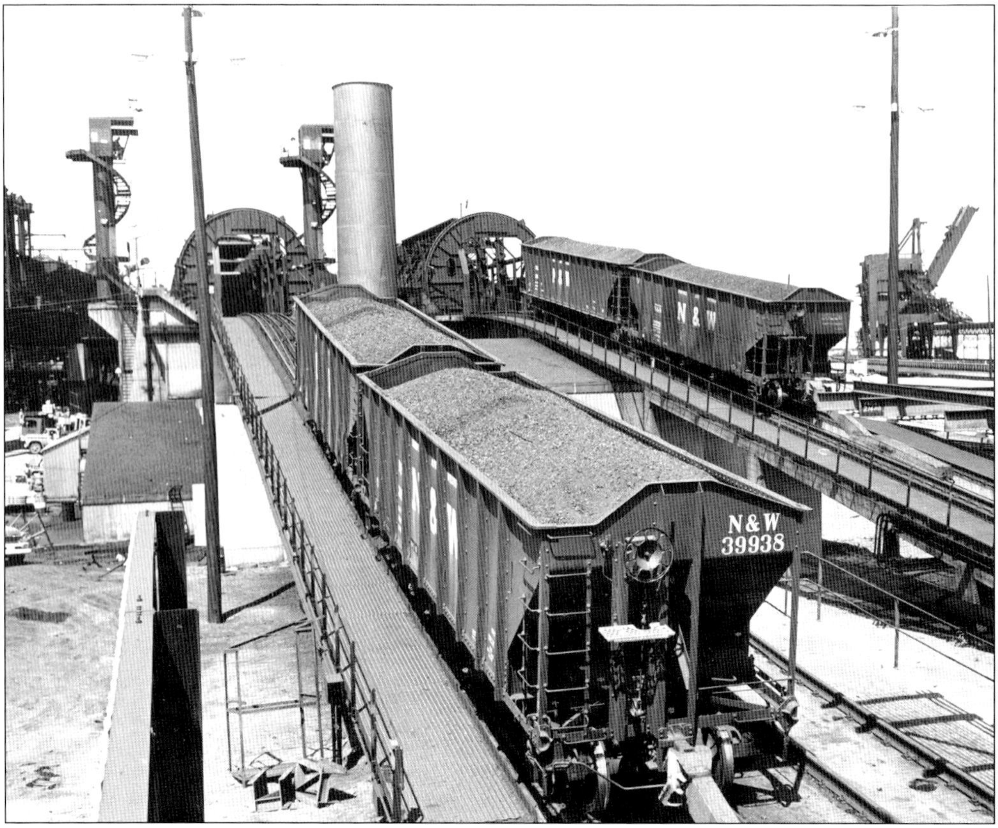

Coal hoppers enter the new Coal Pier 6 in 1963. Opened in December 1962, Coal Pier 6 was completed the following July. The facility was formally dedicated on September 18, 1963, with a gala celebration that included Virginia governor Albertis S. Harrison Jr., Norfolk mayor Roy B. Martin Jr., and representatives from 23 nations that used Norfolk & Western coal. (Courtesy of Norfolk Southern.)

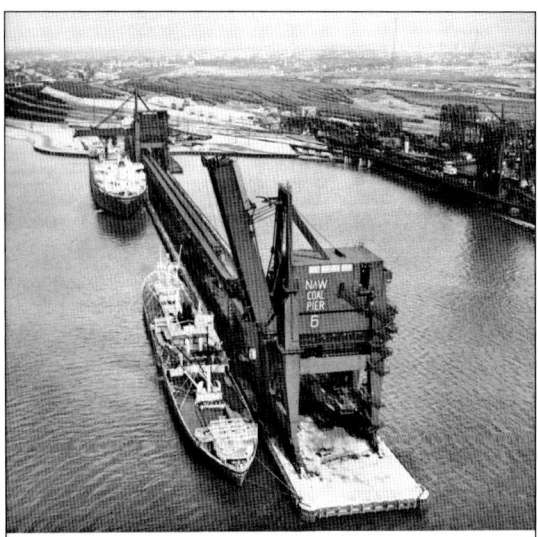

This 1960s advertisement promoted Norfolk & Western's new $25 million Coal Pier 6. At the time, it was the railroad's largest capital outlay for a single facility. (Courtesy of Norfolk Southern.)

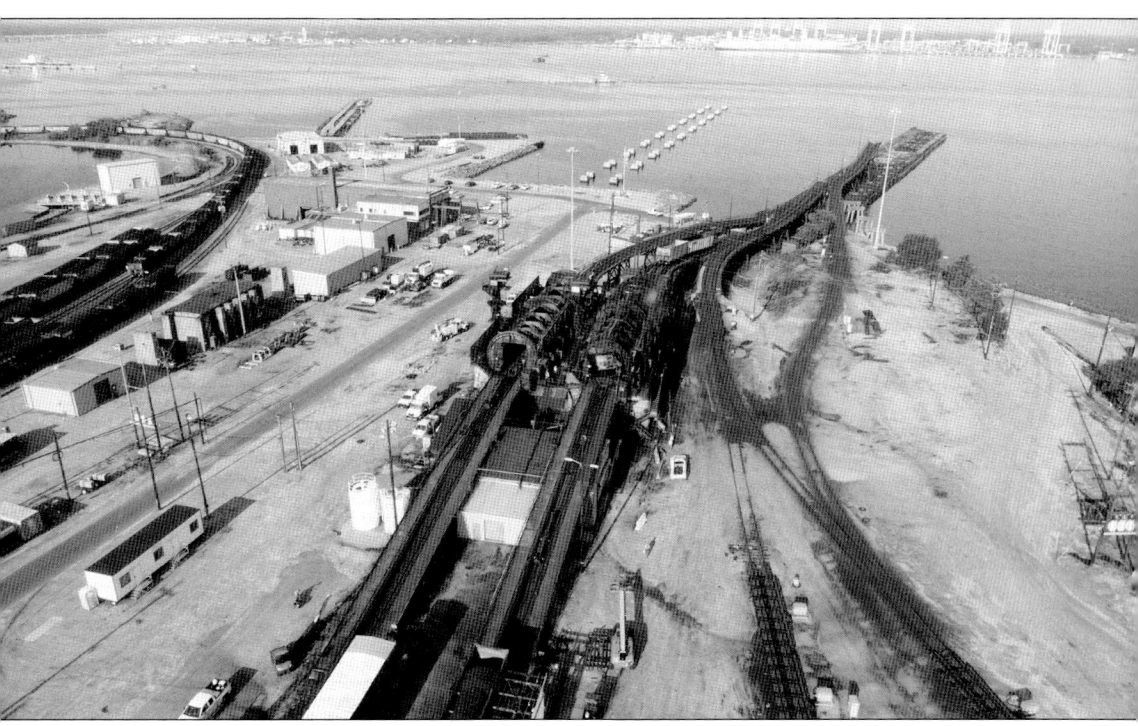

A train carrying coal is headed to Pier 6 at Lamberts Point Coal Terminal. The pier remains the northern hemisphere's largest, fastest, and most efficient transloading facility. Until the space shuttle's moving tower was built, the pier's two 18-story customer loading towers were the largest pieces of moving machinery on earth. (Courtesy of Norfolk Southern.)

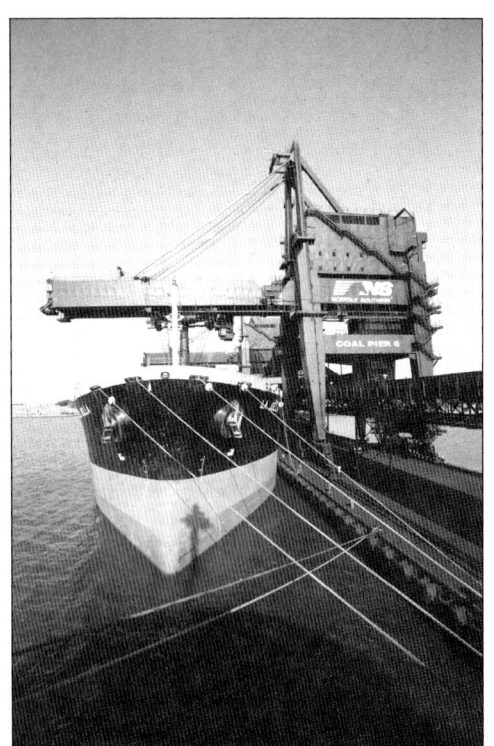

Known as a "pier without peer," the 1,850-foot-long Coal Pier 6 provides matchless quality to the global metallurgical and thermal coal markets. It takes an average of 24 hours to load one ship with a typical 80,000 tons of coal. The pier dumped its billionth ton of coal in 1999, becoming the only facility in the world to reach that milestone. (Courtesy of Norfolk Southern.)

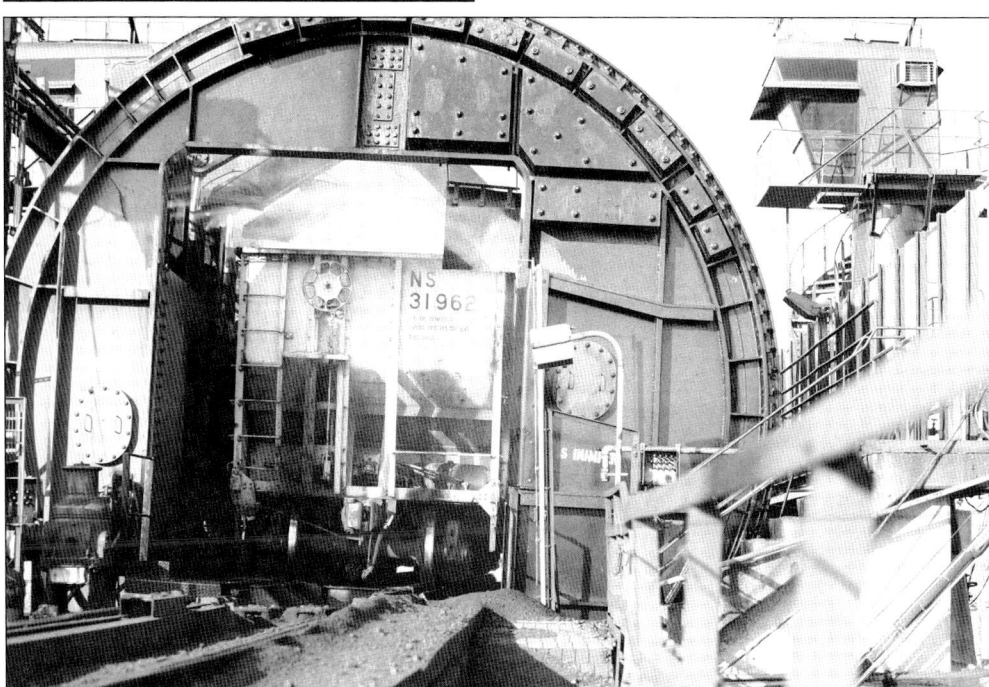

Coal Pier 6 was designed and built mainly to load ships bound for steel mills around the world with high-quality, metallurgical coal from the central Appalachian coalfields. The pier's twin shiploaders rise 182 feet above the Elizabeth River. With both dumpers and shiploaders operating, Coal Pier 6 can handle up to 8,000 tons of coal per hour. (Courtesy of Norfolk Southern.)

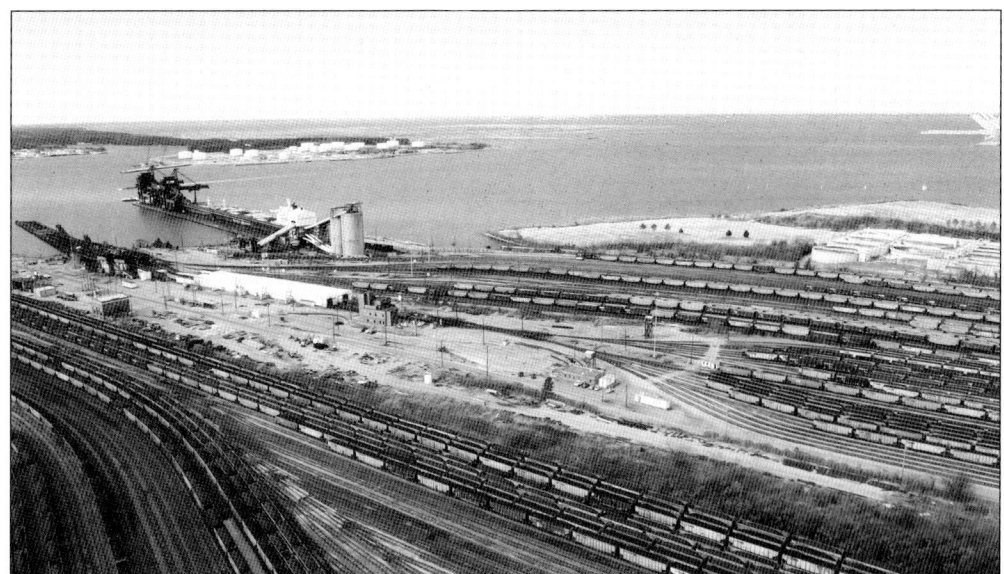

Coal operations at Lamberts Point cover 400 acres, while the entire facility can hold approximately 6,500 railcars on 150 miles of track. During World War II, the US Navy and US Marine Corps leased space at Lamberts Point's piers and warehouses. (Courtesy of Norfolk Southern.)

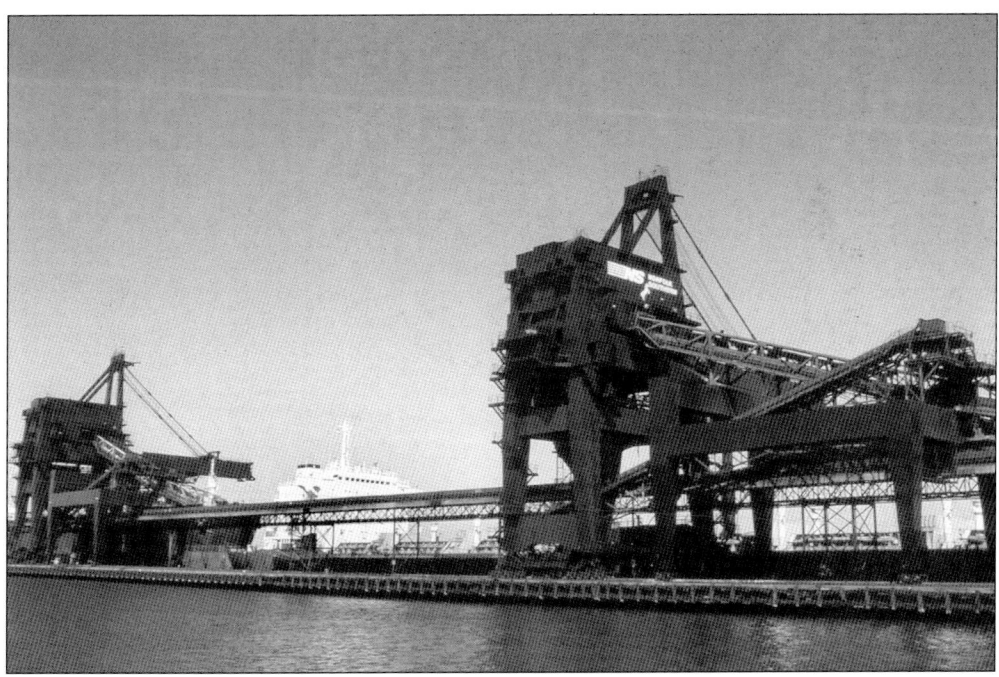

Each of the twin shiploaders on Coal Pier 6 weighs 2,400 tons and rolls on 96 rail wheels. They are among the largest pieces of moving machinery in the world. The pier has access to a deep 50-foot channel in Hampton Roads that allows modern vessels to make productive use of their large holds. (Courtesy of Norfolk Southern.)

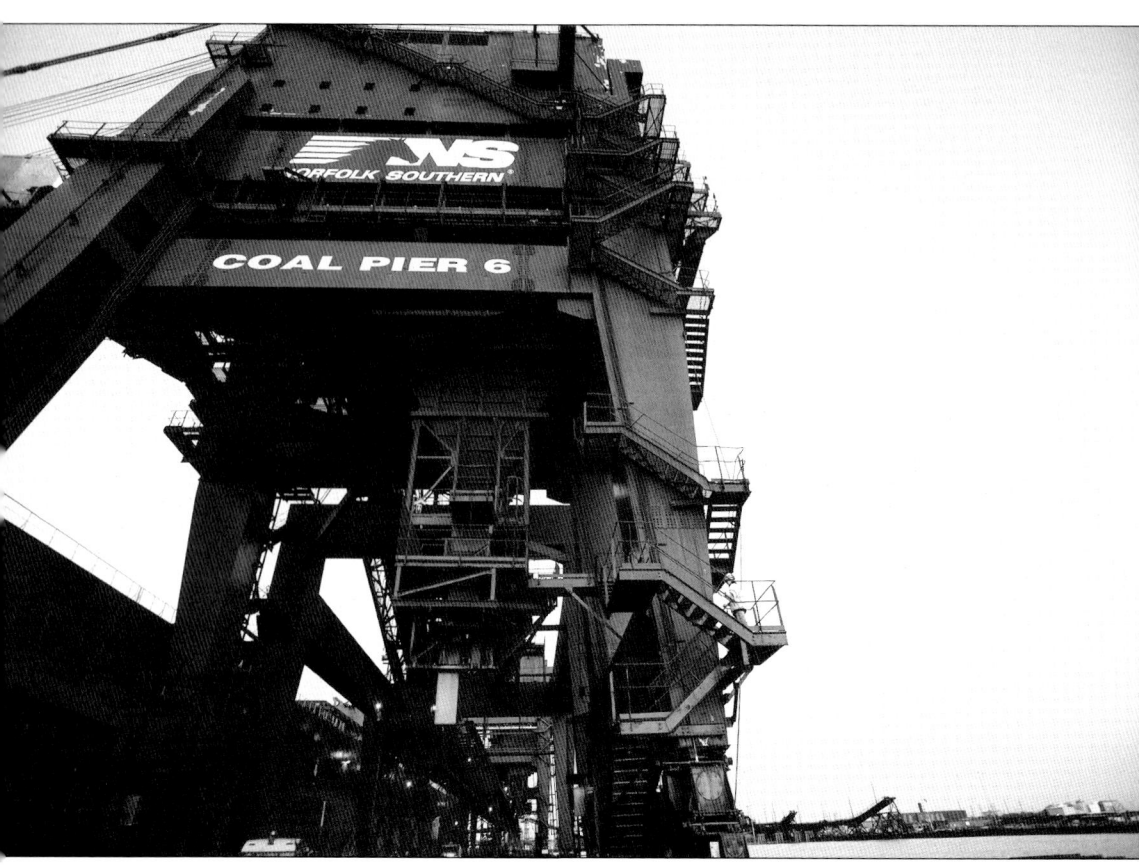

When Coal Pier 6 celebrated its 50th anniversary in September 2013, Norfolk Southern president and CEO Wick Moorman credited the resourcefulness and confidence of those who designed and built the facility. "The people who built this pier didn't make small plans," Moorman said. "They had vision. They had foresight." (Courtesy of Norfolk Southern.)

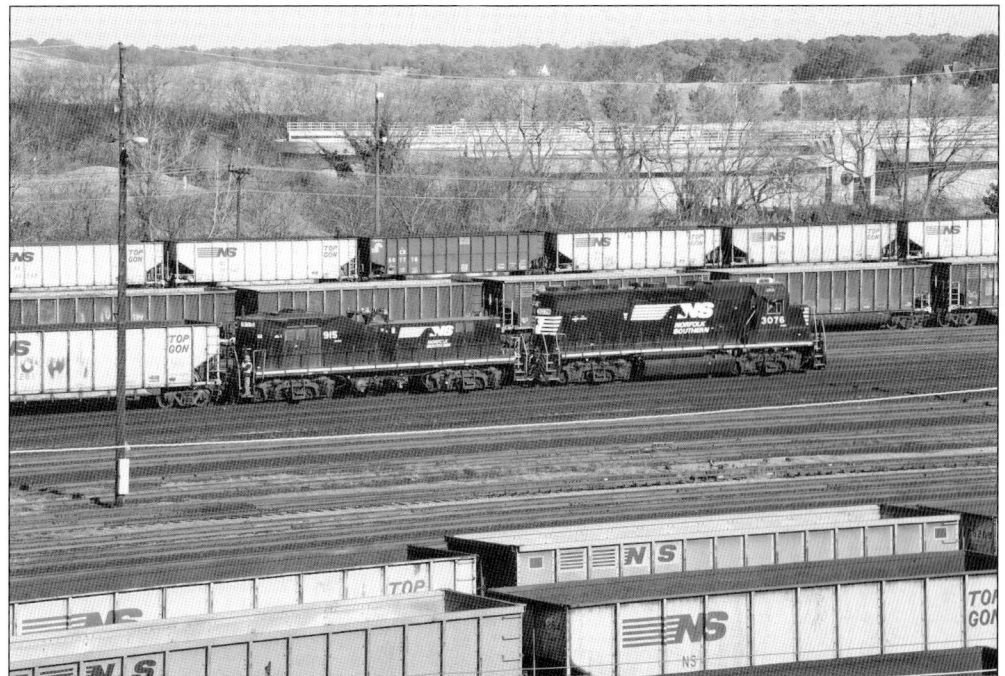

After emptying their contents onto overseas-bound ships, gondolas prepare to make their way from Lamberts Point back to the Pocahontas coalfields led by Norfolk Southern locomotive No. 3076. Norfolk Southern has a fleet of more than 21,000 coal cars, including manual hoppers and gondolas for rotary dump service, high cubic capacity coke hoppers, and air-operated quick discharge hoppers. The railroad rebuilds or replaces its oldest hoppers and gondolas to ensure continued quality. (Courtesy of Norfolk Southern.)

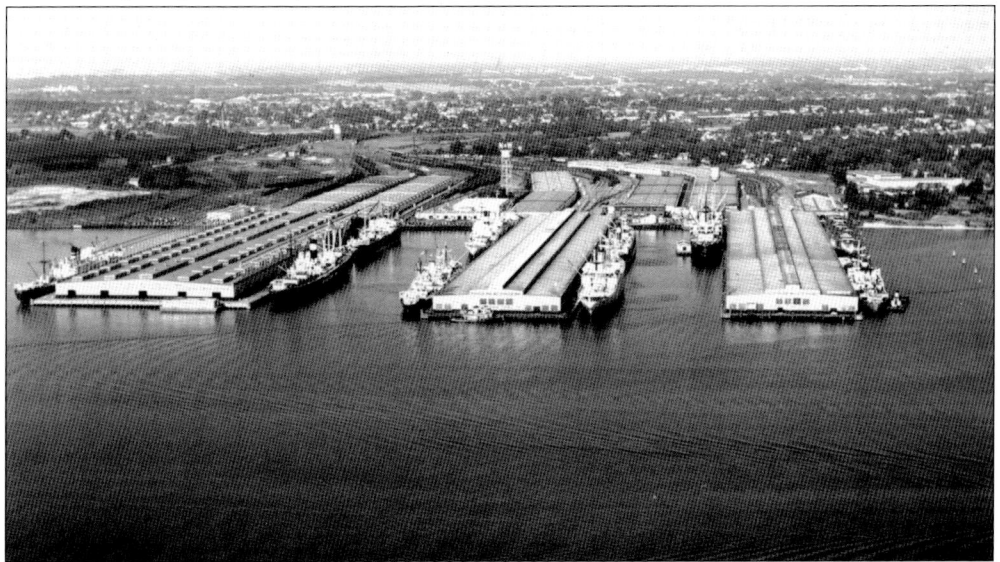

Norfolk Southern's subsidiary, Lambert's Point Docks, is one of Virginia's largest break-bulk marine terminals. The 117-acre, full-service facility specializes in rubber, wood products, machinery, and project freight and can move more than a half million tons of cargo annually. (Courtesy of Norfolk Southern.)

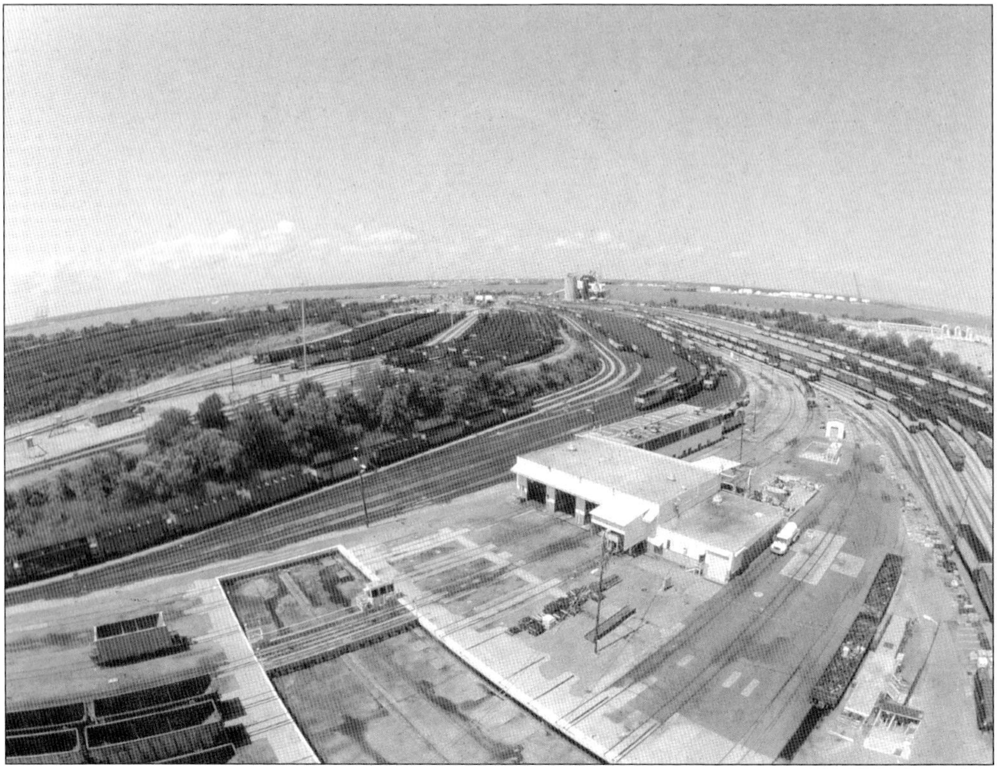

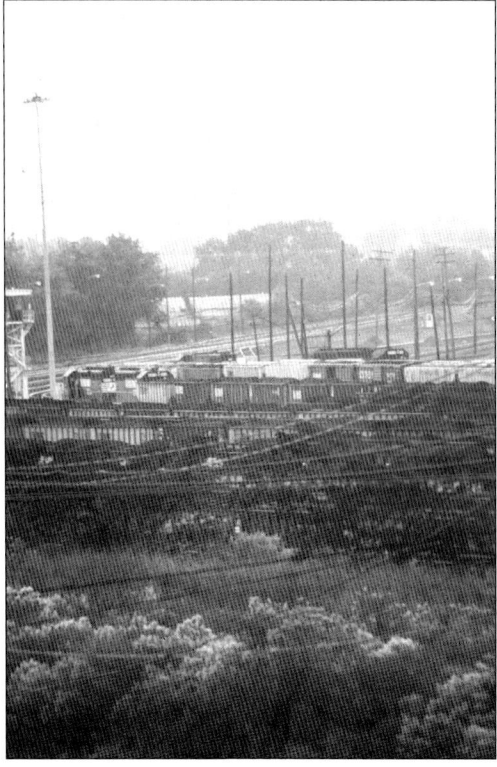

Norfolk Southern's 38th Street Car Shop, built in 1962, is in the foreground in this aerial photograph. The railroad's coal transloading facility is in the background. Carmen employed at the shop inspect Norfolk Southern railcars for defects and make repairs. (Courtesy of Norfolk Southern.)

Downtown Norfolk is seen in the background of this 2007 sunrise photograph of railcars at Lamberts Point. In an effort to ensure safe, environmentally responsible operations at Lamberts Point, Norfolk Southern has adopted innovative practices to minimize impacts to the environment and neighborhoods surrounding the facility. (Courtesy of Norfolk Southern.)

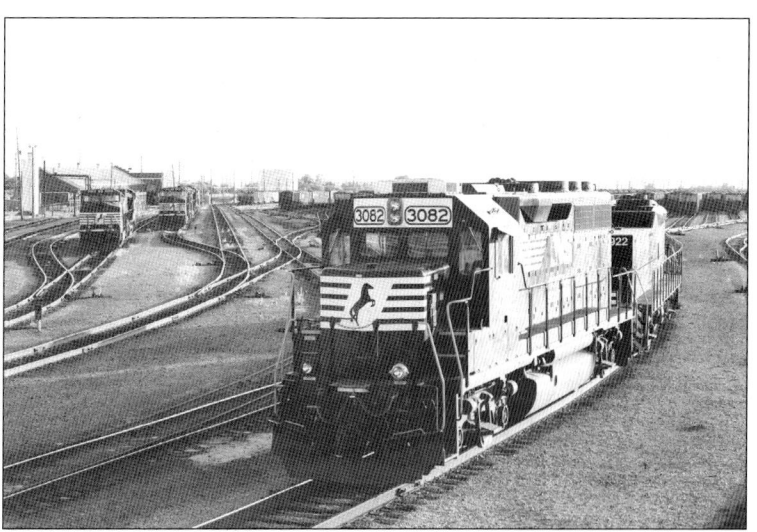

In this 2010 photograph, Norfolk Southern locomotive No. 3082 is pictured in the rail yard at Lamberts Point after delivering coal from the Pocahontas coalfields. The unit has since been retired. (Courtesy of Norfolk Southern.)

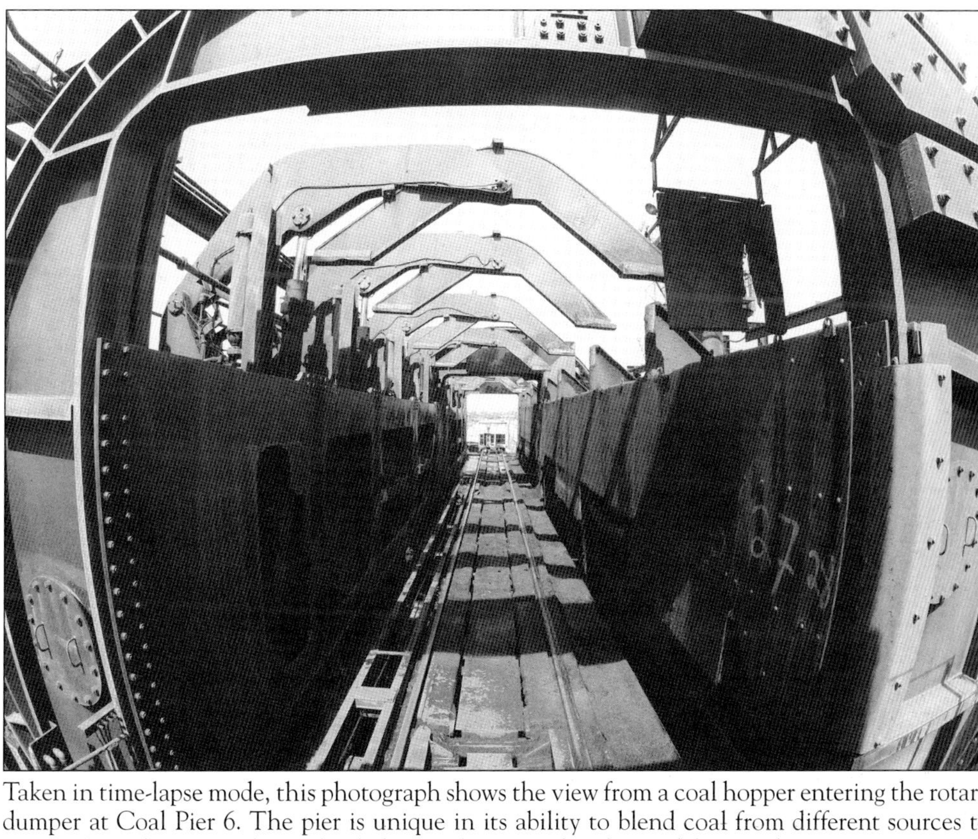

Taken in time-lapse mode, this photograph shows the view from a coal hopper entering the rotary dumper at Coal Pier 6. The pier is unique in its ability to blend coal from different sources to precise formulas as it is being loaded onto ships. Coal is dumped from railcars into a conveyor system feeding directly into ships' holds as opposed to other facilities that store coal on the ground rather than in railcars. This is a valuable service to receivers of metallurgical coal, who have exacting blend requirements and can receive the coal ready to use off the ship. (Courtesy of Norfolk Southern.)

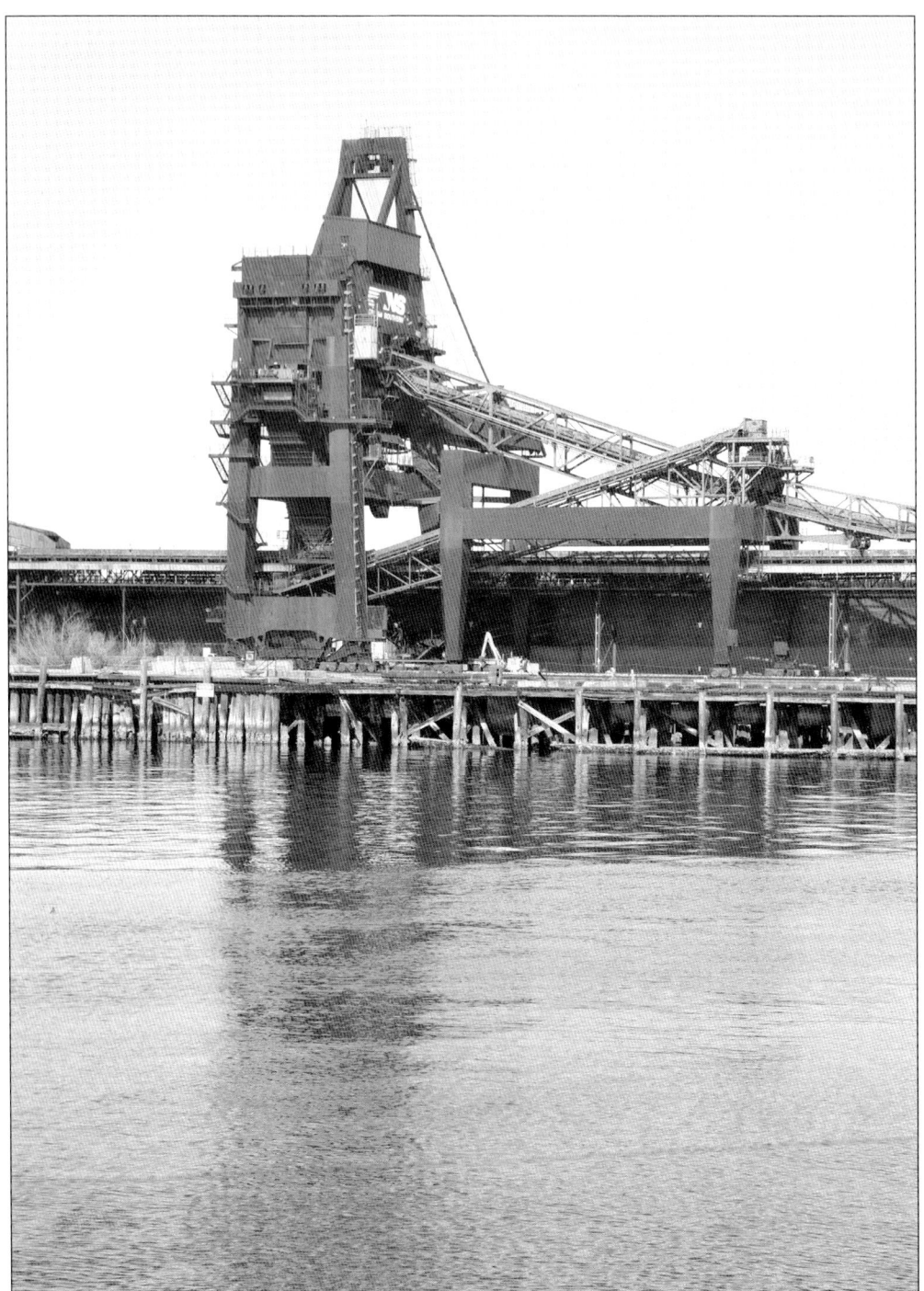

The labyrinthine structure of the massive Coal Pier 6 includes an operations center opened in 2012. Along with implementing innovative practices to minimize the impacts of coal on the environment and neighborhoods surrounding the terminal, Norfolk Southern is also a longtime participant in community endeavors to restore water quality on the Elizabeth River. (Courtesy of Norfolk Southern.)

Three

SOUTHERN RAILWAY AND ITS HAMPTON ROADS LINES

Southern Railway's heritage includes almost 150 predecessor lines, beginning with the South Carolina Canal & Rail Road chartered in 1827. The Southern Railway that merged with Norfolk & Western was formed in 1894 as part of the reorganization of the Richmond & Danville Railroad and the East Tennessee, Virginia & Georgia Railway and absorbed another 68 railroad companies by the turn of the 20th century.

After obtaining trackage rights to the Elizabeth River port from the Atlantic Coast Line Railroad, Southern built a pier at Pinners Point in Portsmouth in 1896. Portsmouth Marine Terminal is now located on the site of Southern's shipping terminal. Southern also had freight houses across the Elizabeth River in Norfolk.

In 1974, the original Norfolk Southern Railway became the last railroad to join Southern's family. That railroad traced its origins to January 1870 when the Elizabeth City & Norfolk Railroad Company was chartered in North Carolina. Organizers then spent a decade convincing northern industrial leaders to provide capital to construct the railroad connecting the two cities. The first train finally took the 46-mile trip on a roadbed running parallel to the Dismal Swamp on May 26, 1881. Later that year, the line was extended to Edenton, North Carolina, and then to Goldsboro, North Carolina. In early 1883, the North Carolina General Assembly provoked the wrath of Elizabeth City residents by changing the railroad's name to Norfolk Southern to more accurately reflect the company's efforts to expand regionally.

Encountering financial difficulties, the company entered receivership and reorganized in 1891 as the Norfolk & Southern Railroad Company and offered rail and steamboat service to southeastern Virginia and northeastern North Carolina. Passengers disembarked at the railroad's Berkley station and traveled by ferry across the Elizabeth River to downtown Norfolk.

In 1900, Norfolk & Southern purchased the Norfolk, Virginia Beach & Southern Railroad, which ran steam trains from Norfolk to the Virginia Beach oceanfront where it played a significant role in the development of the resort area. Following a series of mergers, the railroad ran from Norfolk to Raleigh, with branches to Virginia Beach and Suffolk and southeastern North Carolina. The company went into receivership in 1908, emerging two years later as the Norfolk Southern Railroad Company. The original Norfolk Southern was headquartered in Norfolk until 1961 when the company moved its corporate offices to Raleigh, North Carolina.

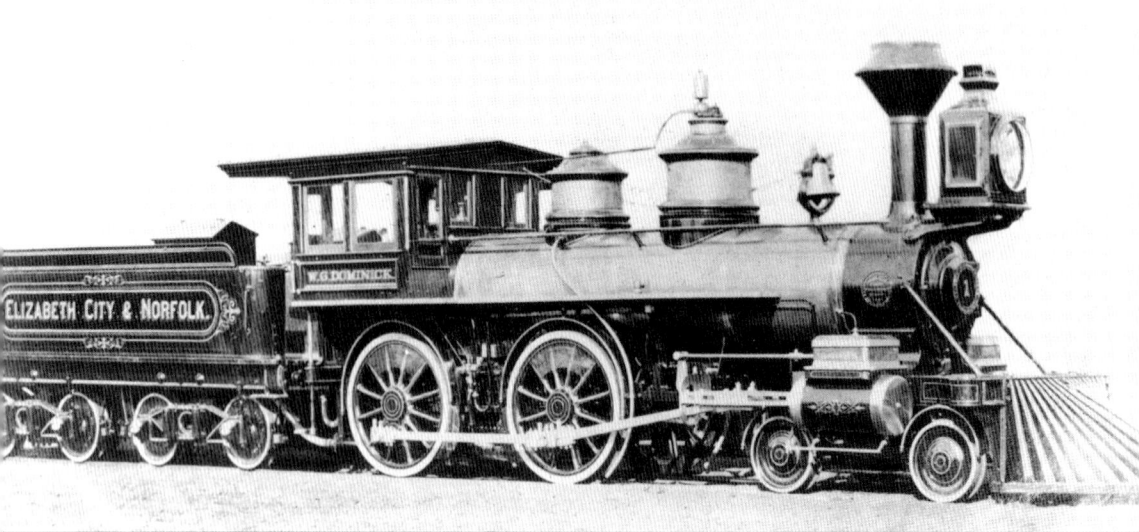

The Elizabeth City & Norfolk Railroad completed tracks from Norfolk to Edenton, North Carolina, in 1881. Two years later, its name was changed to Norfolk Southern. The railroad initially entered receivership in 1889 and was purchased and reorganized in May 1891 as the Norfolk & Southern Railroad. By then, it had acquired Norfolk & Western trackage rights over the Elizabeth River into Norfolk. The Norfolk & Southern also acquired the Albemarle & Pantego Railroad from the John L. Roper Lumber Company in Washington County, North Carolina. (Courtesy of Kurt Reisweber.)

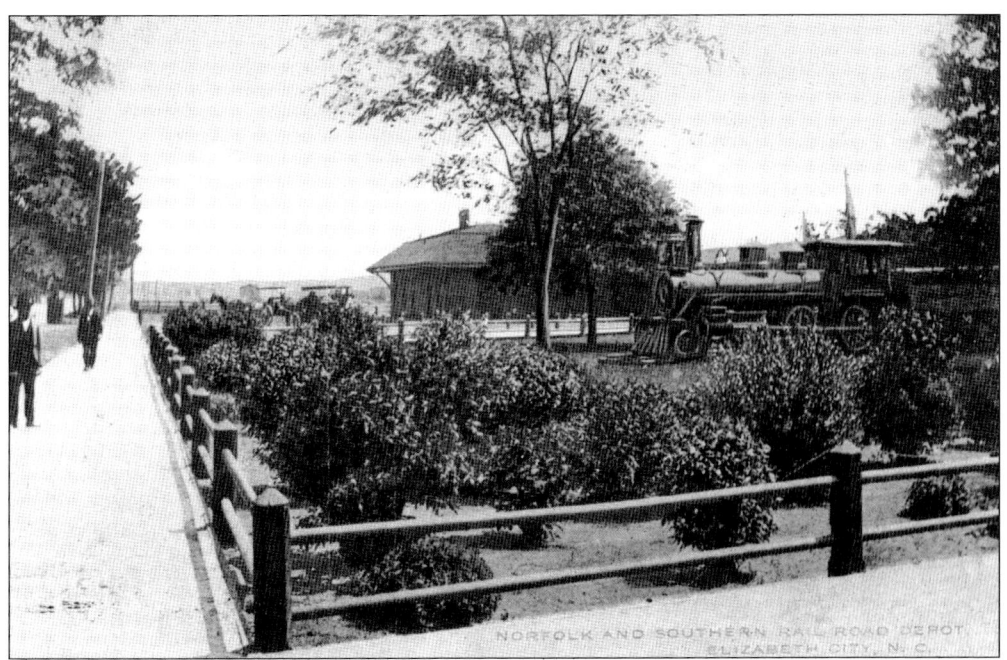

In North Carolina, the Elizabeth City & Norfolk Railroad line passed through Camden County and crossed the Pasquotank River as it entered Elizabeth City. The railroad's main line continued west to Hertford, while a spur ended along the river at what is now North Poindexter Street. In 1882, the railroad contracted with the Old Dominion Steamship Company to provide passenger and freight service between Elizabeth City and New Bern and Washington, North Carolina. (Courtesy of Kurt Reisweber.)

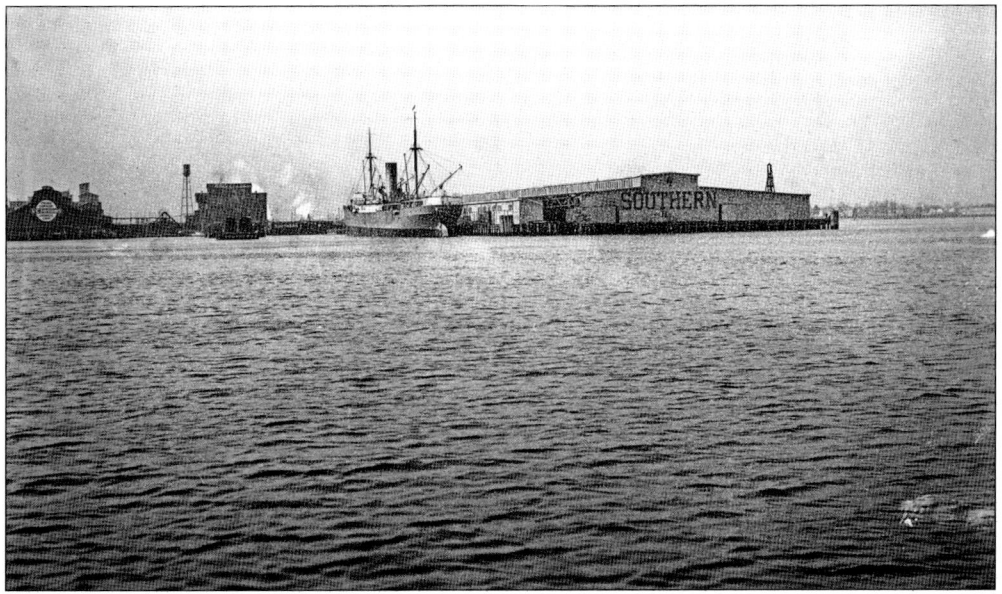

Southern Railway's waterfront warehouses at the foot of Jackson Street in South Norfolk are seen in this February 1935 photograph. The 1936 Norfolk City Directory listed Clifford L. Chandler as general agent, Marion L. Newbill as freight agent, and William A. Wright as commercial agent. (Courtesy of Sargeant Memorial Collection, Norfolk Public Library.)

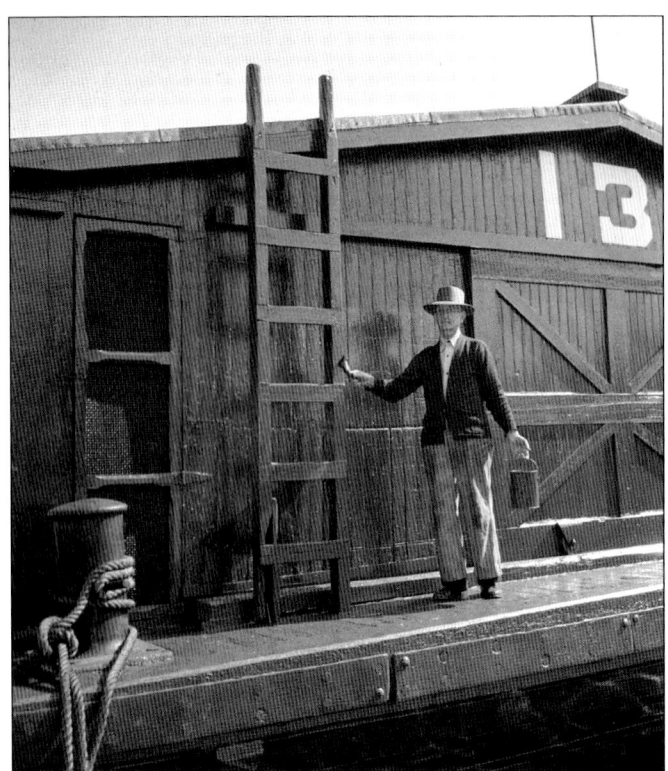

At Southern Railway's Pinners Point facility, incoming freight could be transferred to the Norfolk & Portsmouth Belt Line Railroad, the Atlantic & Danville Railroad, or the Atlantic Coast Line Railroad. Other railcars rolled down tracks to the water to cross a floating bridge onto car floats. A tugboat moved the floats, loaded with up to four freight cars, to warehouses and businesses across the river. Southern employee W.H. Hedrick is painting one of the piers in this 1951 photograph. (Courtesy of Norfolk Southern.)

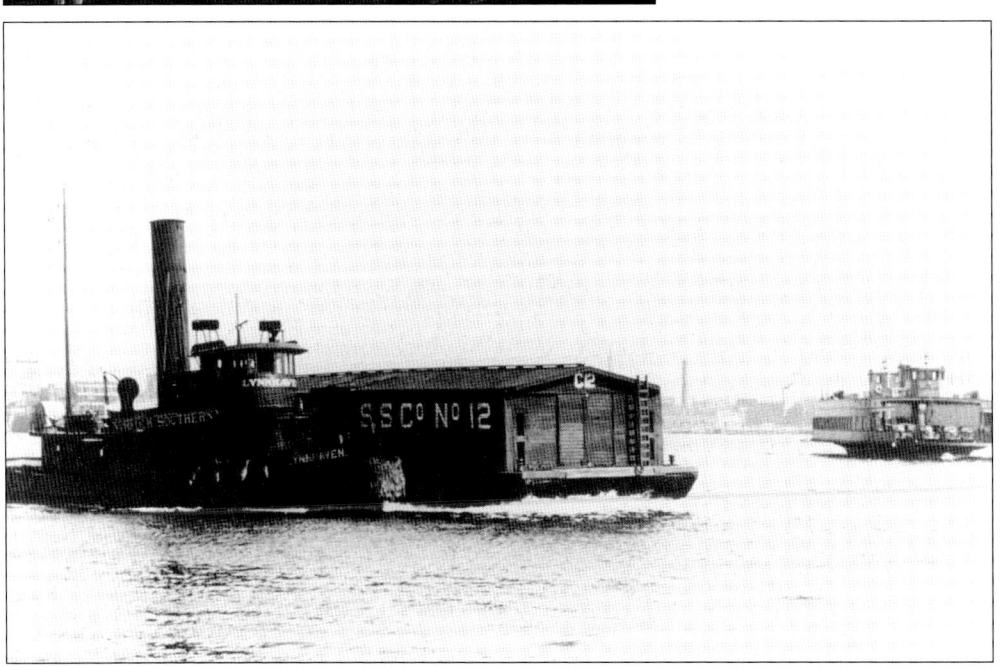

Skinner Shipbuilding and Drydock of Baltimore, Maryland, built the coal-burning tugboat *Lynnhaven* in 1910 for Norfolk's Tugboat Lynnhaven Company. Norfolk Southern acquired the tug in 1925 and used it in towing service on the Lynnhaven River until 1935. (Courtesy of Norfolk Southern.)

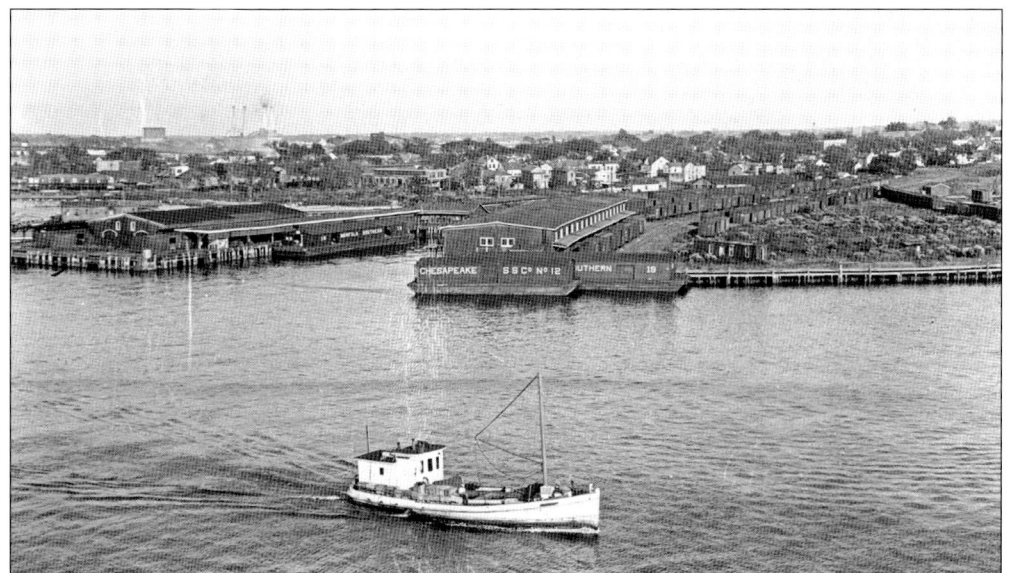

Taken in October 1934, this photograph shows Norfolk Southern Railroad Company piers at the Berkley Terminal in the Berkley section of Norfolk. The terminal at the foot of Pearl Street largely imported and distributed bananas from Cuba. (Courtesy of Sargeant Memorial Collection, Norfolk Public Library.)

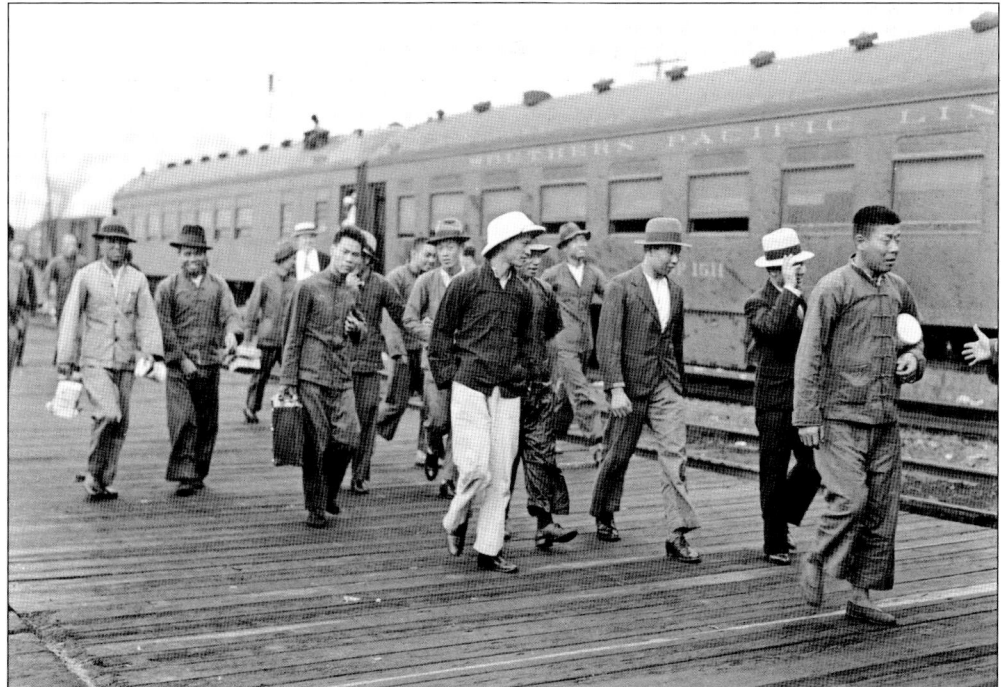

Some of the 77 Chinese merchant seamen who had just arrived at Southern Railway's Pinners Street station and dock in Portsmouth are shown in this September 1937 photograph. The sailors had come from San Francisco to take possession of three merchant ships to run the Japanese blockade of Shanghai, China. They hoped to take supplies, food, and munitions to the long-suffering residents. (Courtesy of Sargeant Memorial Collection, Norfolk Public Library.)

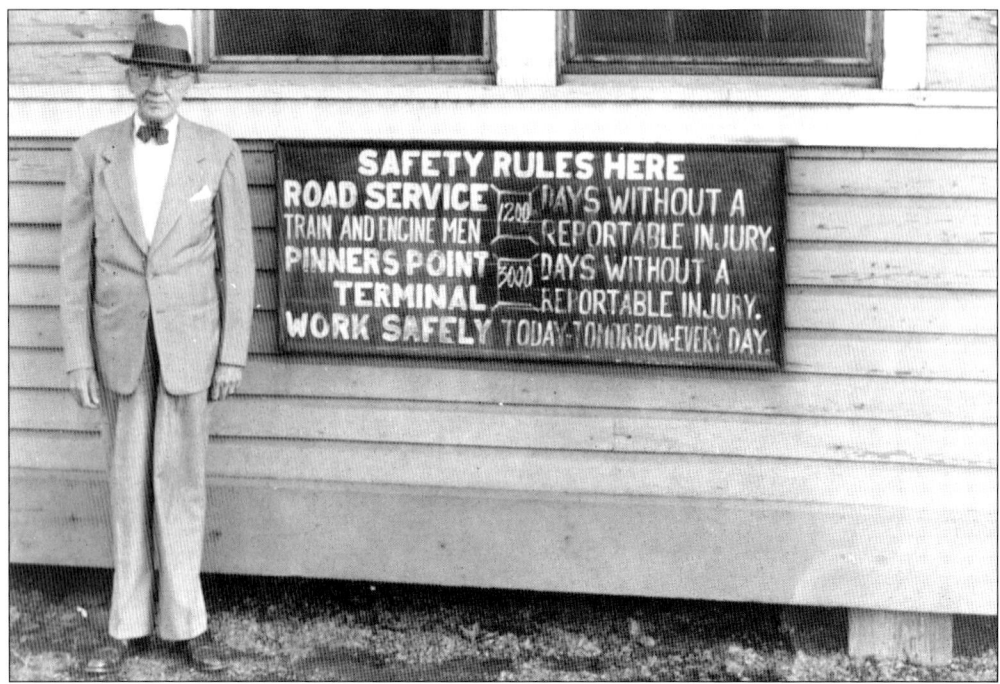

Southern Railway employees at the Pinners Point terminal in Portsmouth celebrated a safety milestone in 1953 with an oyster roast. Employees at the terminal had worked 3,000 days without an injury, while train and engine employees had achieved 1,200 injury-free days. Agent-yardmaster J.A. Sams and the safety committee sponsored what they called a "typical Norfolk celebration" with oysters, Ritz crackers, and potato chips. A sign in the yard reminded employees to "work safely today—tomorrow—every day." (Both, courtesy of Norfolk Southern.)

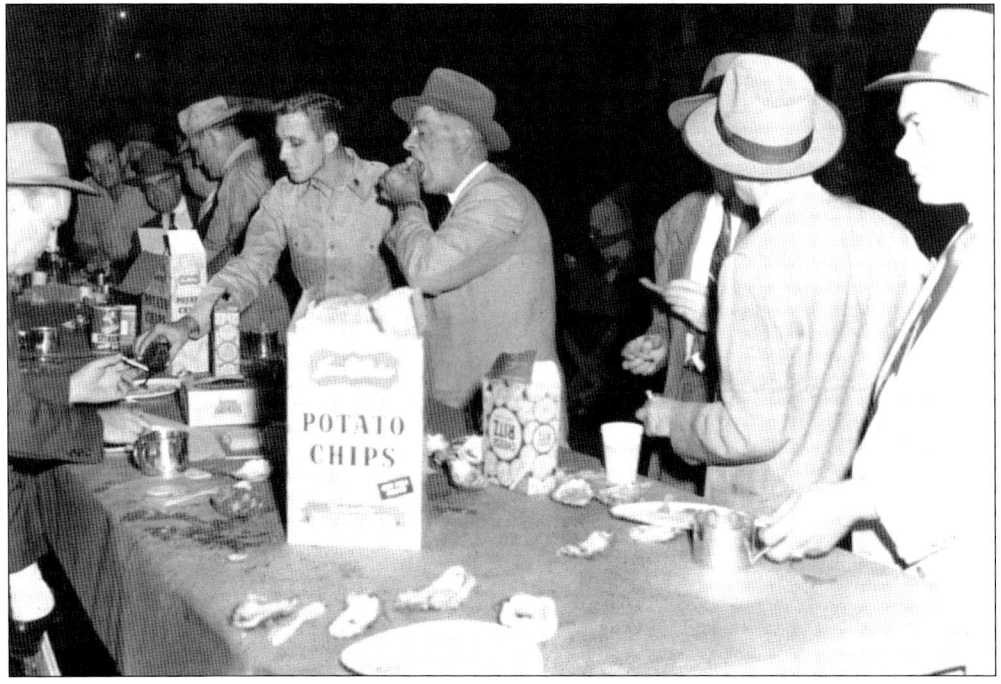

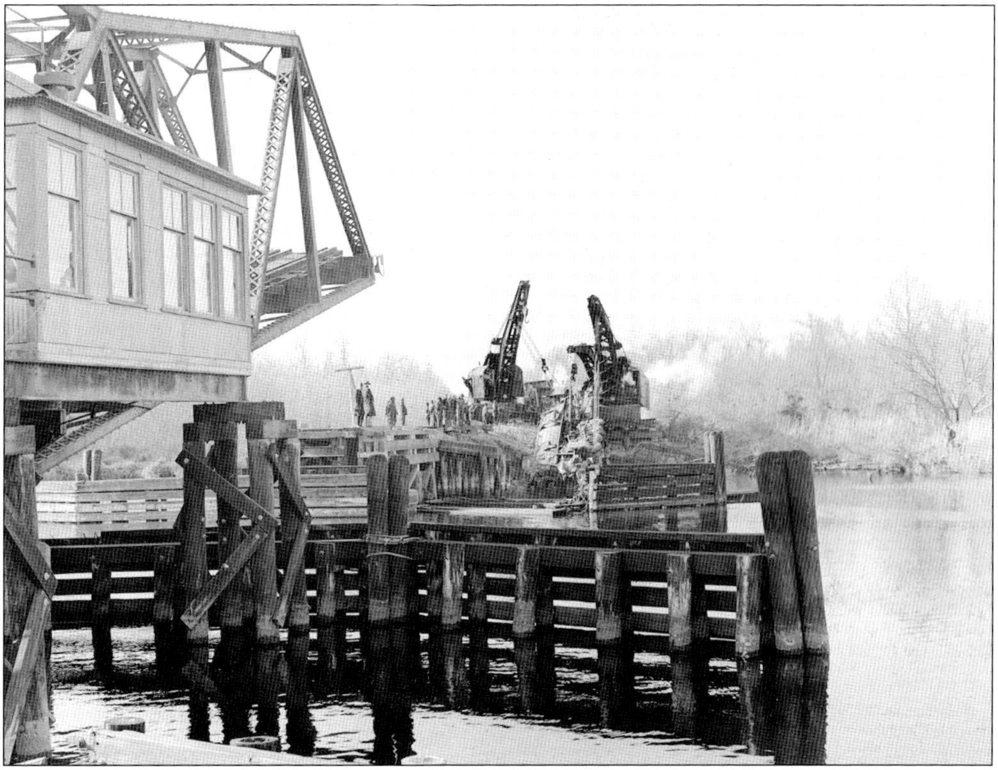

The above photograph shows salvage operations underway to recover a Norfolk Southern locomotive that had gone through an open drawbridge and crashed into the Chesapeake and Albemarle Canal half a mile east of Great Bridge in March 1943. Three crew members on the 33-car train were injured. Below, the engine lies alongside track after being recovered from the canal in early April 1943. (Both, courtesy of Sargeant Memorial Collection, Norfolk Public Library.)

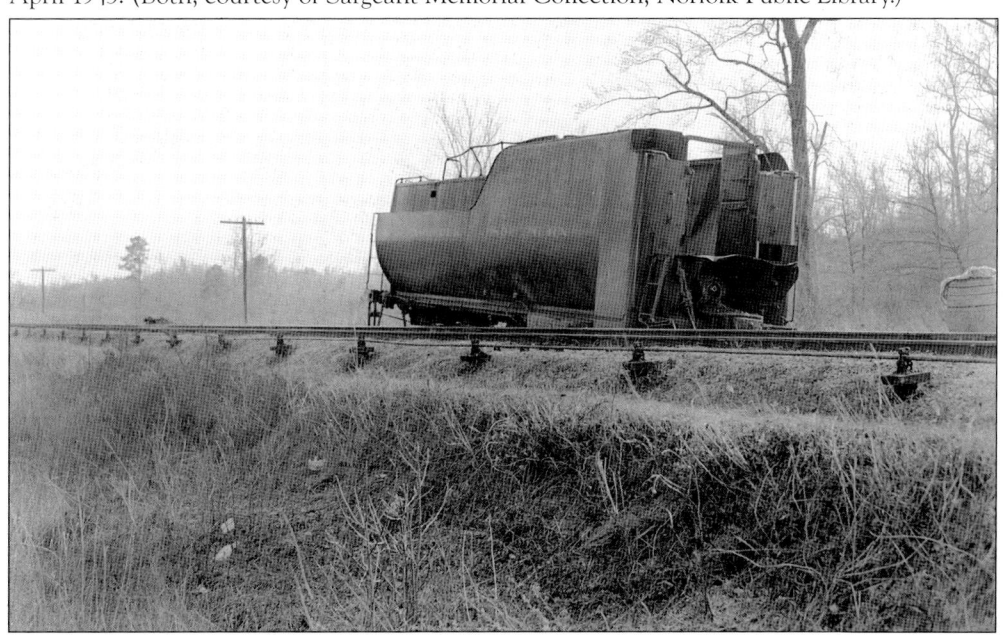

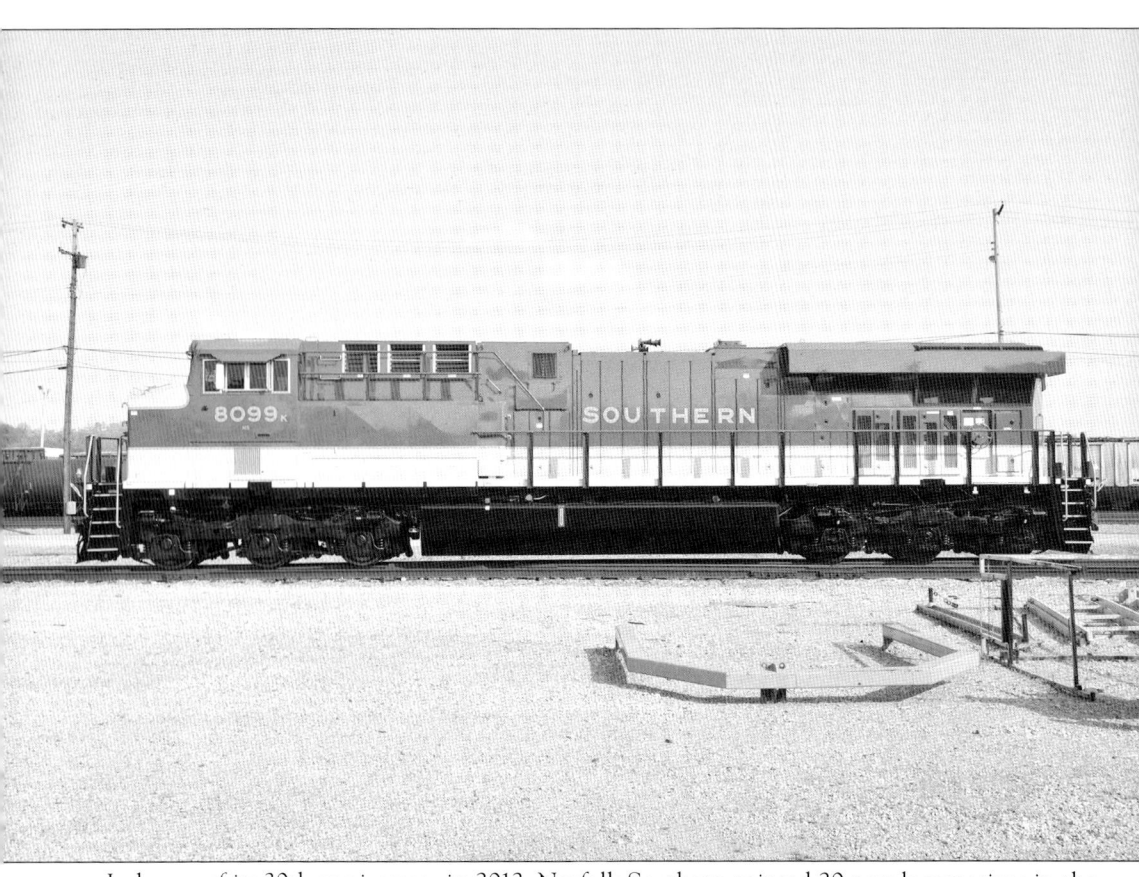

In honor of its 30th anniversary in 2012, Norfolk Southern painted 20 new locomotives in the color schemes of predecessor railroads that played noteworthy roles in its history. The Southern Railway heritage locomotive was decked out in the railroad's green and gold colors. (Courtesy of Norfolk Southern.)

Four
Building a Resort at Virginia Beach

Nearly 40 miles of beaches along the Atlantic Ocean and Chesapeake Bay made Princess Anne County a prime spot for development as a major East Coast resort in the late 19th century, with a Norfolk Southern predecessor playing an integral role in the area's evolution.

In 1872, Norfolk businessman Marshall Parks formed the Norfolk & Sewell's Point Railroad Company to build a rail line from Norfolk to either the Chesapeake Bay or the Atlantic Ocean in Princess Anne County. Parks wanted to develop the area into a seaside resort but was unable to find investors. After becoming president of the Seaside Hotel and Land Company, he reorganized the railroad as the Norfolk & Virginia Beach Railroad and Improvement Company and built the Virginia Beach Hotel, the oceanfront's first large hotel.

In July 1883, the railroad began running steam trains along a 19-mile narrow-gauge track. The trains carried passengers as well as seafood and agricultural products from truck farms in Princess Anne County.

Financial issues forced the Norfolk & Virginia Beach Railroad and Improvement Company to undergo several reorganizations. In 1896, it was sold at auction to investors who formed the Norfolk, Virginia Beach & Southern Railroad Company. Major stockholders in the new railroad included members of the Vanderbilt family and the New York Central & Hudson River Railroad.

The Norfolk & Southern Railroad acquired the Norfolk, Virginia Beach & Southern in 1900. Eight years later, Norfolk & Southern entered receivership, emerging in 1910 as the Norfolk Southern Railroad Company. Today, a portion of that railroad operates as the Chesapeake & Albemarle Railroad, a short line running from Chesapeake to Edenton, North Carolina.

Passenger service to the oceanfront lasted until the late 1940s when it was discontinued as travelers increasingly preferred to take their trips in automobiles.

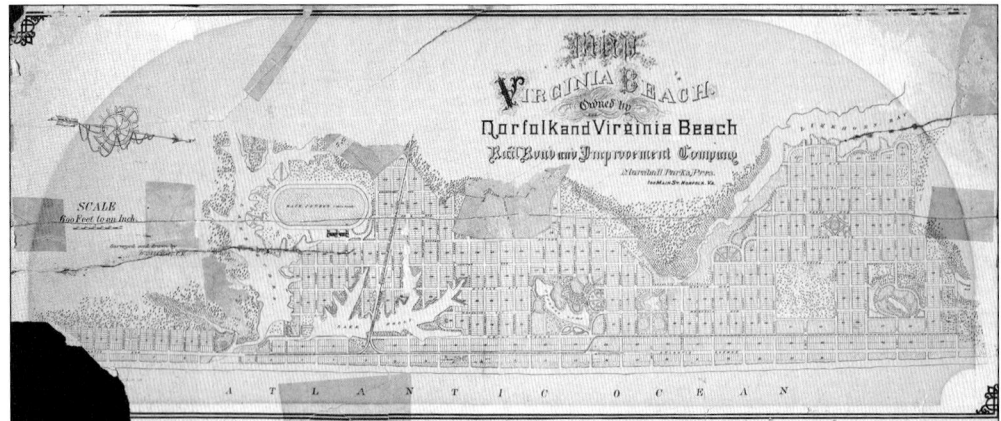

This c. 1883 map created by the Norfolk & Virginia Beach Railroad and Improvement Company shows the Virginia Beach oceanfront: north to Forty-Eighth Street, east to the Atlantic Ocean, south to South Eleventh Street, and west to Courtright Avenue. (Courtesy of Sargeant Memorial Collection, Norfolk Public Library.)

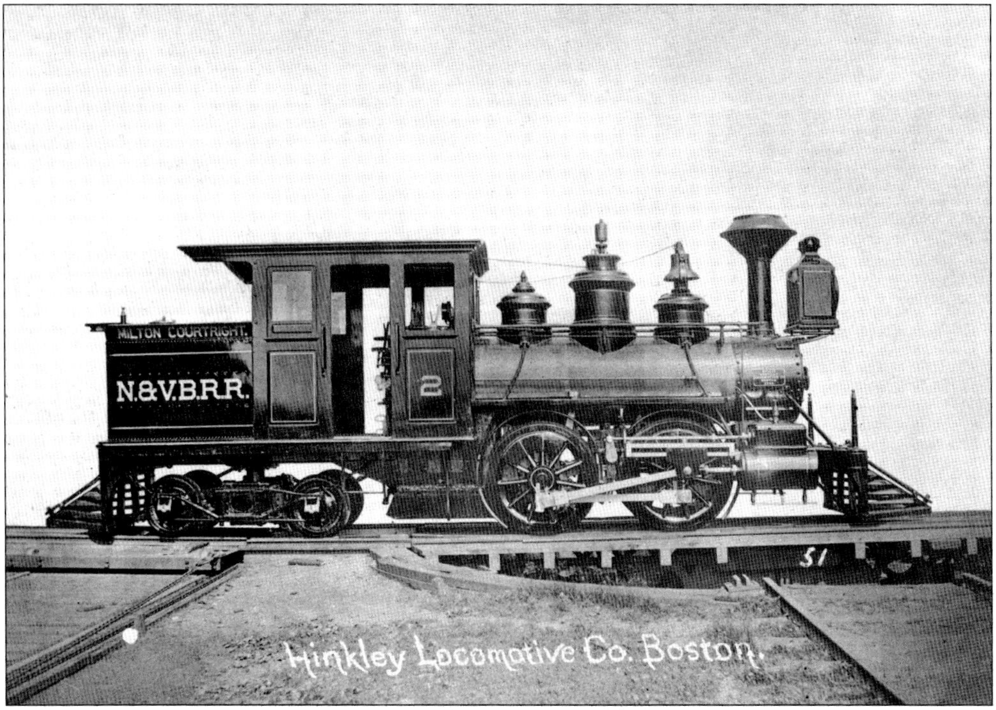

The Norfolk & Virginia Beach Railroad and Improvement Company's locomotive is shown in this 1884 photograph. Including "Improvement" in the name signaled the company's plans to build and operate a railroad as well as develop Virginia Beach as a summer resort. (Courtesy of Virginia Beach Public Library.)

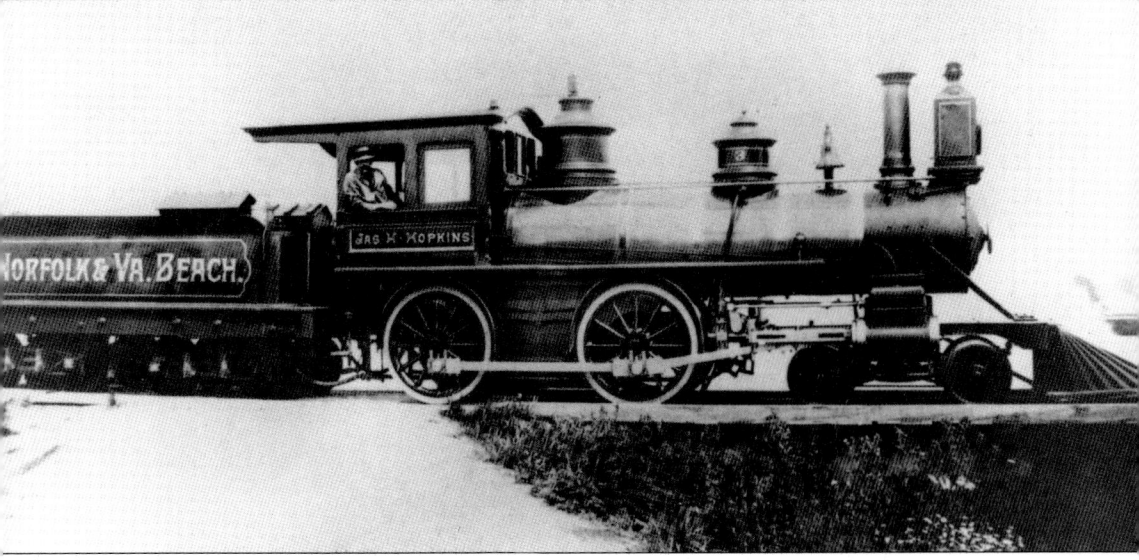

This late-19th-century photograph shows a Norfolk & Virginia Beach Railroad steam locomotive built by Hinkley Locomotive Company in Boston. Trains traveled from Broad Creek in Norfolk to the Virginia Beach oceanfront. Since passengers had to take a boat across Broad Creek to reach the westernmost track, the railroad soon built a bridge across the waterway and extended the rails into the Norfolk & Western station at the end of East Main Street in downtown Norfolk. (Courtesy of Kurt Reisweber.)

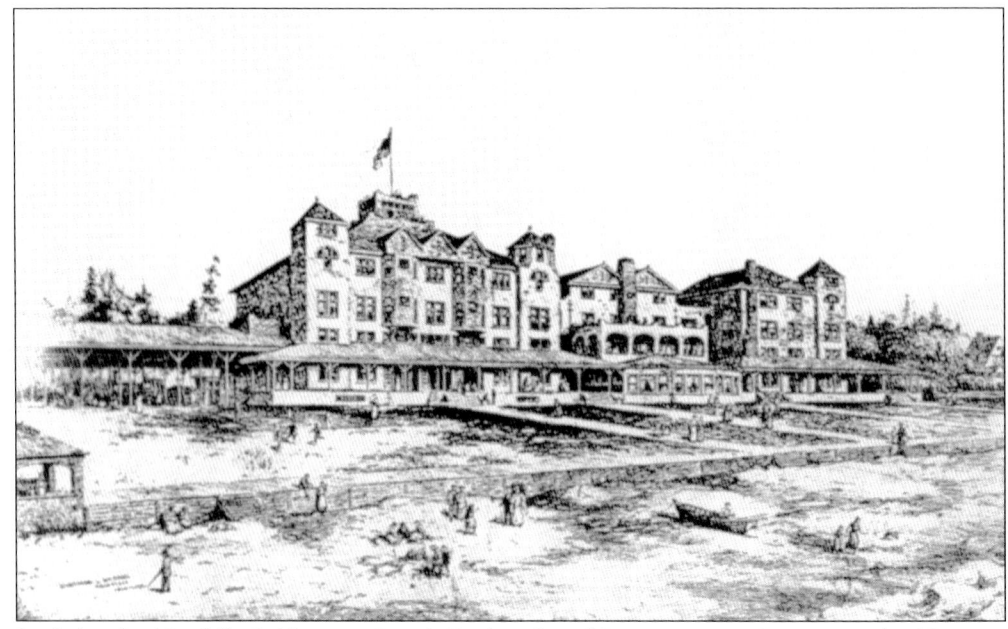

Built by the Norfolk & Virginia Beach Railroad and Improvement Company, the Virginia Beach Hotel opened in July 1884 on 1,600 acres of shoreline. It was the first large hotel on the oceanfront and extended from what is now Fourteenth Street to Sixteenth Street. (Courtesy of Norfolk Southern.)

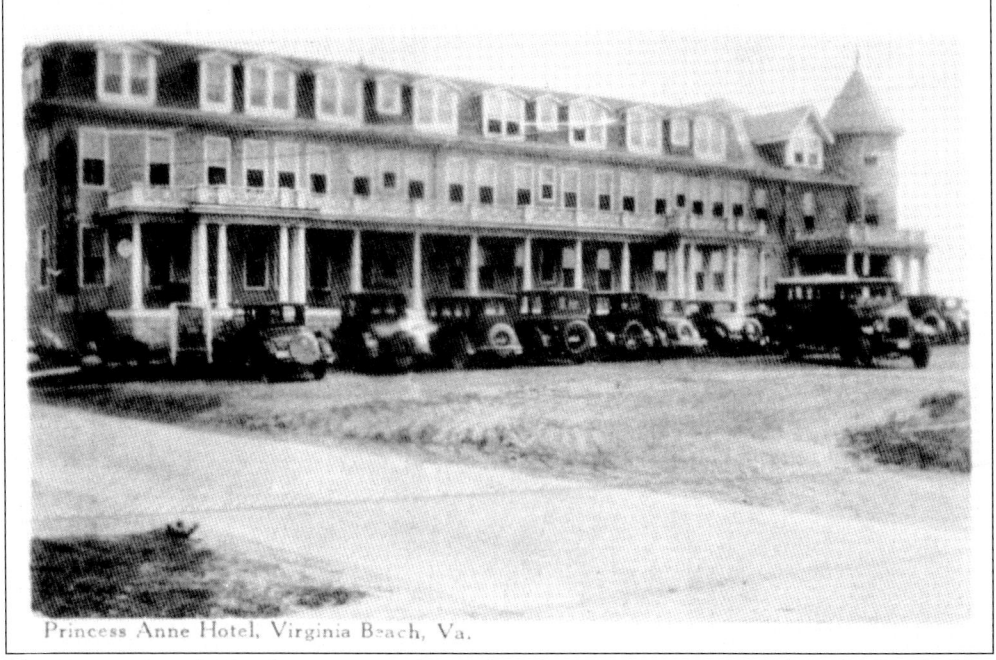

The Virginia Beach Hotel's name was changed to the Princess Anne Hotel, and a fourth floor was added to the property in 1888. Renovations also included a remodeled ballroom and dining room as well as an electrical plant, believed to be the first in Virginia. (Courtesy of Virginia Beach Public Library.)

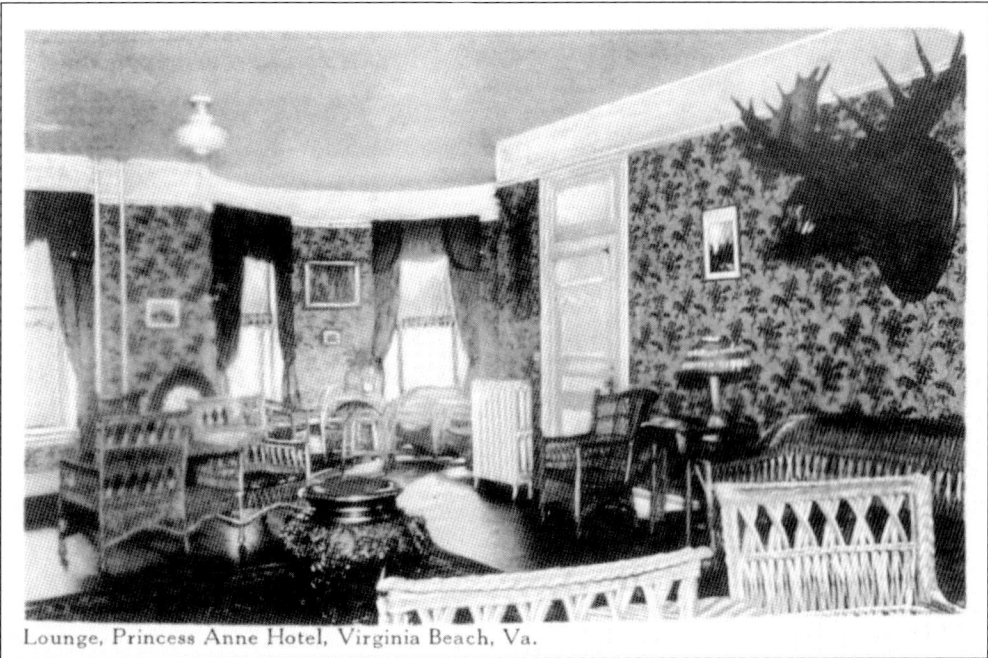

Lounge, Princess Anne Hotel, Virginia Beach, Va.

Epitomizing the Gay Nineties era, the Princess Anne Hotel could accommodate 400 guests and boasted amenities that included a post office, a bowling alley, dance halls, a casino, and a private walkway to the Virginia Beach boardwalk. (Courtesy of Virginia Beach Public Library.)

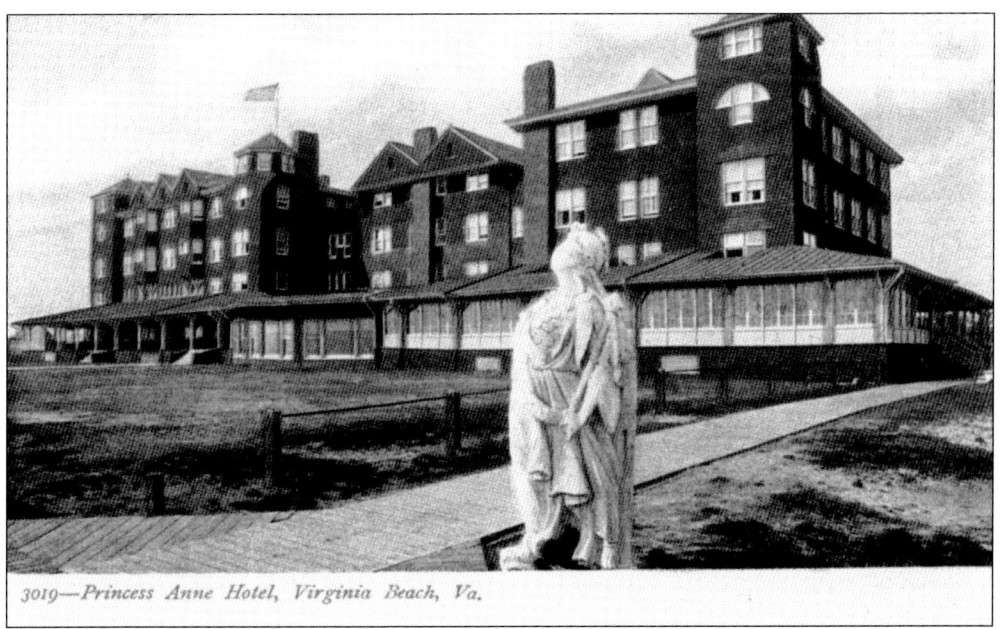

3019—Princess Anne Hotel, Virginia Beach, Va.

Featuring steam heat and elevator service, the Princess Anne attracted wealthy Northern families during the winter months. Famous guests included US presidents Benjamin Harrison and Grover Cleveland, railroad and shipping magnate Cornelius Vanderbilt, and Alexander Graham Bell. A fire destroyed the hotel in July 1907. (Courtesy of Kurt Reisweber.)

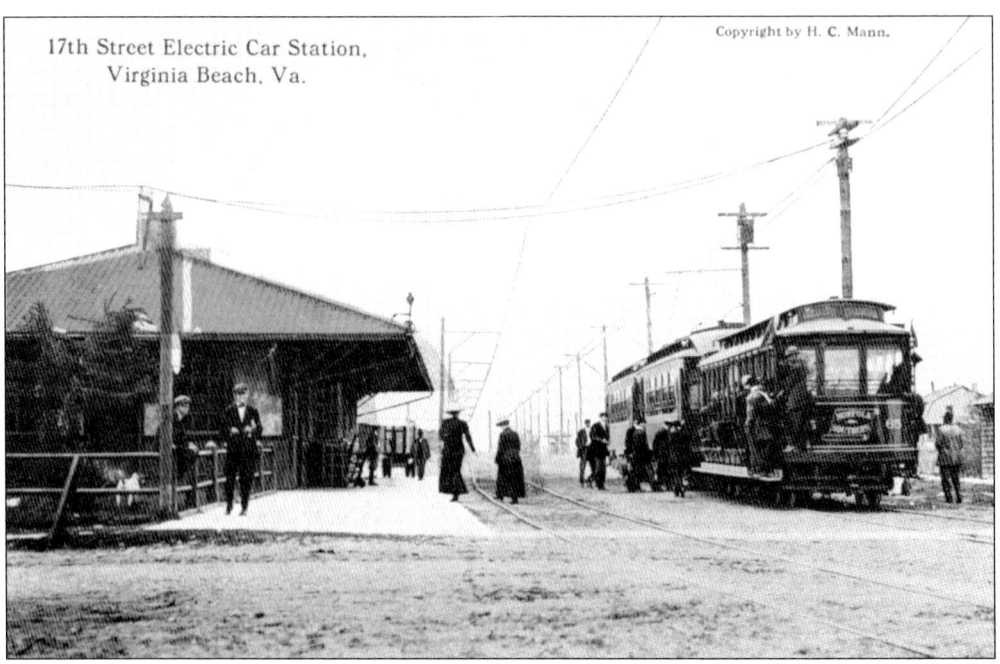

The Norfolk & Southern depot was so close to the Princess Anne Hotel that some said trains almost ran into the lobby. Like the hotel, the depot was reduced to ashes in a July 1907 fire. (Courtesy of Kurt Reisweber.)

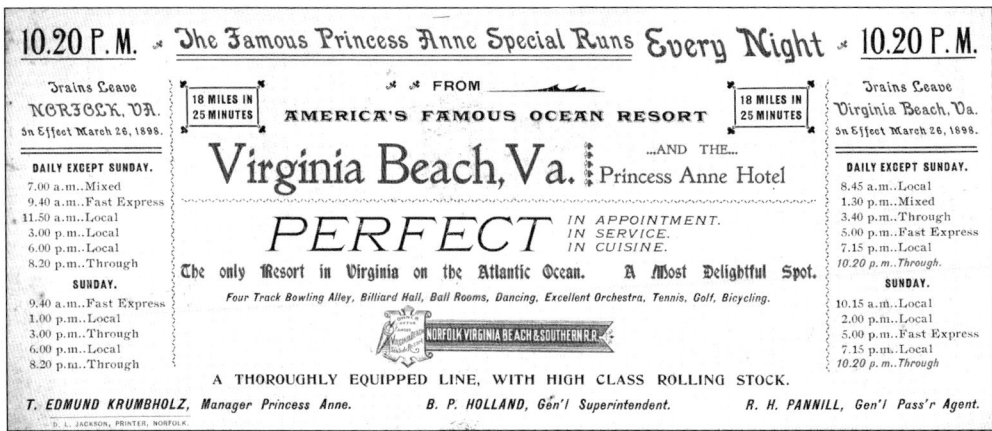

An 1898 Norfolk, Virginia Beach & Southern Railroad schedule advertised the nightly "Famous Princess Anne Special Runs" from Norfolk to Virginia Beach. The schedule also listed Bernard P. Holland as general superintendent. Holland, who later became superintendent of Norfolk & Southern's electric service, served as Virginia Beach's first mayor following its incorporation as a town in 1906. (Courtesy of Virginia Beach Public Library.)

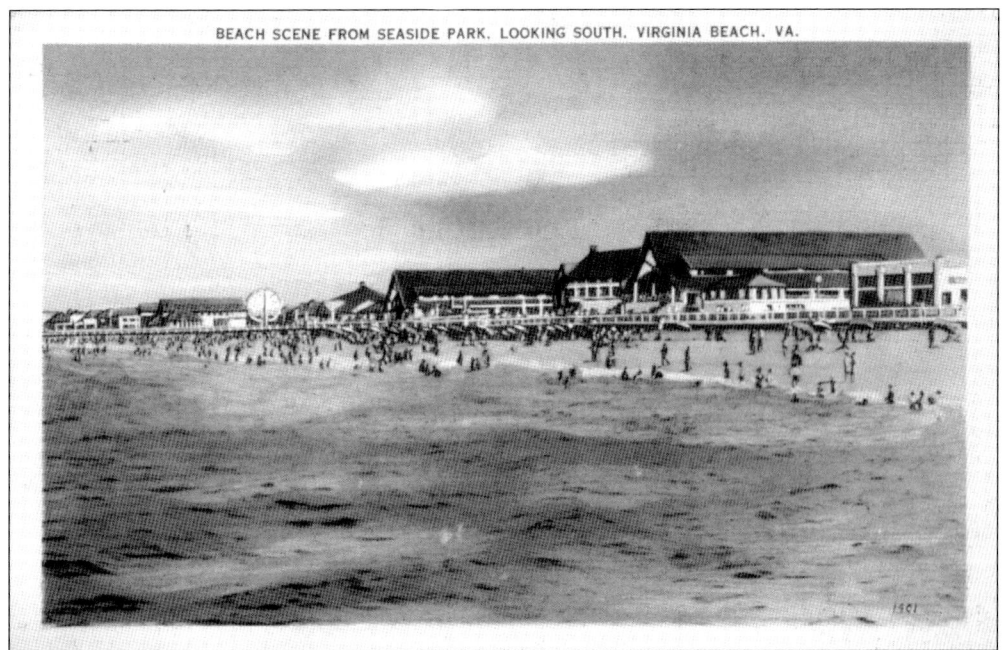

Its revenues negatively affected by the loss of the Princess Anne Hotel, the Norfolk & Southern Railroad negotiated with the Virginia Beach Development Company to buy a large parcel of land for an amusement park. Seaside Park opened in 1912 on the Norfolk & Southern rail line, with railcars dropping off visitors at the park's entrance. (Courtesy of Virginia Beach Public Library.)

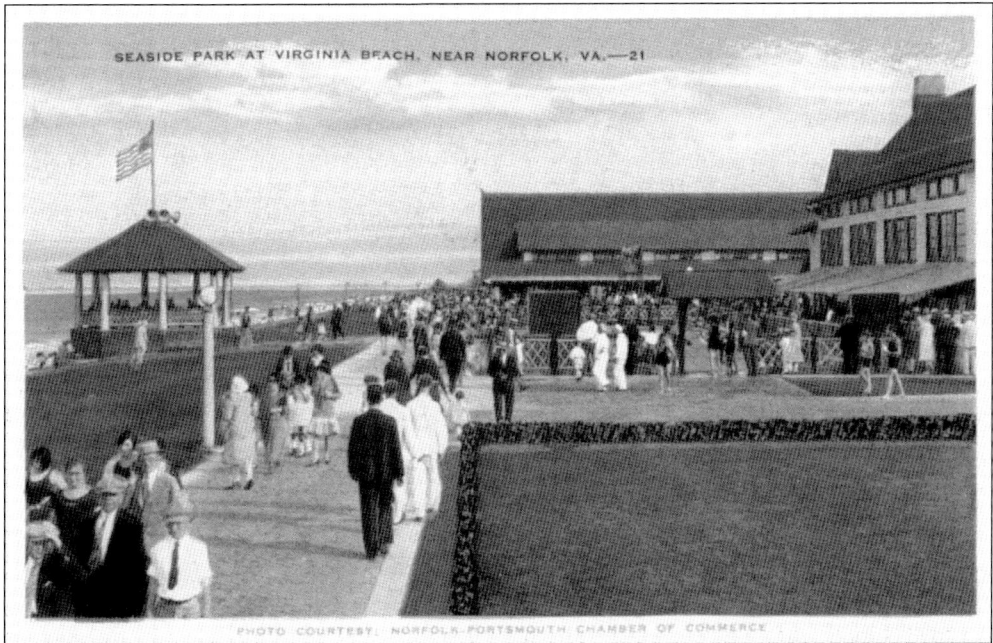

Virginia Beach visitors could ride on Seaside Park's merry-go-round, swim in the saltwater pool, and listen to musicians perform on the bandstand. Norfolk Southern sold Seaside Park in 1926. Damaged by a fire in 1956, the park's last remaining section was torn down in 1986 and replaced with hotels. (Courtesy of Virginia Beach Public Library.)

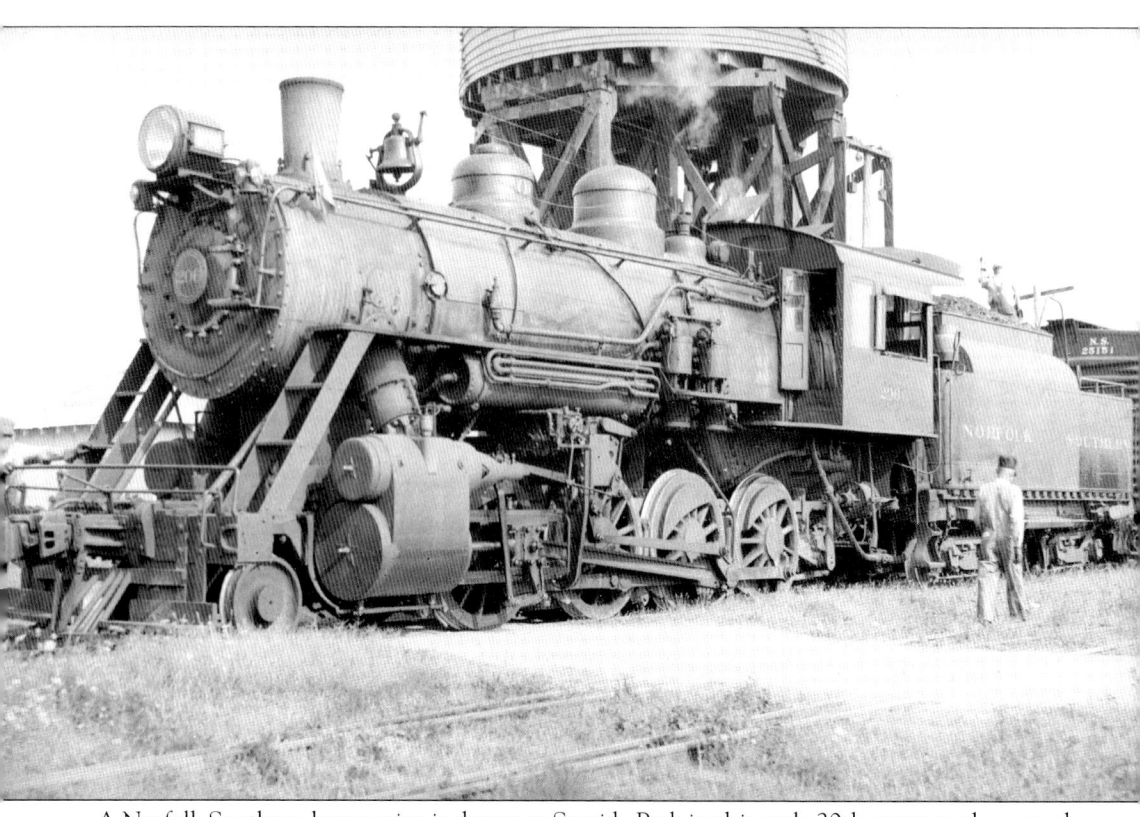

A Norfolk Southern locomotive is shown at Seaside Park in this early-20th-century photograph. The amusement park was situated between Thirtieth and Thirty-Third Streets, 1.5 miles north of the former Princess Anne Hotel. Ornate walkways connected the railroad's station with the park's Peacock Ballroom, restaurants, bathhouses, and picnic pavilions. (Courtesy of Edgar T. Brown Collection, Virginia Beach Public Library.)

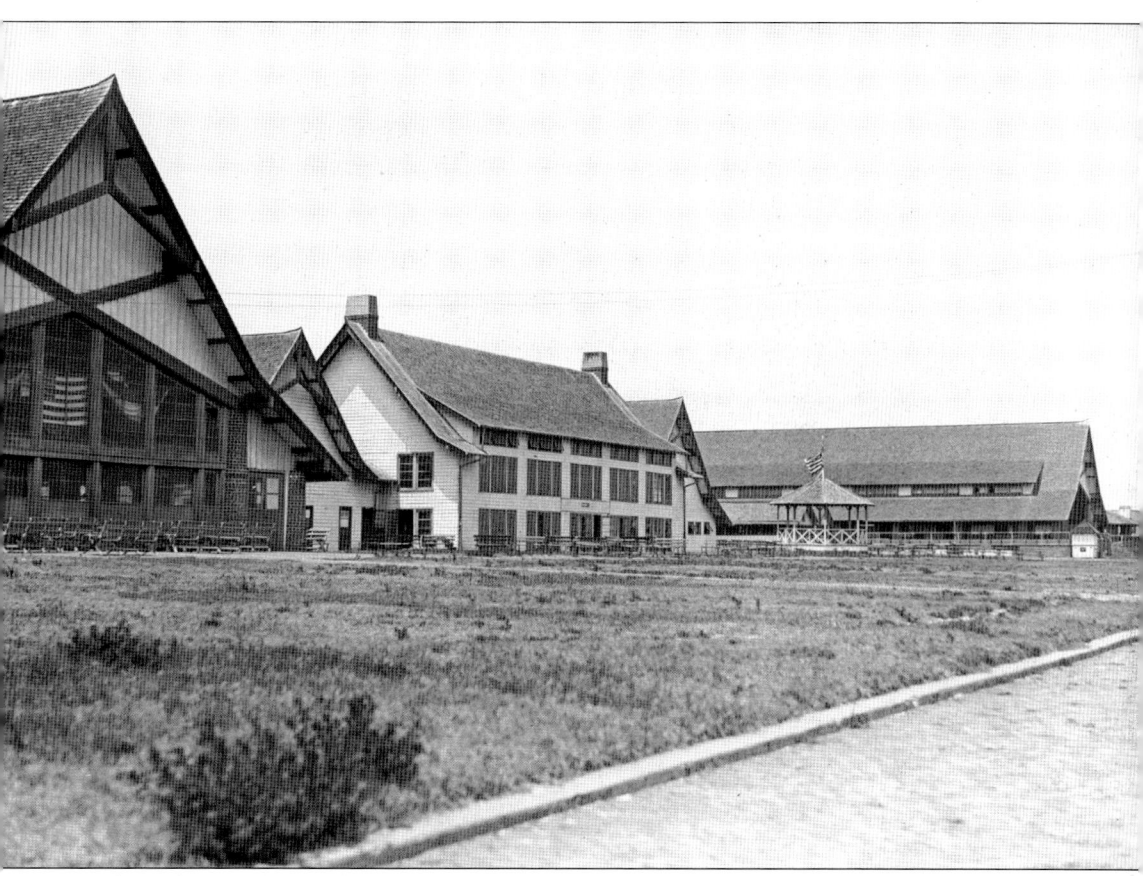

Seaside Park is seen from the ocean side in this c. 1920s photograph. The Peacock Ballroom, which hosted nationally known dance bands in the 1920s and 1930s, was in the building on the left. The middle building, which contained a restaurant, was torn down in 1982. (Sargeant Memorial Collection, Norfolk Public Library.)

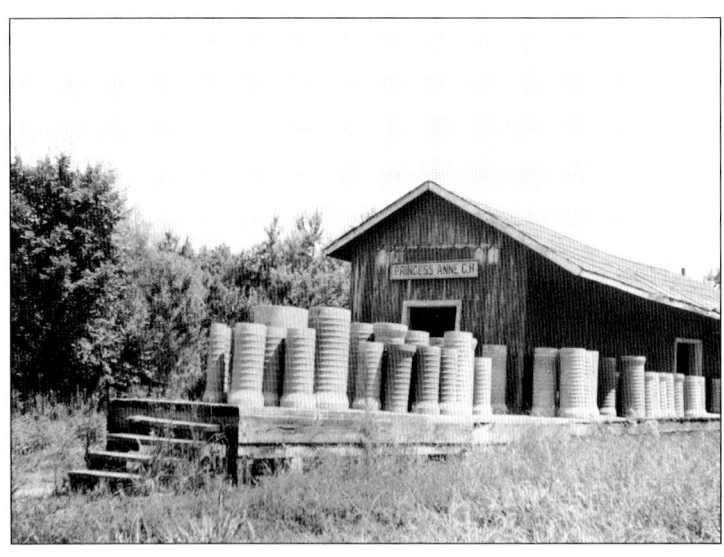

In the late 1890s, the Norfolk, Virginia Beach & Southern Railroad opened a spur on its rail line from Norfolk to the oceanfront with the first stop at the Princess Anne Courthouse station. Later, the original Norfolk Southern Railroad ran on the tracks until abandoning the line in 1955. The line followed the route of what is now Princess Anne Road. (Courtesy of Kurt Reisweber.)

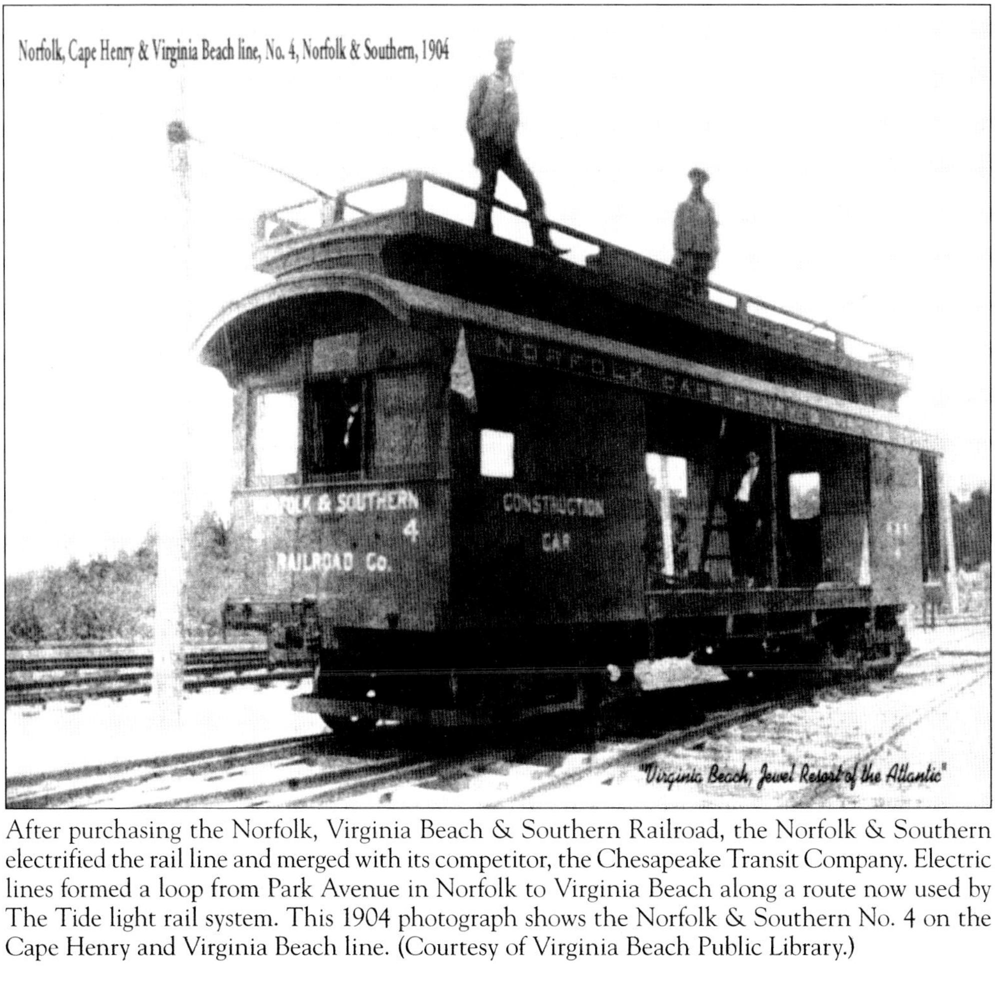

After purchasing the Norfolk, Virginia Beach & Southern Railroad, the Norfolk & Southern electrified the rail line and merged with its competitor, the Chesapeake Transit Company. Electric lines formed a loop from Park Avenue in Norfolk to Virginia Beach along a route now used by The Tide light rail system. This 1904 photograph shows the Norfolk & Southern No. 4 on the Cape Henry and Virginia Beach line. (Courtesy of Virginia Beach Public Library.)

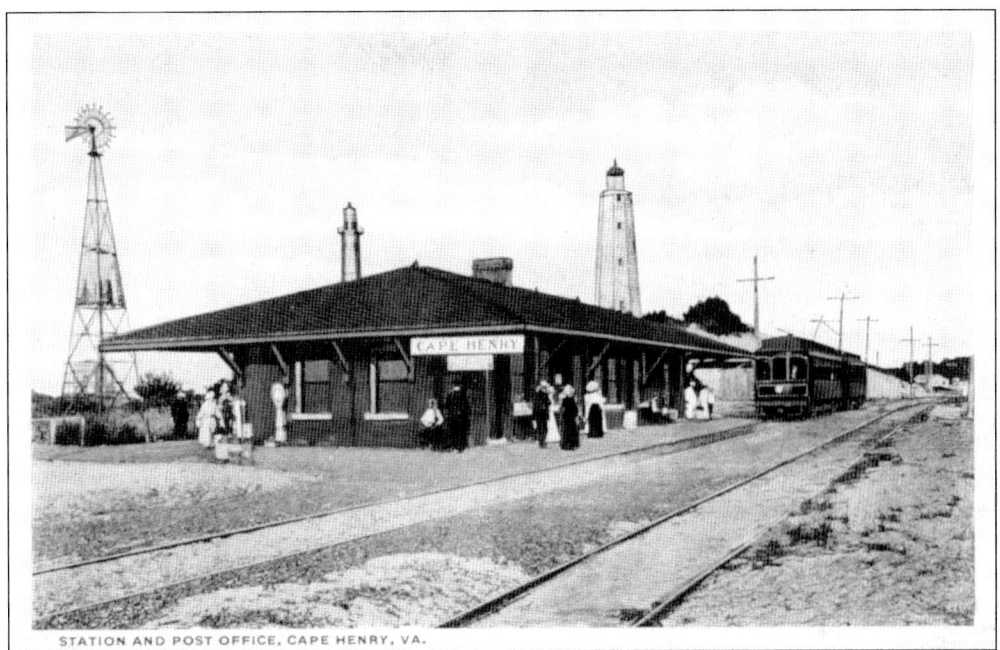

Norfolk & Southern built a passenger station at Cape Henry in 1902. After the US Army built Fort Story in 1914, Norfolk Southern began transporting military passengers and freight to the Cape Henry Lighthouse. The railroad also installed a spur to what is now Camp Pendleton for trains to carry National Guard troops from Rifle Range Junction to the camp for training. The former passenger station later became Fort Story's education center. (Courtesy of Kurt Reisweber.)

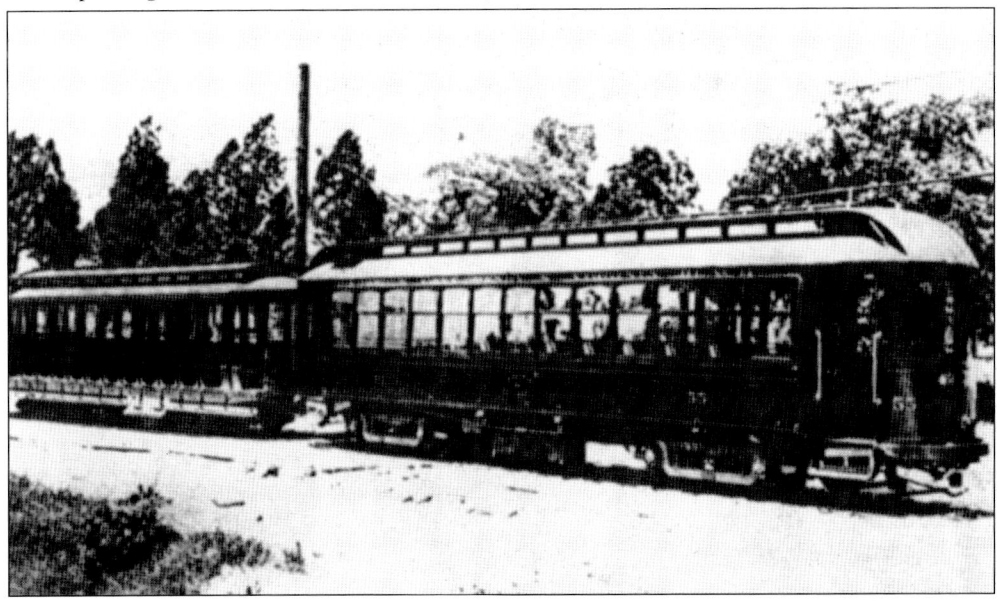

This c. 1917 photograph shows Norfolk & Southern electric railcar No. 55, followed by an open trailer car. Open cars contained wooden seats and running boards. Canvas curtains provided protection during inclement weather. At one time, the railroad had 39 electric motor cars and trailers with closed and open passenger cars. The track right-of-way ran approximately parallel to today's Virginia Beach Boulevard. (Courtesy of Virginia Beach Public Library.)

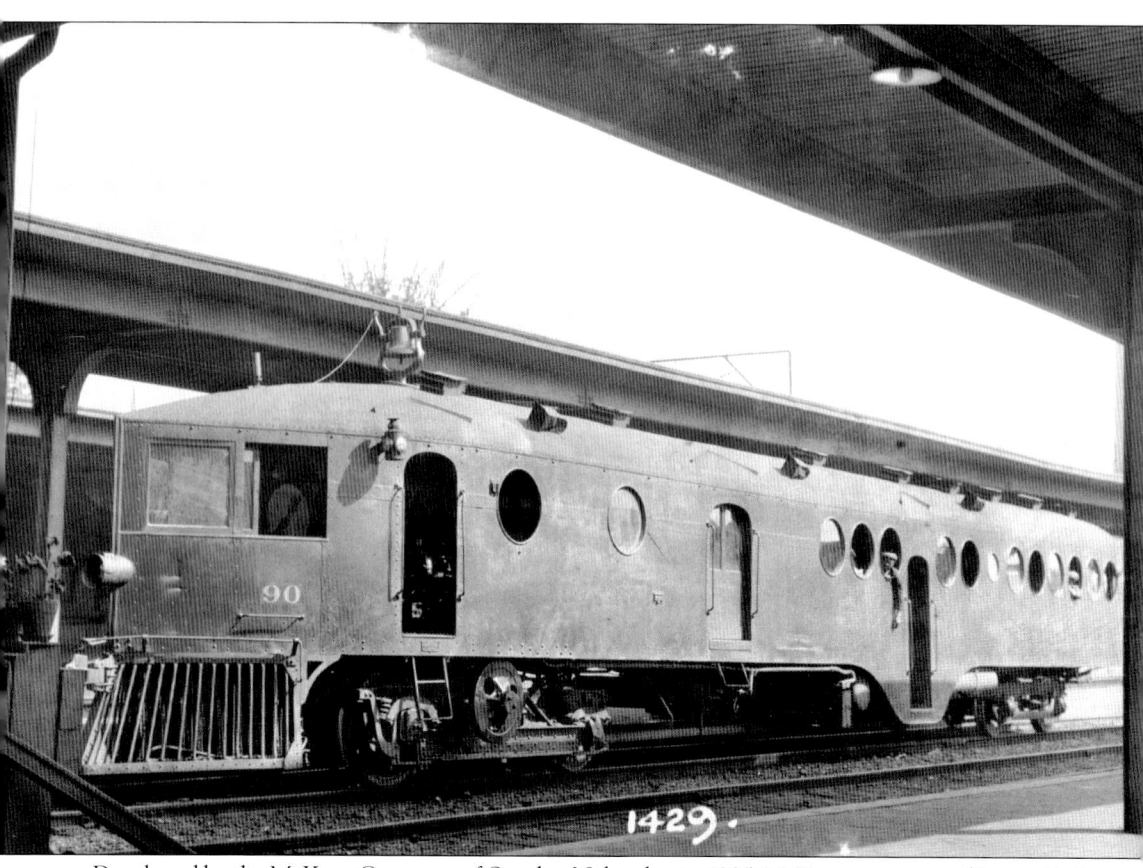

Developed by the McKeen Company of Omaha, Nebraska, in 1905, McKeen cars were self-propelled railcars with a gasoline-powered motor. Most McKeen cars featured a pointed aerodynamic front end and rounded tail as well as porthole windows. The precursor of railbuses, McKeen cars were the first attempt to replace steam trains. Norfolk Southern's McKeen car, seen here around World War I, traveled from Norfolk to Munden Point on Virginia Beach's North Landing River. (Courtesy of Kurt Reisweber.)

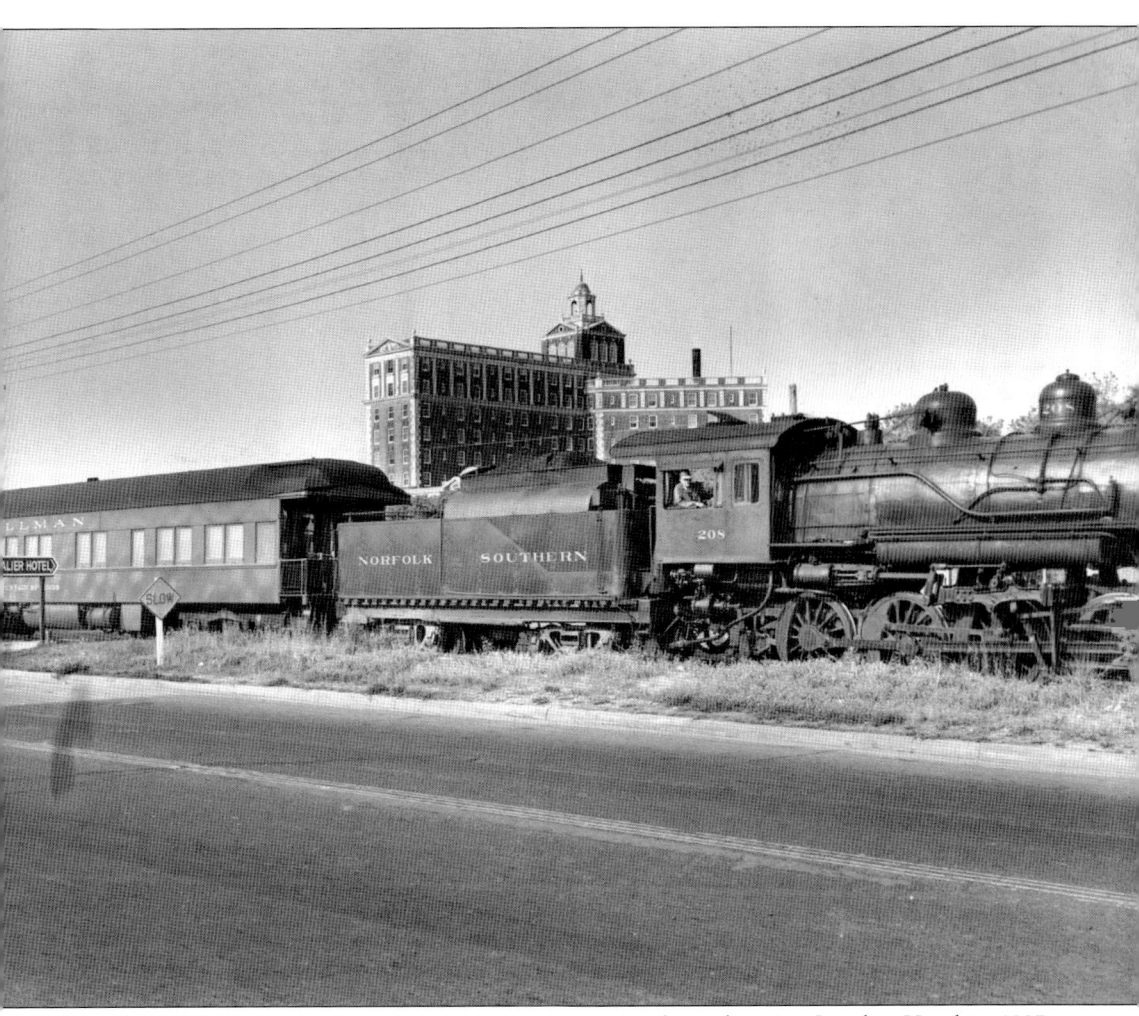

The Norfolk Southern Railroad opened a station across from the new Cavalier Hotel in 1927, offering direct service from New York to Virginia Beach, including Pullman car runs. The service was operated in conjunction with the Pennsylvania Railroad and Norfolk & Western. It continued until World War II when the US Navy used the Cavalier as a training facility. (Courtesy of Kurt Reisweber.)

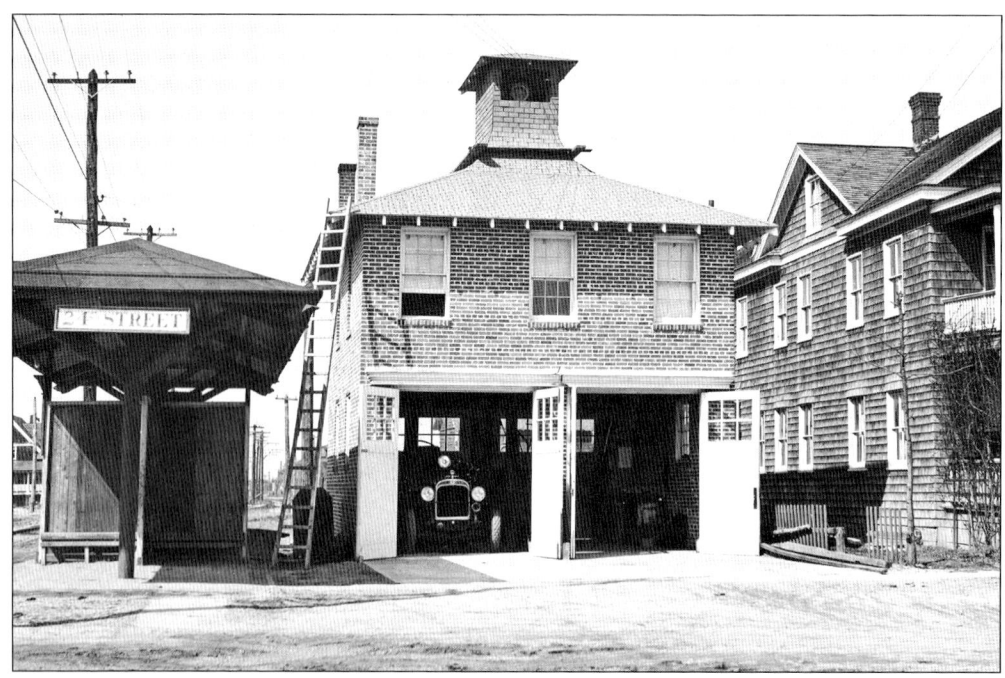

The Virginia Beach Fire Department's first police and fire station at 211 Twenty-Fourth Street was built in 1924. Norfolk Southern's Twenty-Fourth Street Station is shown adjacent to the department's station in this 1920s photograph. Restored by Virginia Beach firefighters in 2013, the station now houses the Virginia Beach Firefighters Museum. (Courtesy of Sargeant Memorial Collection, Norfolk Public Library.)

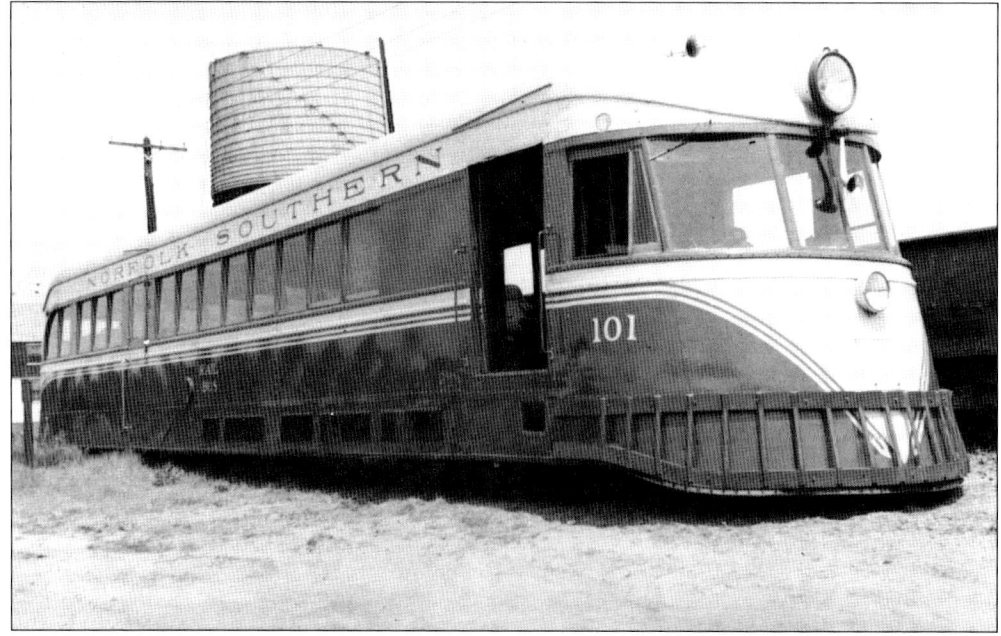

Railbuses replaced passenger trains after Norfolk Southern ended electric operations on its Virginia Beach route in the mid-1930s. The first railbus arrived in 1934 and was operated by the Norfolk Southern Bus Company. (Courtesy of Kurt Reisweber.)

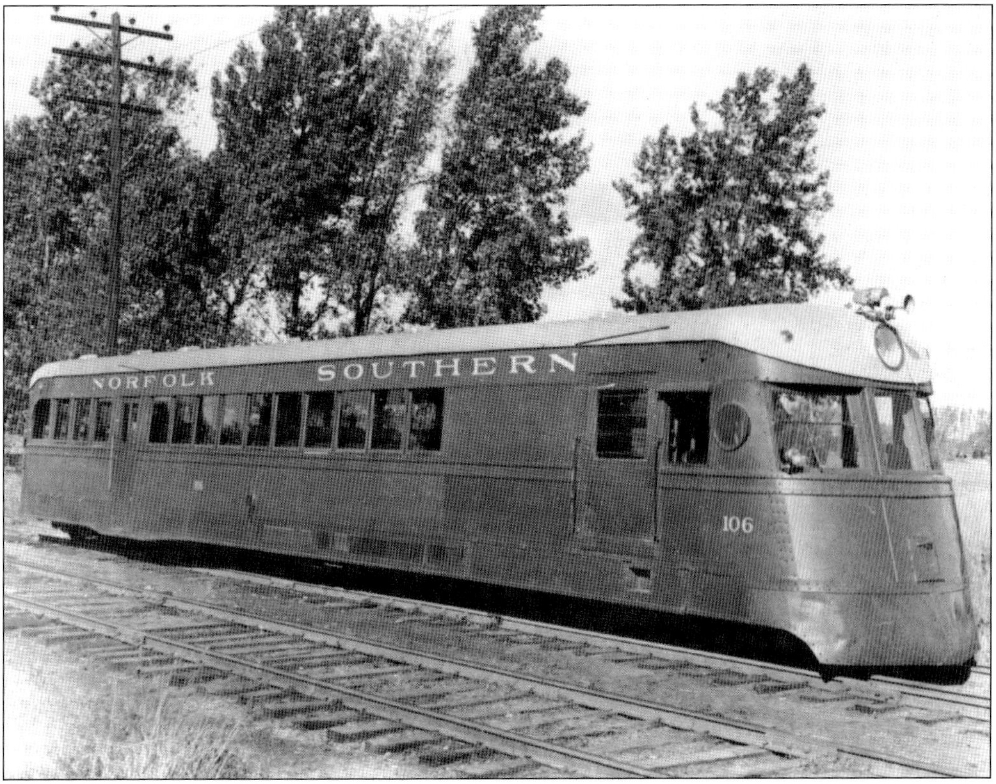

Norfolk Southern ran its last railbus in November 1947. Abandoned rail lines remain visible on Northampton Boulevard from Diamond Springs Road east and along Cape Henry Drive and Cape Henry Trail. (Courtesy of Kurt Reisweber.)

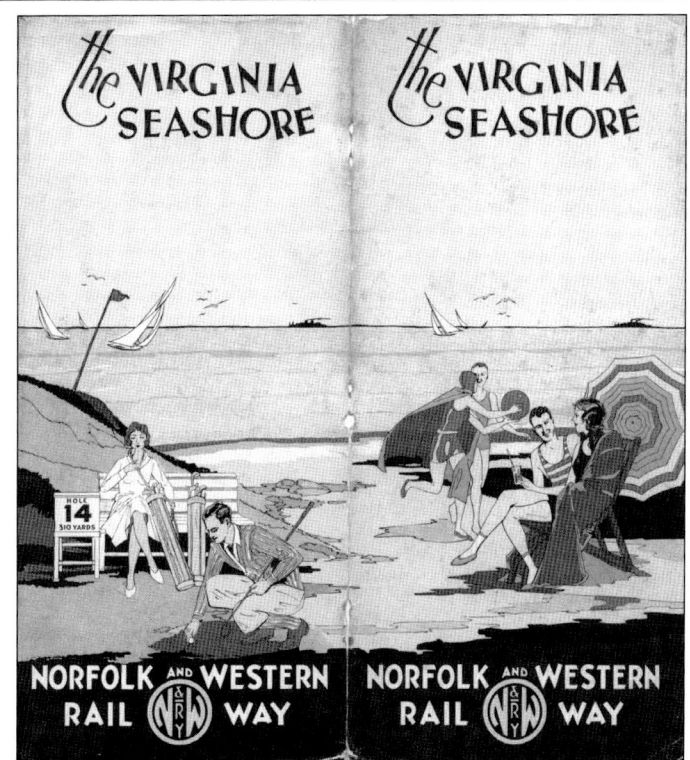

This 1930 advertisement depicts some of the activities potential visitors could enjoy after traveling on a Norfolk & Western train to the Virginia coast. Norfolk & Western began offering overnight passenger service from Midwestern cities to Norfolk in the late 1920s. (Courtesy of Norfolk Southern.)

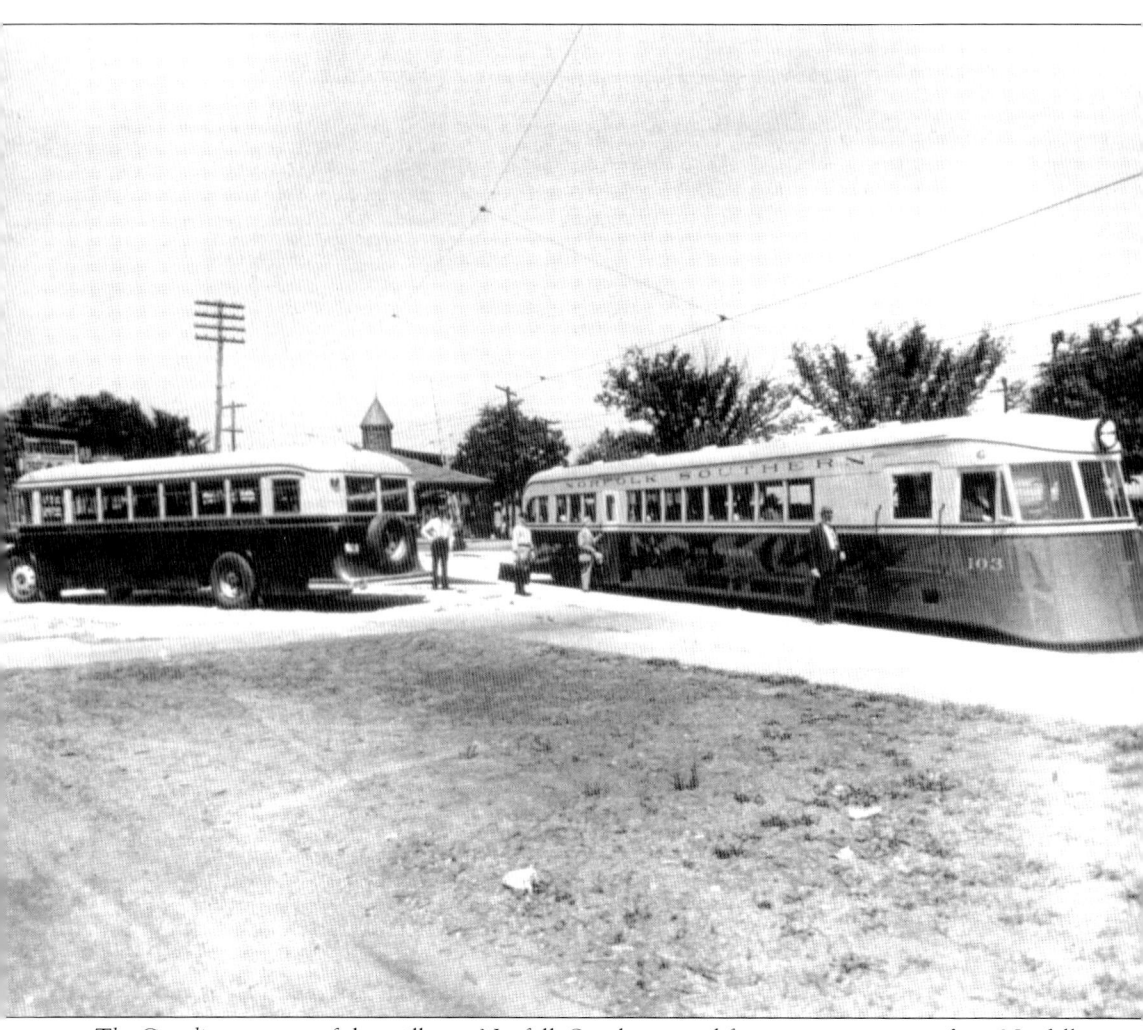

The Cavalier was one of the railbuses Norfolk Southern used for passenger service from Norfolk to Virginia Beach in the 1930s. Other buses included the *Carolinian* and the *Princess Anne*. (Courtesy of Virginia Beach Public Library.)

In the 1930s and 1940s, travelers could take a streamliner passenger train to Norfolk where they could catch a railbus to the Virginia Beach oceanfront. This Norfolk Southern advertisement enticed passengers with fast, streamlined service from Norfolk Terminal Station to the Virginia Beach and Cape Henry Stations. (Courtesy of Virginia Beach Public Library.)

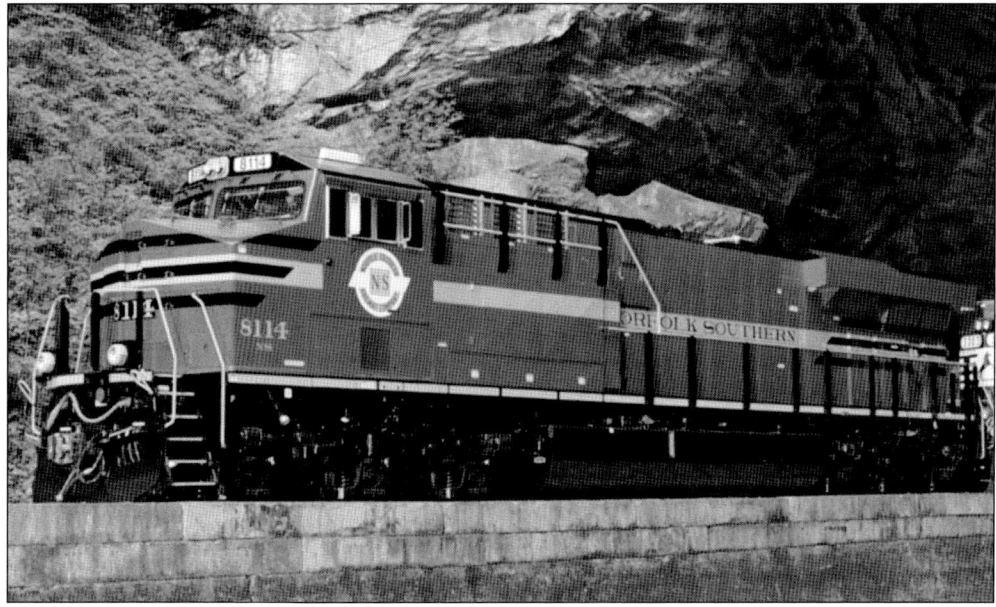

The original Norfolk Southern Railway was one of the predecessors Norfolk Southern honored during its 30th anniversary year in 2012 by painting 20 new locomotives in commemorative schemes reflecting its forebears' heritage. The representative railroads were chosen based on the significant roles they played in Norfolk Southern's heritage. These locomotives continue to haul freight throughout the Norfolk Southern network. (Courtesy of Norfolk Southern.)

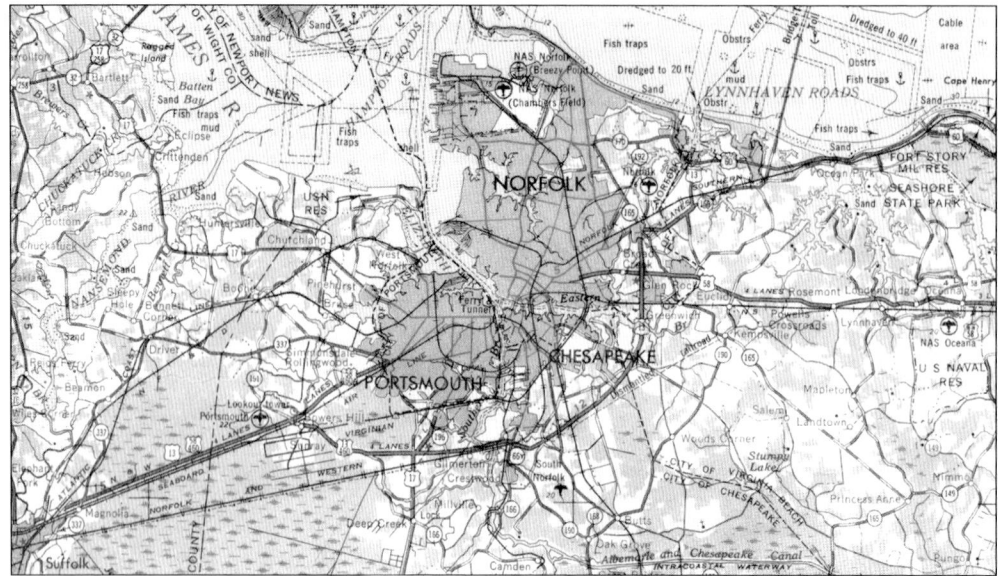

This 1950s map of Hampton Roads shows the original Norfolk Southern rail lines out of Norfolk into Virginia Beach, including the oceanfront, Fort Story, and Cape Henry. Today, abandoned lines are beneath sections of Pacific and Atlantic Avenues. (Courtesy of Kurt Reisweber.)

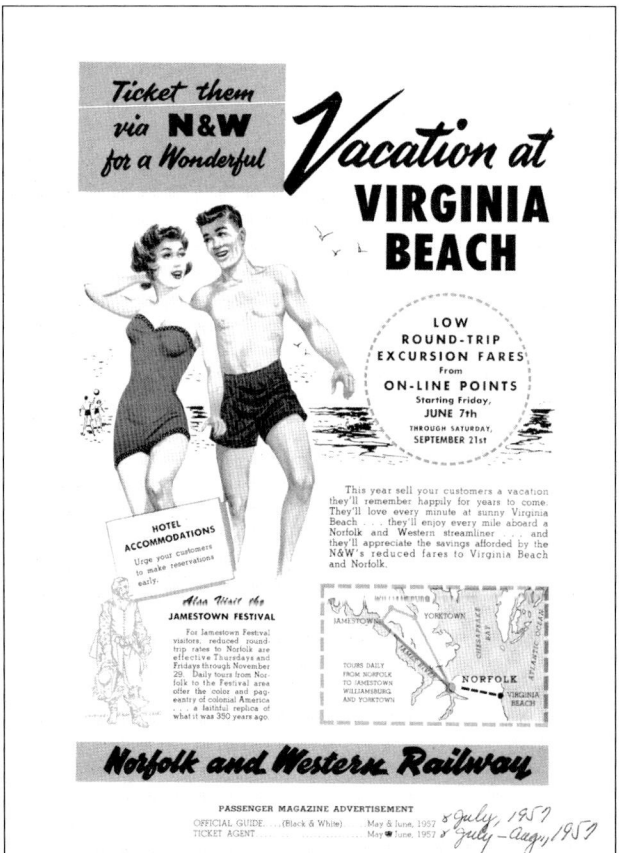

Norfolk & Western placed this advertisement in travel magazines in 1957 to encourage travel agents to book their clients a memorable vacation to Virginia Beach aboard one of the railroad's streamliner passenger trains. Along with frolicking in the Atlantic Ocean, visitors could take advantage of reduced fares to visit the Jamestown Festival. (Courtesy of Norfolk Southern.)

Five

THE VIRGINIAN RAILWAY

Known for its massive locomotives, oversize railcars, and long trains, the Virginian Railway was a leader in the development of motive power and equipment, operating some of rail's largest and best steam, electric, and diesel engines from the coalfields of southern West Virginia to the Norfolk port.

One of the last Class 1 railroads built in the eastern United States, the Virginian was the only major US railroad financed by one man, oil magnate Henry Huttleston Rogers. In the early 20th century, the Standard Oil Trust executive invested in entrepreneur Col. William N. Page's fledgling Deepwater Railway, a short line formed to haul coal out of the mountains of southern West Virginia to the coast. When the Norfolk & Western and Chesapeake & Ohio railroads refused to charge reasonable rates to interchange coal traffic, Rogers and Page created the intrastate Tidewater Railway, which extended to Hampton Roads. By 1907, they combined the Deepwater and the Tidewater to form the Virginian Railway.

Construction of the Virginian's line into Norfolk was expected to be ready for the 1907 Jamestown Exposition celebrating the 300th anniversary of the Jamestown settlement. The 441-mile main line from Sewells Point in Norfolk to Deepwater, West Virginia, was completed in January 1909, following a route across Virginia that avoided most of the state's largest cities. That April, Rogers's old friend Mark Twain joined him at a banquet in Norfolk celebrating the "Mountains to the Sea" railroad.

Traveling a route less than 1,000 miles long, the Virginian was nicknamed "the Richest Little Railroad in the World" as it earned a reputation for quality, reliability, and profitability. Its corporate offices were based at the Norfolk Terminal Station.

Throughout its 50-year existence, the Virginian was almost entirely dependent on coal traffic. The railroad's Sewells Point yard, which it built from 1907 to 1909 on land across from the Jamestown Exposition site, included two coal piers. However, by the 1950s, the Virginian's business had weakened due to coal strikes, a reduced demand for coal in Europe, and inflation, leaving the railroad ripe for a merger with Norfolk & Western. On December 1, 1959, Norfolk & Western acquired the Virginian. Norfolk & Western eventually retired the Sewells Point yard and coal piers and sold the facility to the US Navy in 1976. Today, a large portion of the Virginian's line remains in service as part of Norfolk Southern.

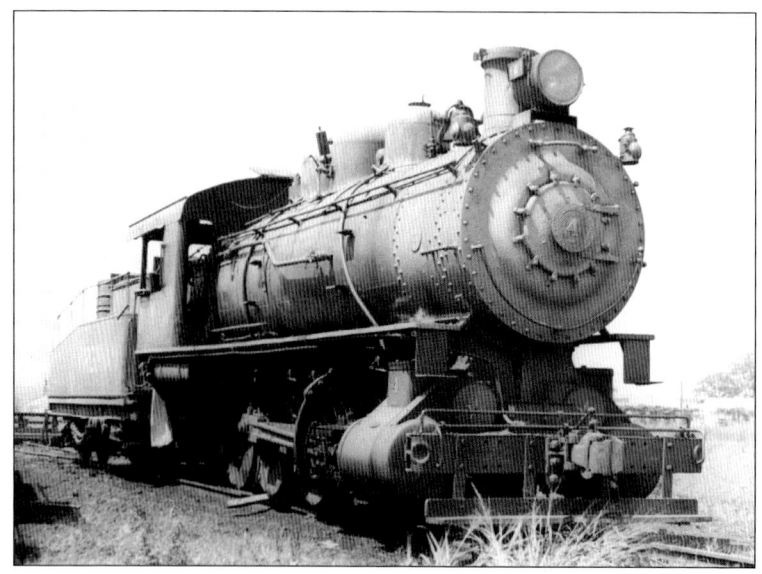

Built in 1910 for the Virginian Railway, this locomotive was retired in 1957. Now housed in the Virginia Transportation Museum in Roanoke, it is the last remaining steam engine from the Virginian. (Photograph by George E. Votava; courtesy of Kurt Reisweber.)

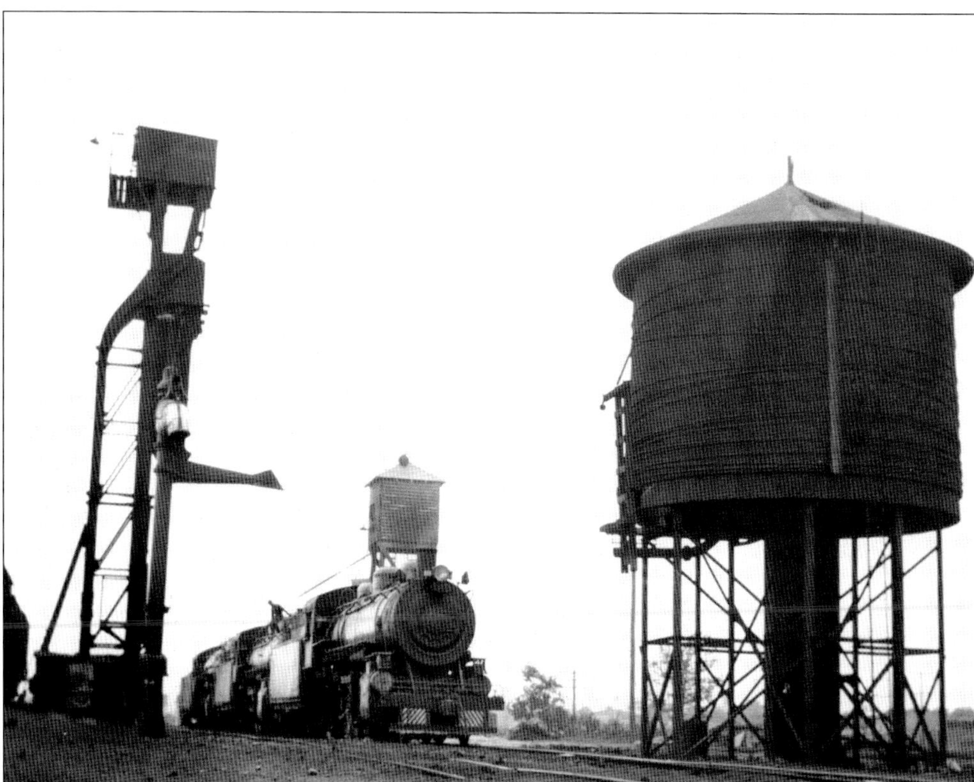

Locomotive No. 428 leads a line of three Virginian MB 2-8-2 steam engines in this May 1947 photograph taken near the wooden water tank at Sewells Point. The Virginian Railway used the fleet of Mikako steam locomotives from 1909 to 1956. (Courtesy of Kurt Reisweber.)

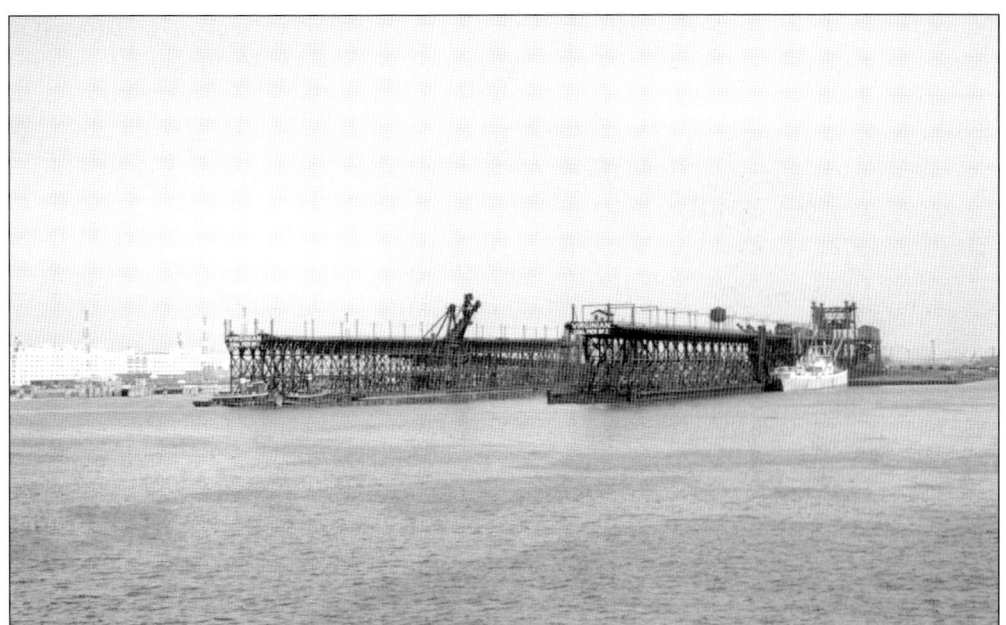

The Virginian Railway's $2.5 million Coal Pier 1 opened at Sewells Point in 1909 with a capacity of 5,400 tons of coal per hour. The $2 million Coal Pier 2 began operations in 1925. Electric pier cars carried coal from car dumpers to chutes on the piers where it was funneled into ship holds. The piers were also equipped with Seal-tite de-dusters to keep coal dust down during the dumping process. (Courtesy of Kurt Reisweber.)

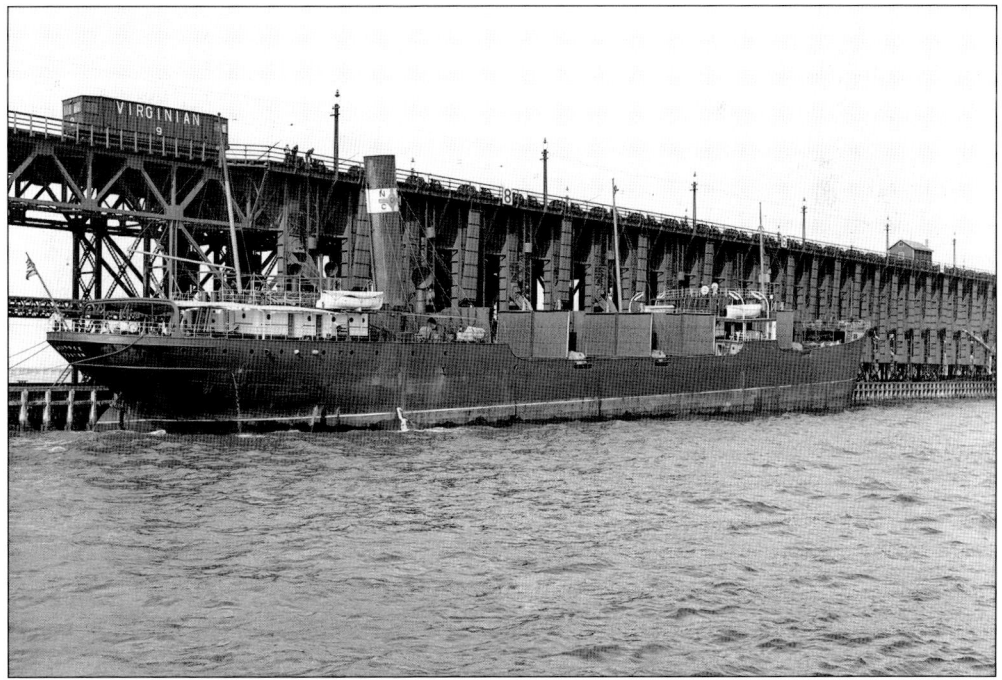

Coal is loaded onto the cargo ship *Melrose* at the Virginian Railway's Coal Pier 1 in this 1920 photograph. A cable-operated barney shoved loaded coal cars up an incline to a rotary dumper. The pier was rebuilt in 1939. (Courtesy of Norfolk Southern.)

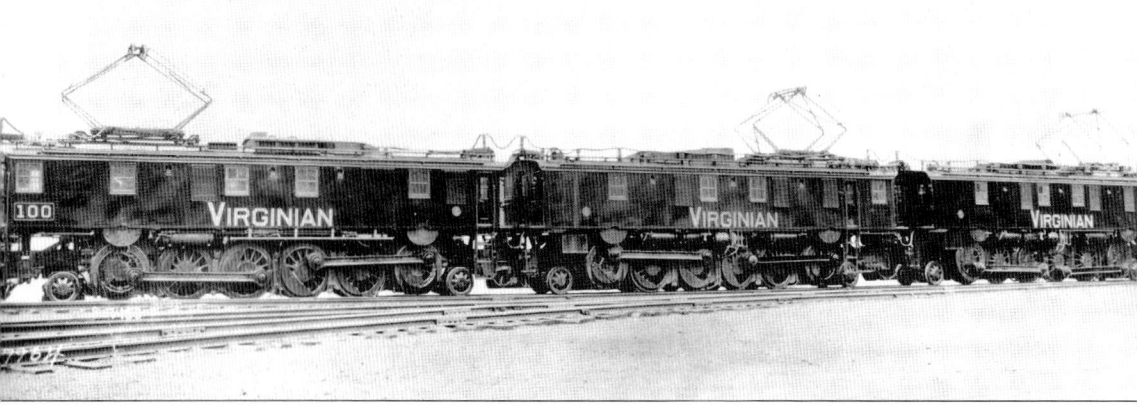

Seen in this 1926 photograph, the Virginian Electric Unit No. 100 was one of the 36 original ALCO/Westinghouse overhead electric units built for the Virginian Railway and used for 3,000-ton coal trains. The 152-foot locomotive was built in three sections to allow it to round curves. Each section contained two motors. (Courtesy of Norfolk Southern.)

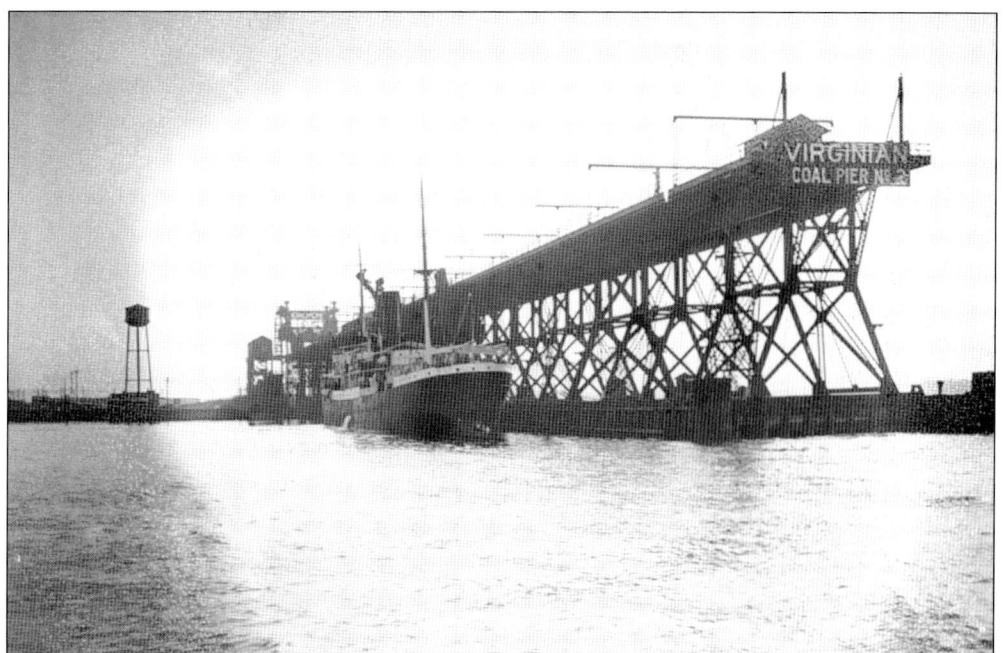

The Virginian Railway Coal Pier 2 is shown in this 1935 photograph. The pier had a capacity of 7,200 tons of coal per hour. It was upgraded in the late 1950s to include a rotary car dumper. Norfolk & Western officials were so impressed with that machinery that they used the design in the construction of Coal Pier 6, which opened in 1962 at Lamberts Point. (Courtesy of Sargeant Memorial Collection, Norfolk Public Library.)

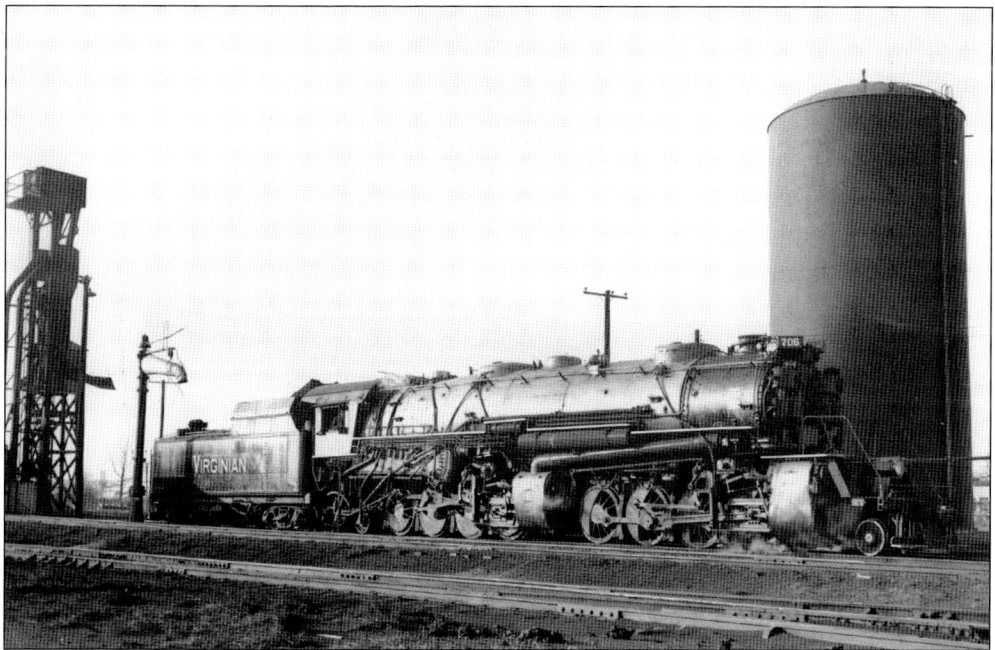

A Virginian Railway train arrives at Sewells Point in this 1948 photograph. Located on 611 acres adjacent to a naval base, Sewells Point was the railroad's eastern terminus. (Courtesy of Kurt Reisweber.)

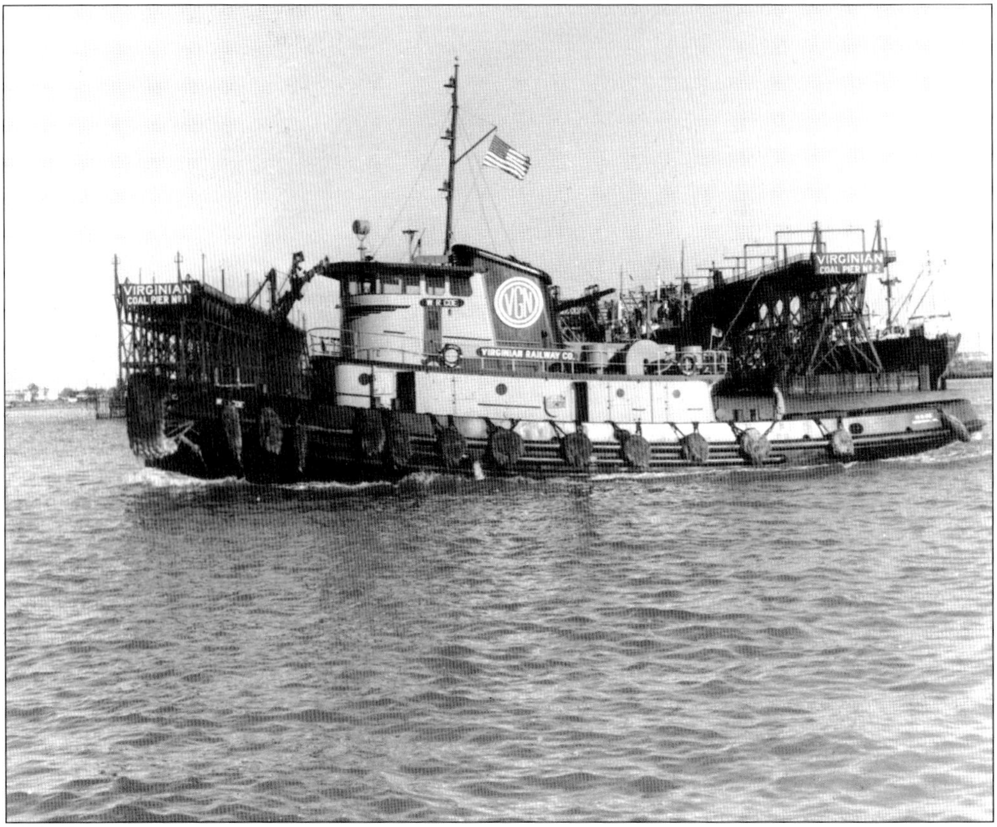

Virginian Railway tugboat the *W.R. Coe* is shown in front of the railroad's coal piers at Sewells Point in the late 1950s. The tugboat was named for William Robertson Coe, an insurance, railroad, and business executive who served on the Virginian board of directors from 1910 until his death in 1955. Coe was also briefly chairman of the board during World War II. (Photograph by Bob Lilgistrand; courtesy of Kurt Reisweber.)

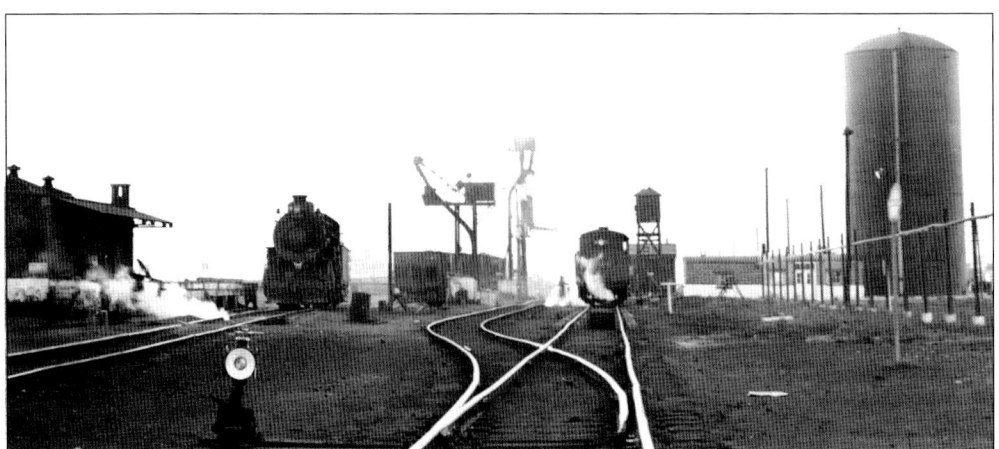

Taken at dusk, this 1950 photograph shows the Virginian Railway's yard at Sewells Point. The yard, coal piers, track, and other facilities were built from 1907 to 1909 and had storage space for about 5,000 railcars. (Courtesy of Kurt Reisweber.)

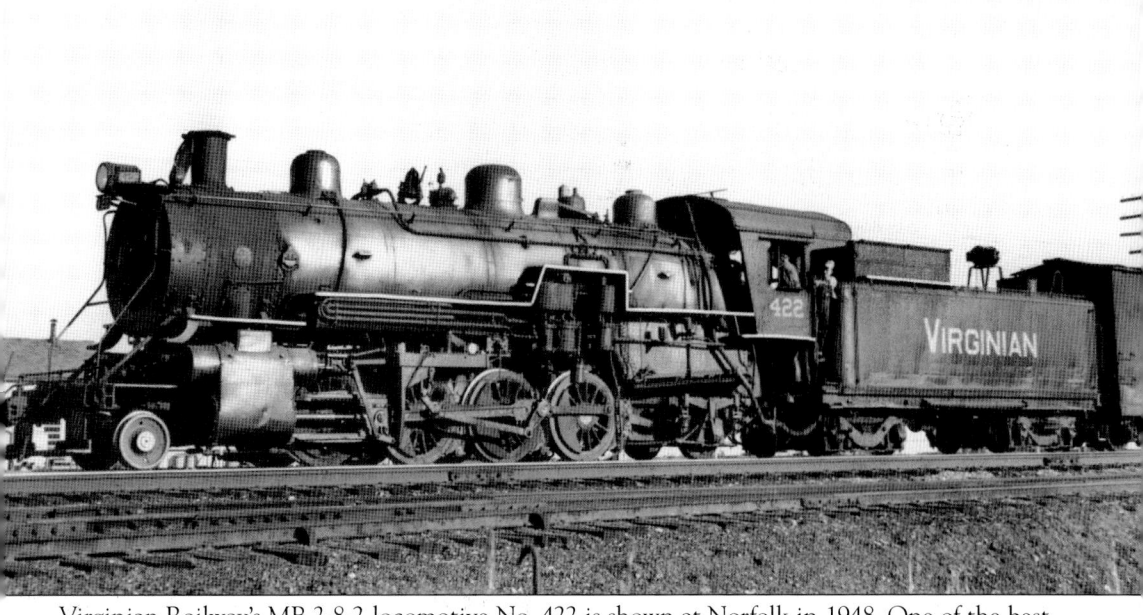

Virginian Railway's MB 2-8-2 locomotive No. 422 is shown at Norfolk in 1948. One of the best known of the Virginian's steam power, the MB 2-8-2 was designed in 1909 by George Halstead, the railroad's chief draftsman, and is considered the first example of the 2-8-2 wheel arrangement. Baldwin Locomotive Works built 42 of these locomotives for the Virginian during 1909–1910. (Photograph by H. Reid; courtesy of Kurt Reisweber.)

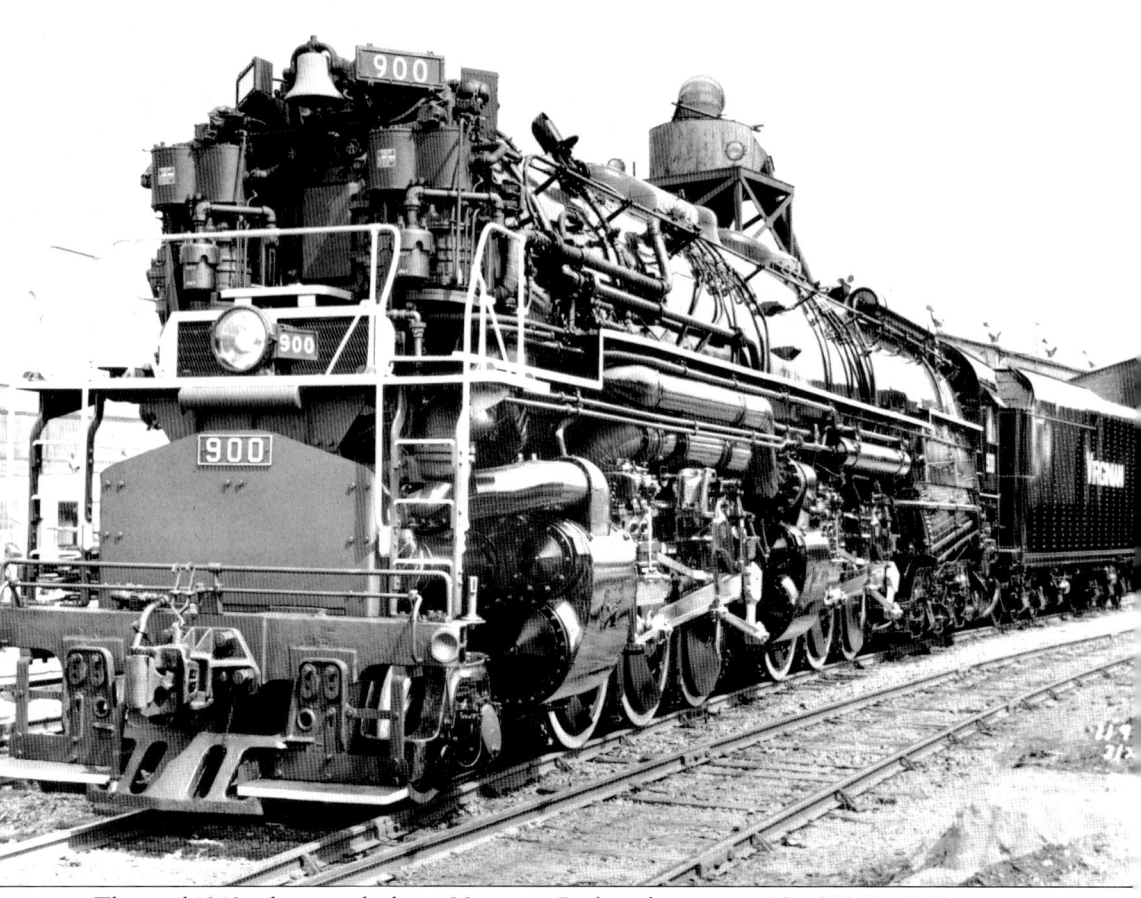

This mid-1940s photograph shows Virginian Railway locomotive No. 900. In 1945, an engineer was driving a short freight train out of Norfolk when its injector began to leak and water trickled into the firebox. The engineer ran to a nearby general store and bought a 10-pound sack of cornmeal, which he poured into the injector. The train then continued on its journey. (Courtesy of Norfolk Southern.)

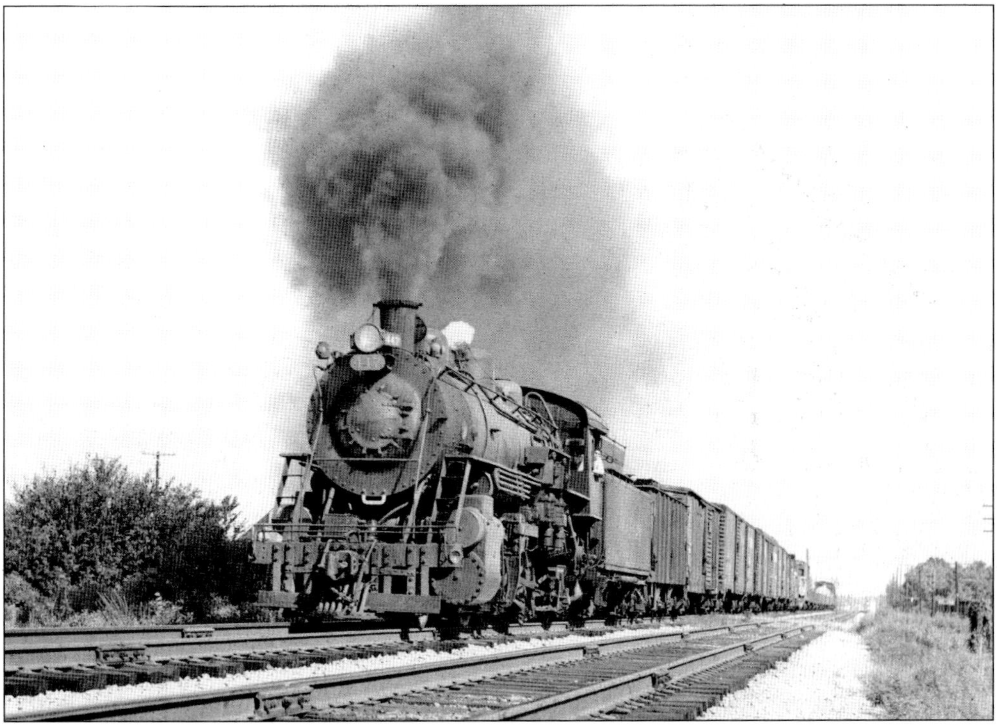

A Virginian Railway freight train is seen approaching Norview Avenue in Norfolk in 1951. Although the Virginian merged with Norfolk & Western in 1959, the two railroads actually operated in conjunction with each other during World War I when the US Railroad Administration took control of the roads. (Photograph by H. Reid; courtesy of Kurt Reisweber.)

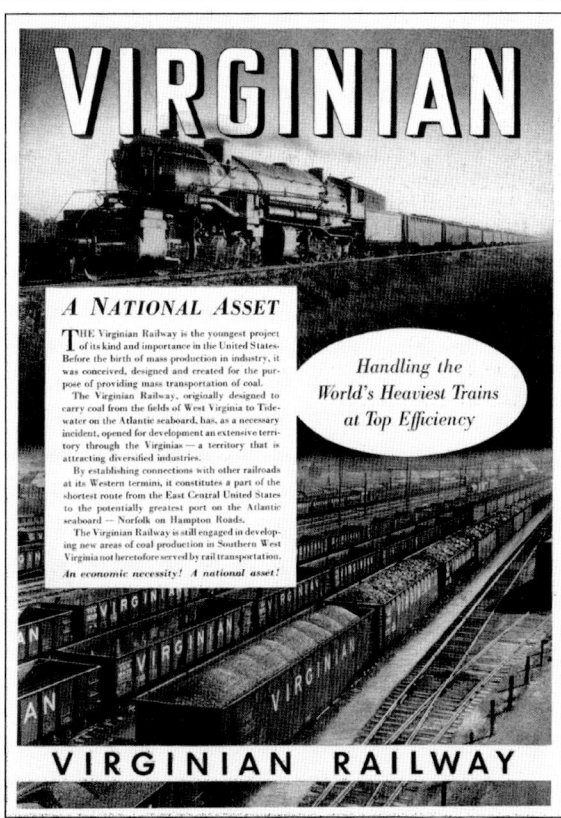

This 1940 advertisement for *Railway Age* magazine noted that the Virginian Railway had opened extensive areas for industrial development throughout Virginia and West Virginia while "handling the world's heaviest trains at top efficiency." Throughout its 50-year history, the Virginian continually achieved best operating efficiencies in the mountains, piedmont, and the coastal terrain. (Courtesy of Norfolk Southern.)

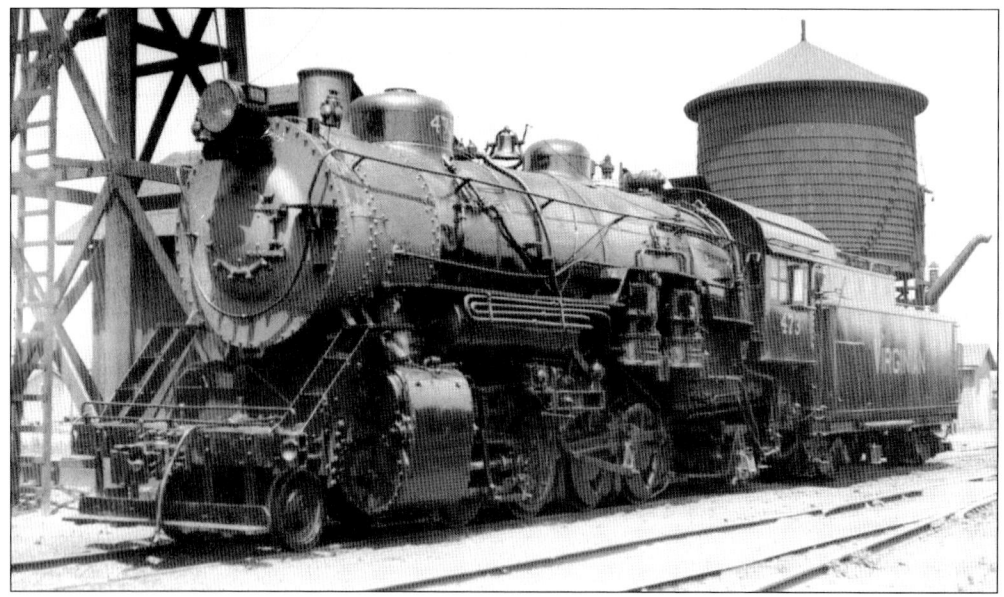

A Virginian Railway locomotive is pictured at Sewells Point in 1936. The Baldwin locomotive was built around 1912. The Virginian and Sewells Point provided critical support to the US Navy during the 20th century. The Virginian hauled the bituminous coal used for naval ships, while its former Sewells Point yard is now part of Naval Station Norfolk, the world's largest naval base. (Courtesy of Kurt Reisweber.)

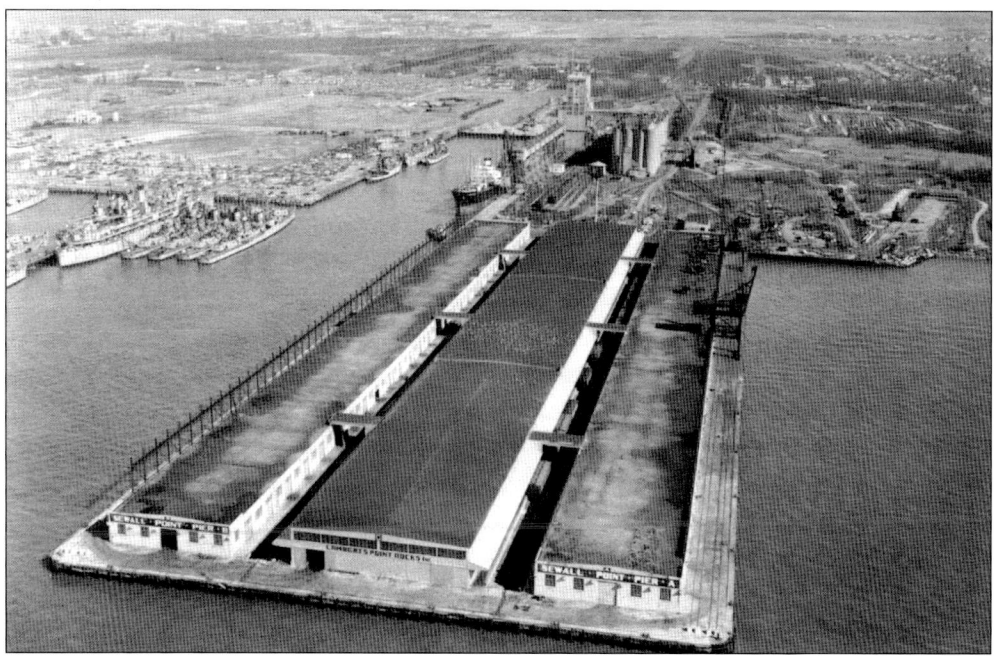

This aerial photograph of the Sewells Point piers was taken in February 1960, two months after the Virginian merged with Norfolk & Western. The following year, Norfolk & Western sold the Virginian's two merchandise piers along with three of its merchandise piers at Lamberts Point to the Virginia State Port Authority. The port authority then began construction on a $13.3 million merchandise pier that Norfolk & Western would later lease. (Courtesy of Norfolk Southern.)

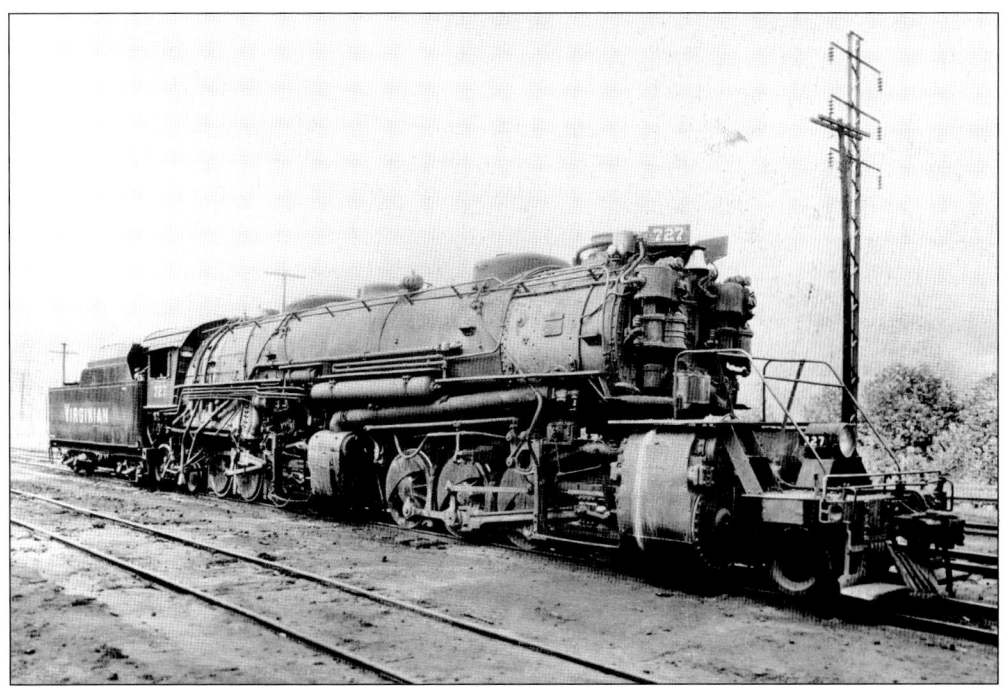

Virginian locomotive No. 727, a steam engine, is shown in October 1961, nearly two years after the railroad merged with Norfolk & Western. Although the Virginian mainly hauled coal, it offered passenger service on all of its lines during its early years. Its final passenger service between Roanoke and Norfolk ended in 1956. (Courtesy of Norfolk Southern.)

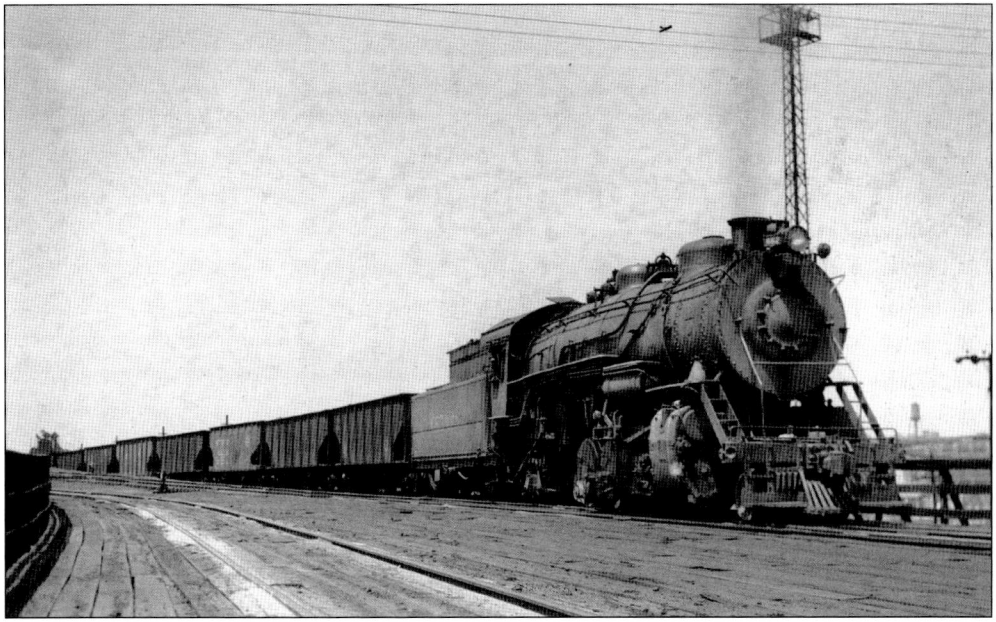

A Virginian Railway coal train is seen crossing Hampton Boulevard in this 1949 photograph. The Virginian was the youngest of the three Pocahontas railroads—Norfolk & Western and Chesapeake & Ohio were the other two—that carried coal from Appalachian coal mines, and the first to end operations. (Photograph by Wally Johnson; courtesy of Kurt Reisweber.)

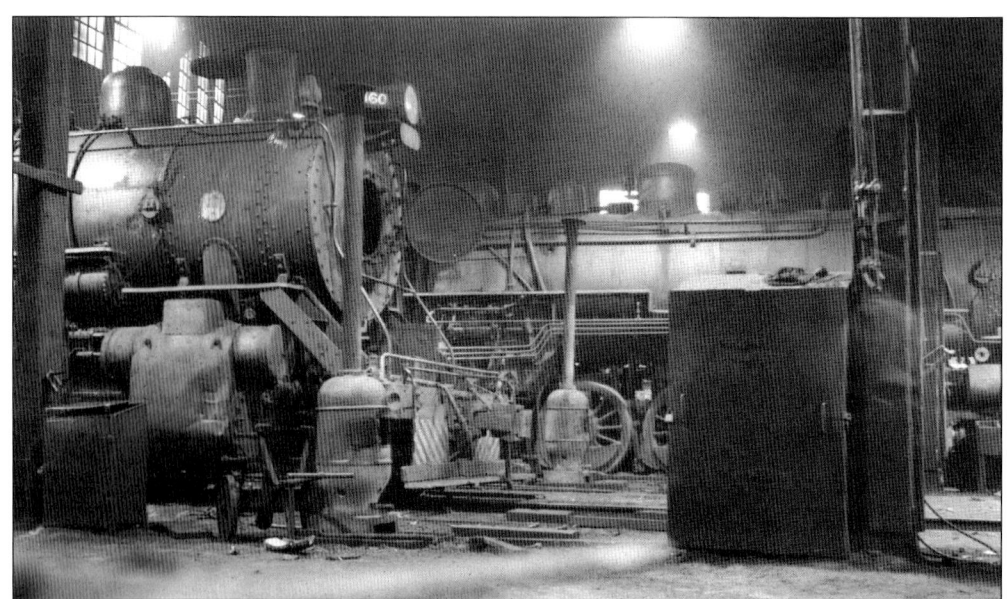

Several Virginian Railway engines are shown undergoing repairs in this May 1953 photograph taken inside the roundhouse at Sewells Point. Engine No. 460 in the foreground was built by Baldwin Locomotive Works in 1910 and was part of the railroad's fleet of steam locomotives until 1956. (Photograph by H. Reid; courtesy of Kurt Reisweber.)

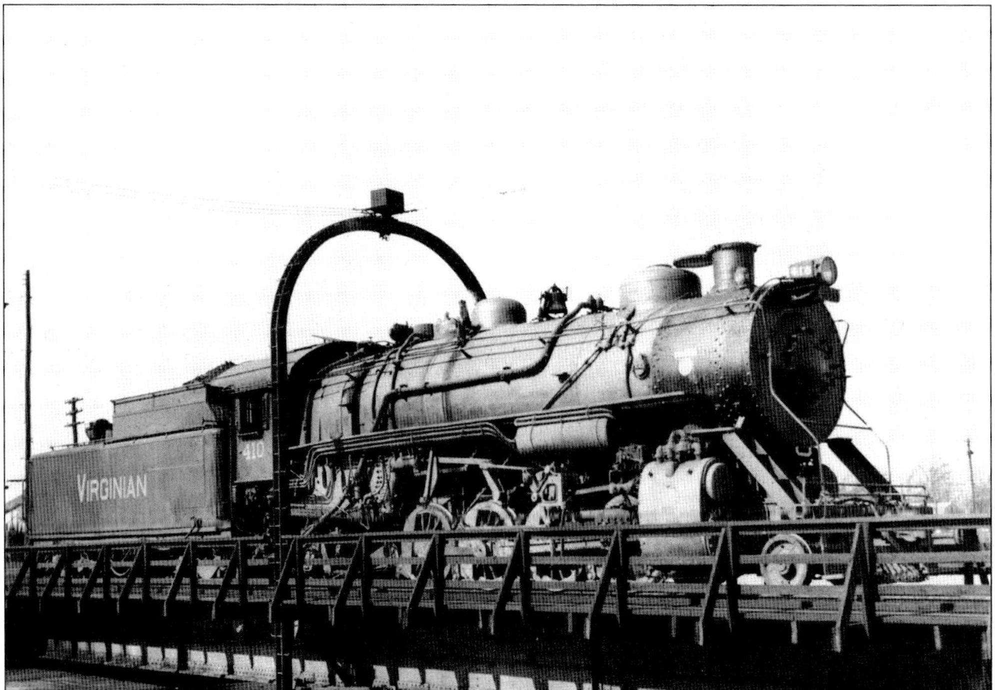

The Virginian No. 410 is shown on the turntable at Sewells Point in June 1949. The 130-foot turntable was installed in 1945, replacing an 80-foot turntable. (Photograph by H. Reid; courtesy of Kurt Reisweber.)

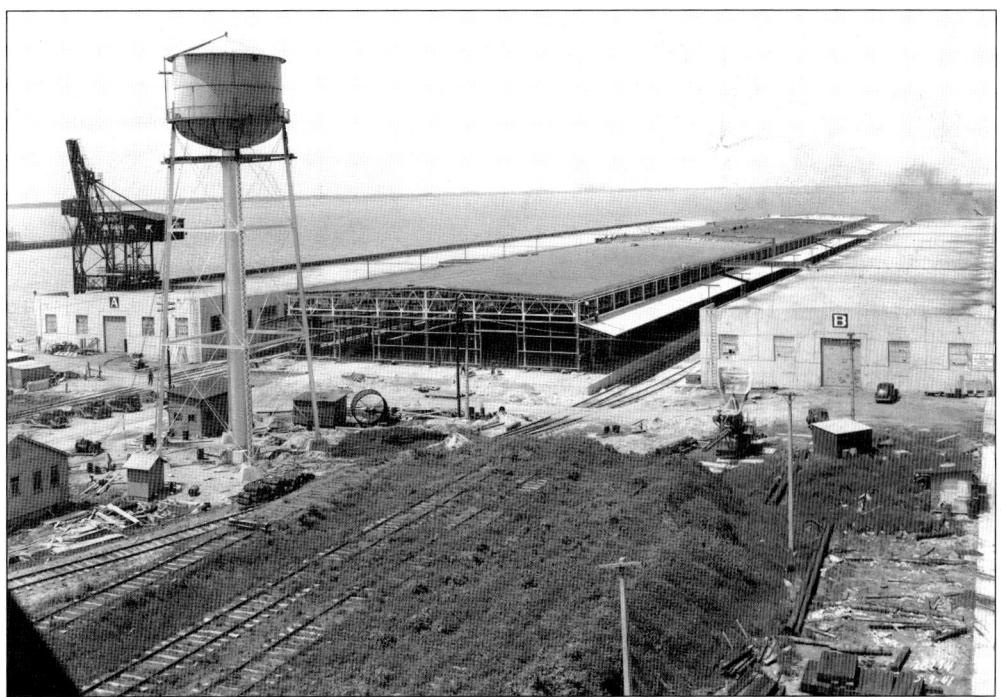

Warehouse G at Sewells Point is seen in this 1941 photograph. The Virginian Terminal Railway Company initially owned the yard and port and warehouse facilities at Sewells Point before merging into its parent company, Virginian Railway, in 1936. (Courtesy of Norfolk Southern.)

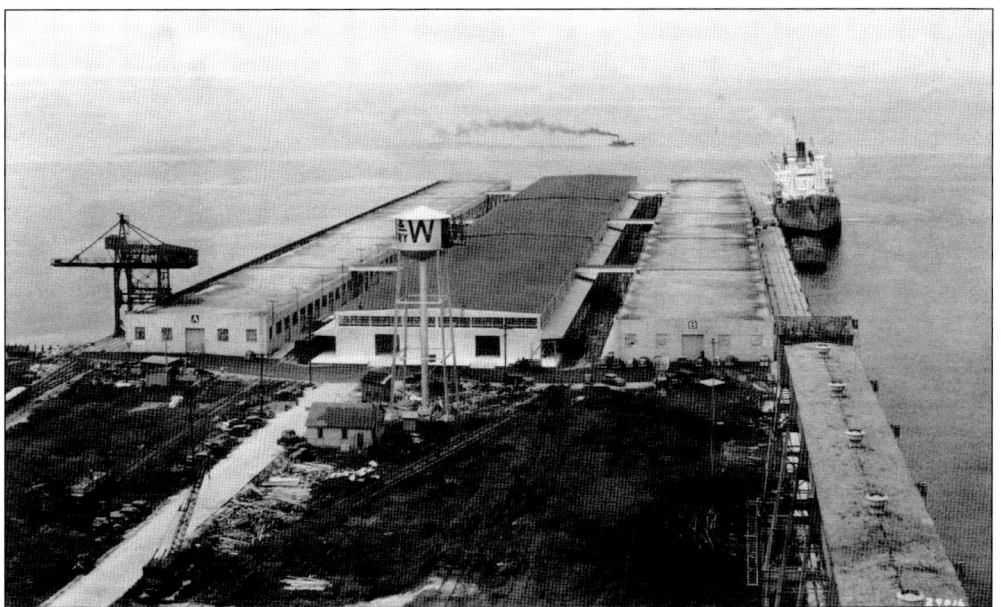

This photograph was taken from the top floor of the grain elevator at Sewells Point shortly after the merger between the Virginian and Norfolk & Western. Norfolk & Western reduced operations at Sewells Point in the mid-1960s, removing the coal piers and mainly using the yard to store loaded coal cars until 1974. The railroad sold the facility to the US Navy in 1976. (Courtesy of Norfolk Southern.)

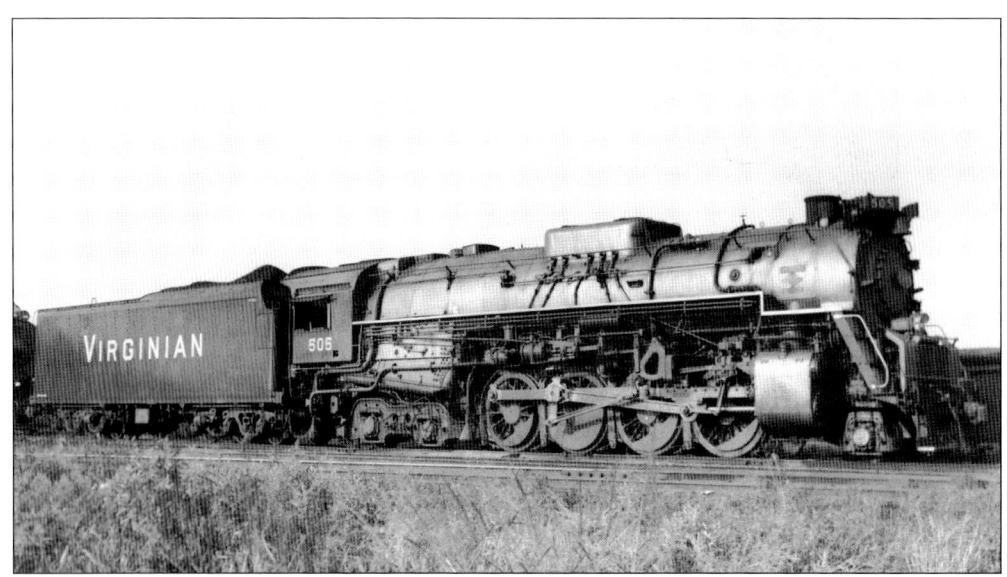

Virginian steam locomotive No. 505 heads into Sewells Point from Roanoke in this 1946 photograph. Built by Lima Locomotive Works of Lima, Ohio, with a 2-8-4 wheel arrangement, the 505 was a workhorse. It was claimed the engine once hit 87 miles per hour as it pulled a 3,500-ton train. (Courtesy of Kurt Reisweber.)

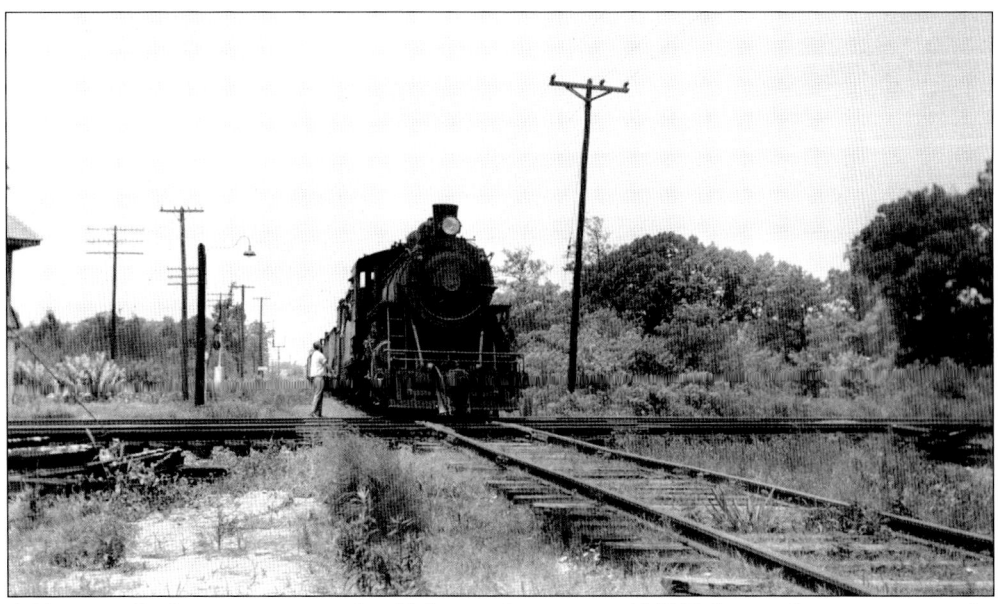

A Virginian Railway train approaches Tidewater Junction in 1947. Tidewater Junction was on the Virginian's main line between Sewells Point and South Norfolk. (Courtesy of Kurt Reisweber.)

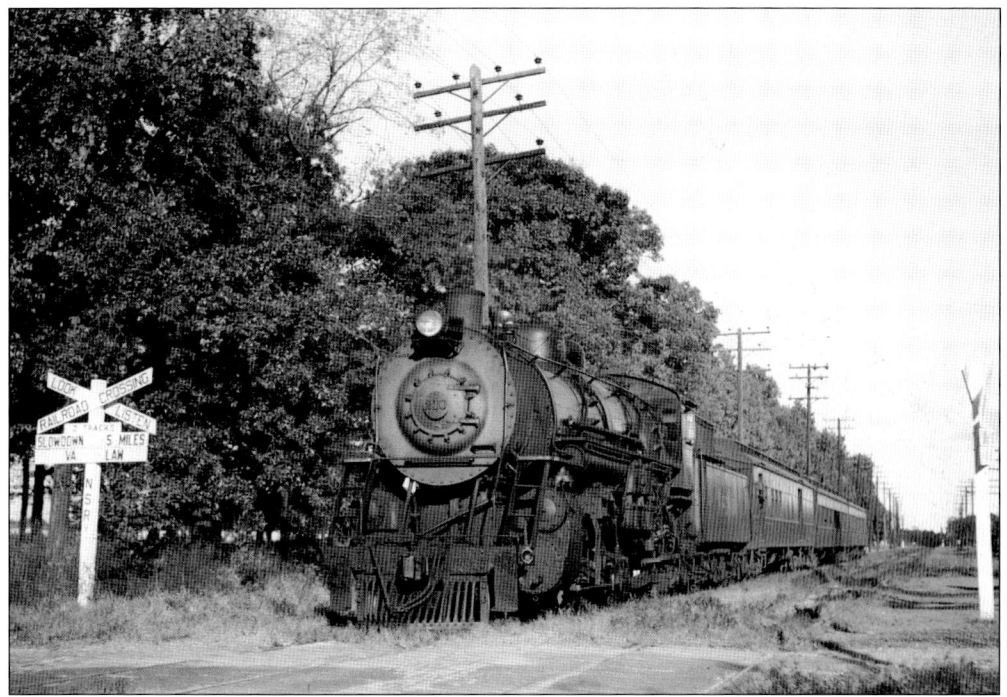

Powered by locomotive No. 210, this Virginian Railway train was photographed on the old Norfolk Southern line traveling east of Norfolk State University in 1949. Today, much of The Tide light rail system follows the Virginian's former right-of-way. (Courtesy of Kurt Reisweber.)

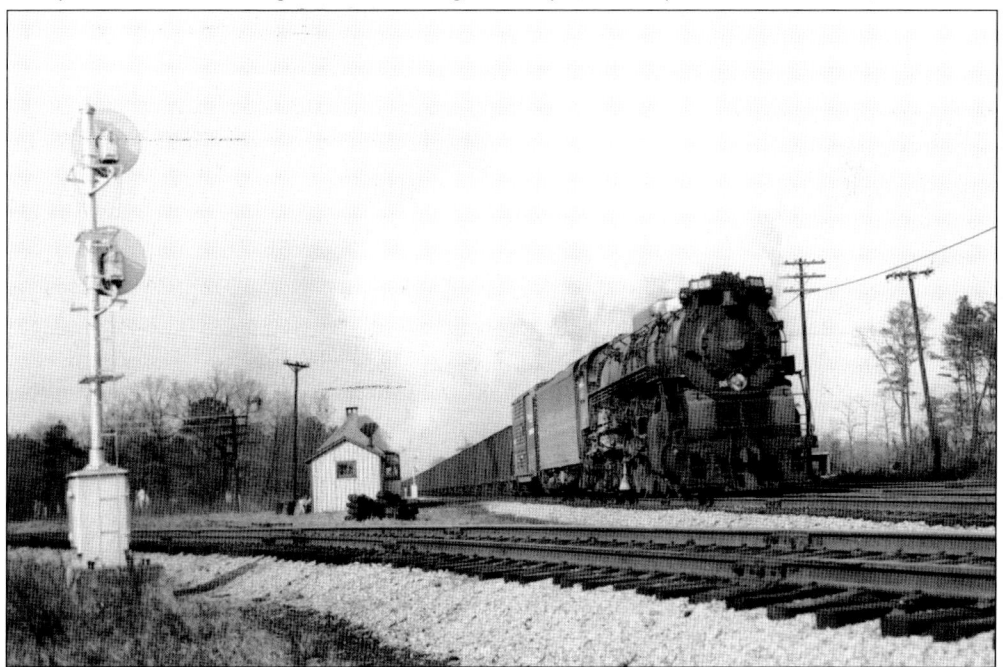

A Virginian Railway train approaches Tidewater Tower in 1954. The track in the foreground is a Virginian track that connected with the old Norfolk Southern track leading to Norfolk Terminal Station. (Courtesy of Kurt Reisweber.)

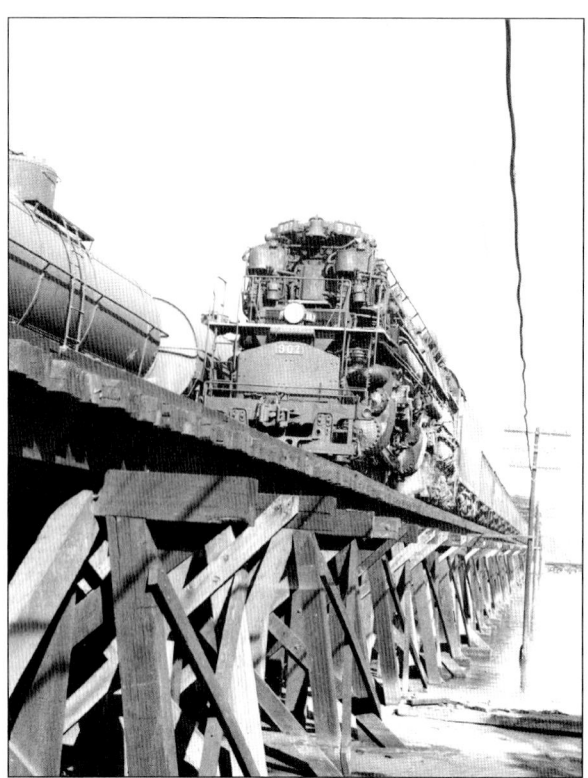

A Virginian Railway train, powered by locomotive No. 907, travels on the Eastern Branch Bridge crossing the trestle over the Elizabeth River in 1951. The locomotive was part of the Virginian's Blue Ridge class of engines, among the most powerful and heaviest steam locomotives ever built. (Courtesy of Kurt Reisweber.)

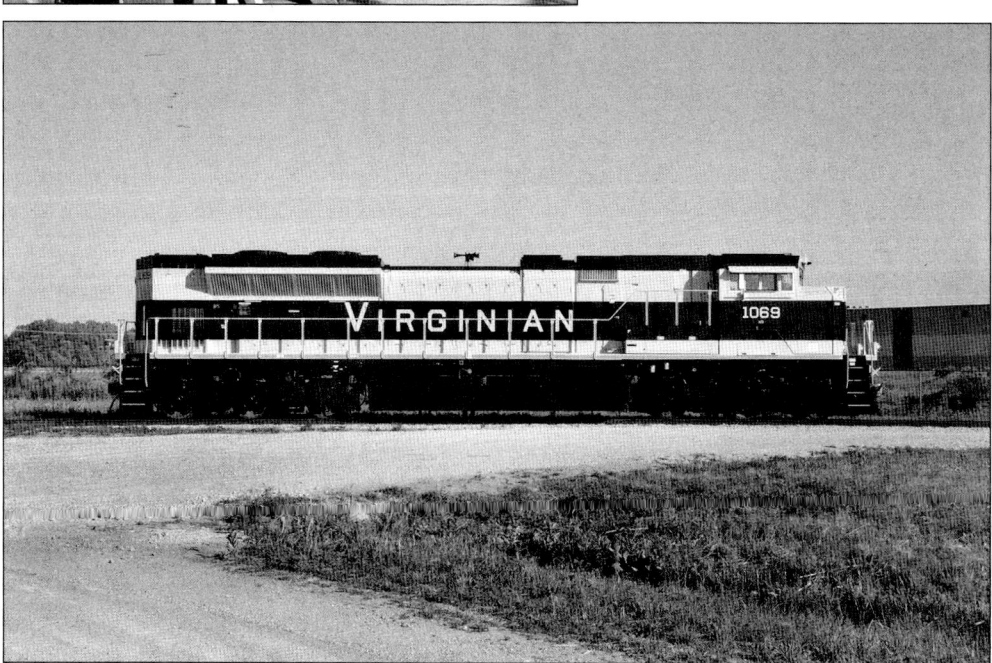

The Virginian Railway was one of 20 predecessor railroads Norfolk Southern honored during its 30th anniversary celebration in 2012. The EMD SD-70ACe unit was painted at the Progress Rail Services facility in Muncie, Indiana, in a commemorative scheme representing the Virginian. (Courtesy of Norfolk Southern.)

Six

The Railroad in Downtown Norfolk

Norfolk Southern's emerald green office tower has been a prominent part of the downtown Norfolk skyline for more than three decades, but the railroad and its predecessor lines have been a fixture on the city's bustling waterfront since the late 1850s.

In 1856, officials of the Norfolk & Petersburg Railroad purchased a site on the eastern end of Main Street to bring the line into Norfolk across the Eastern Branch of the Elizabeth River. Known as Bramble's Point, the parcel bordered Newton's Creek, the mouth of which Norfolk & Petersburg chief engineer William Mahone filled to create a strip of land for the railroad's Norfolk terminal and yard. Tracks from the terminal gave Norfolk & Petersburg trains direct access to waterfront warehouses and wharves. By the 20th century, Newton's Creek was completely filled in for residential development.

Norfolk & Petersburg descendent Norfolk & Western continued to have a large presence on the Elizabeth River in the late 1800s, building warehouses for cotton and other freight, a coal pier, and lumber and train sheds. In 1882, Norfolk & Western opened a large passenger station in downtown Norfolk, the eastern terminus of the railroad. After the station was destroyed in an October 1909 fire, the Norfolk Terminal Railway Company was formed to build a new facility serving Norfolk & Western, the Virginian Railway, and Norfolk Southern Railroad. Completed in 1912 near the old Norfolk & Petersburg yard, Norfolk Terminal Station was an eight-story brick building trimmed with gray stone. Passenger waiting rooms were on the ground level, while the three railroads had offices on the upper floors, with the Virginian's general offices covering the top three floors. The station closed in 1962 and was demolished the following year.

In 1982, the newly formed Norfolk Southern Corporation set up temporary headquarters in downtown Norfolk's Virginia Bank building, which later became Bank of America before being renovated into an upscale apartment building known as ICON in 2017. Ground was broken for the railroad's office tower in 1986.

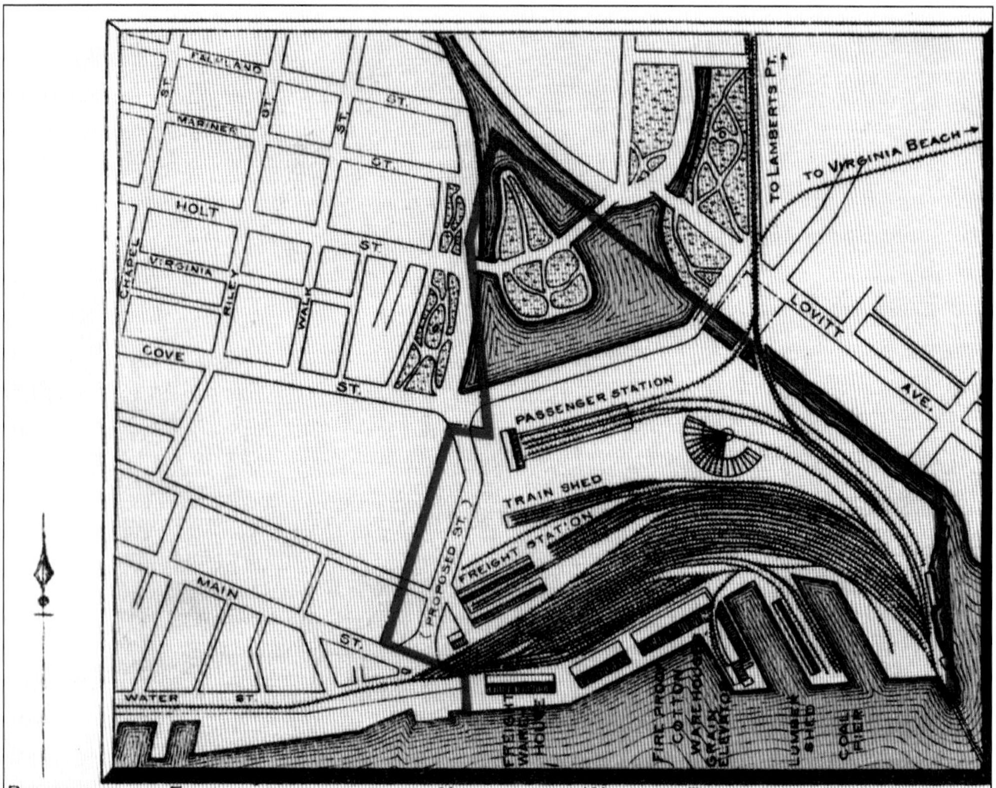

This late-1800s drawing shows Norfolk & Western's facilities in downtown Norfolk. Along with coal and cargo piers, warehouses, and a grain elevator, the railroad's passenger station was based in the downtown district. (Courtesy of Kurt Reisweber.)

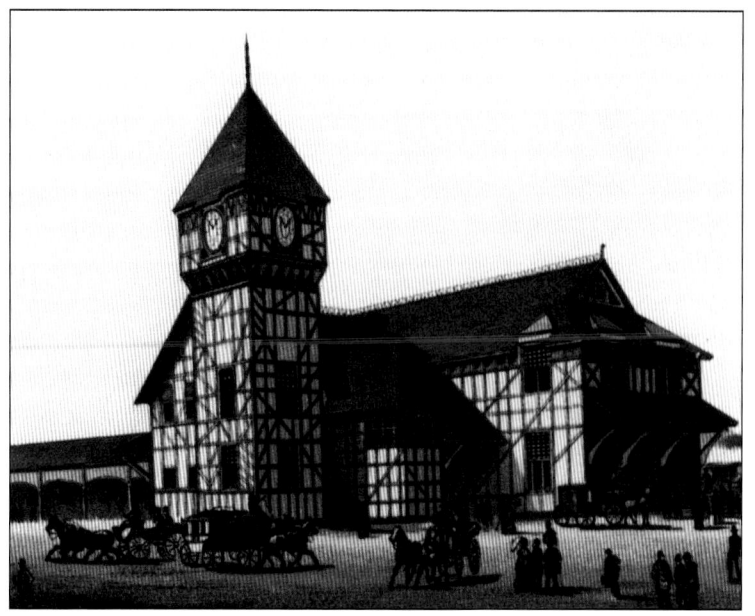

Norfolk & Western's passenger station fronted Main Street. The wooden structure featured a pyramidal roof and an 80-foot-tall tower adorned with a four-faced clock. It was destroyed in a fire on October 13, 1909. (Courtesy of Norfolk Southern.)

Published in Norfolk & Western's 1891 annual report, this map shows the railroad's lines in Norfolk. A proposed beltline crossing the Southern Branch of the Elizabeth River is also shown, as is the Atlantic & Danville Railroad line into Portsmouth. (Courtesy of Kurt Reisweber.)

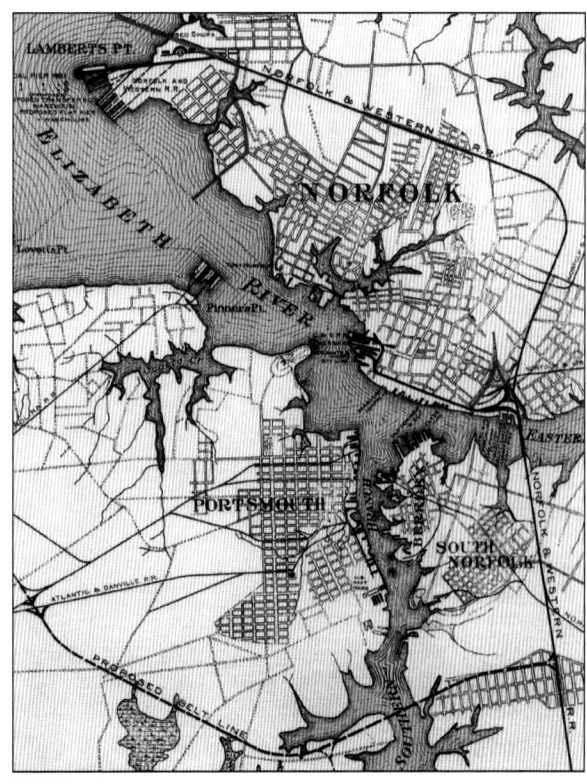

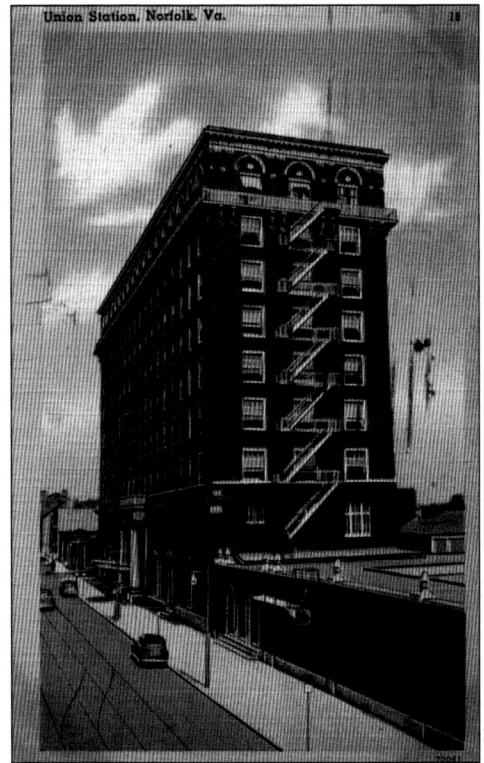

After the Main Street passenger station burned down, Norfolk Terminal Railway Company was formed in 1910 to build a new brick facility for the city's three passenger railroads: Norfolk & Western, Virginian Railway, and Norfolk Southern. Union Station, also known as Terminal Station, opened in 1912 at 1200 East Main Street in the vicinity of what is now Harbor Park. (Author's collection.)

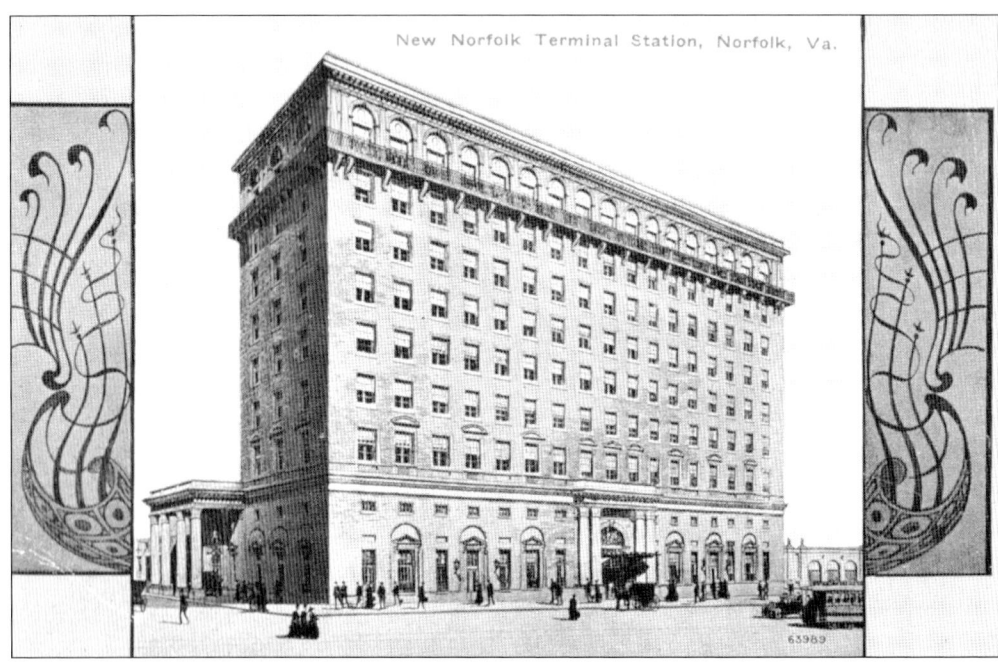

Designed by architectural firm Reed and Stem, which drew up the plans for New York's Grand Central Terminal, the eight-story Norfolk Terminal Station was an impressive site. A metal balcony encircled the top floor, which was marked by alcoves with round arches. When it opened in May 1912, the *Virginian-Pilot and Norfolk Landmark* noted that the station "contains the latest equipment in train sheds with umbrella roofs, handsome and commodious lobby and waiting rooms, separate rest rooms for women and smoking rooms for men." (Courtesy of Norfolk Southern.)

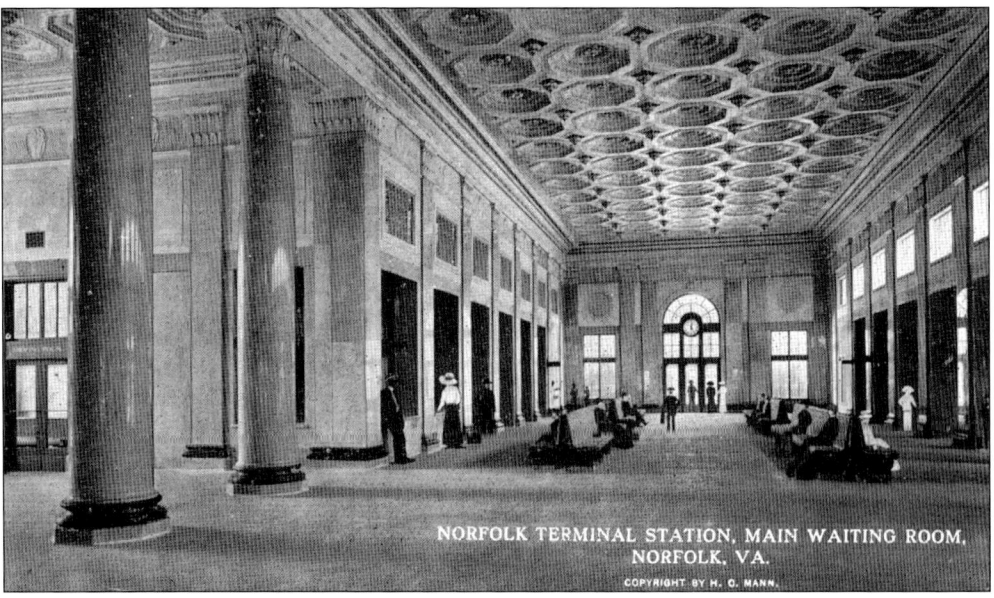

Norfolk Terminal Station's main waiting room was decorated with marble Corinthian columns and featured terrazzo flooring and an ornate stucco ceiling. However, by the 1940s, the once elegant station had fallen into disrepair, marked by scarred benches, messy ash stands and cuspidors, and leaking radiators. (Courtesy of Kurt Reisweber.)

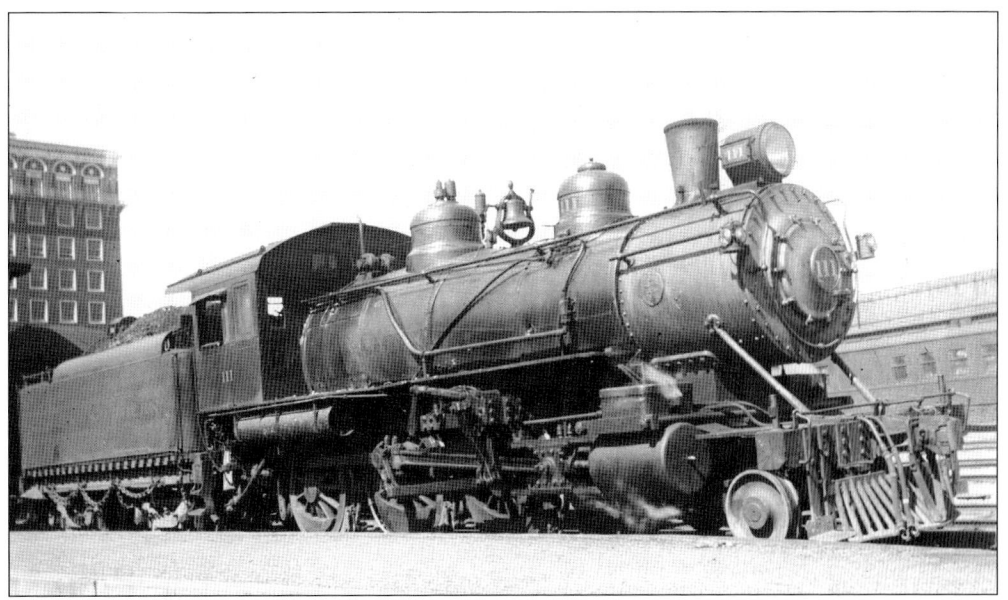

A steam-powered Norfolk Southern train pulls out of Terminal Station in this 1932 photograph. Offices of the Virginian Railway, Norfolk & Western, and Norfolk Southern occupied the upper levels of the building, while passenger facilities were on the ground floor. (Courtesy of Kurt Reisweber.)

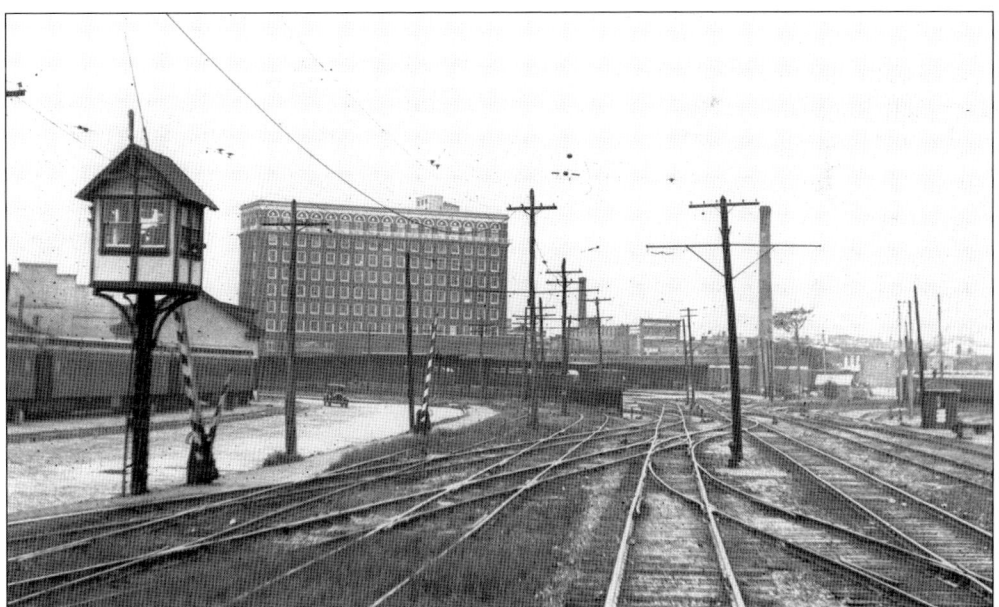

Tracks leading into Terminal Station are shown in this photograph. Norfolk Southern stopped running trains into the station in the late 1940s, while the Virginian Railway continued using the station until 1956 when it ended passenger service. Norfolk & Western used Terminal Station until 1962 when it built a new passenger station at Lamberts Point. Terminal Station was demolished in 1963. (Courtesy of Kurt Reisweber.)

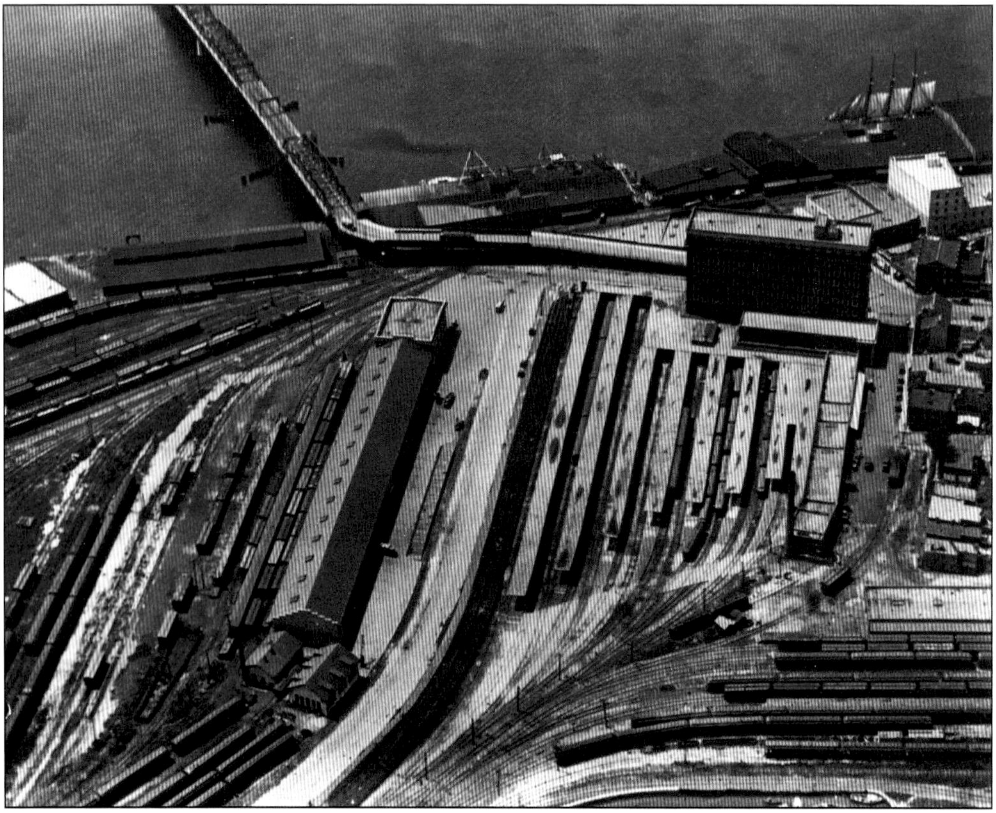

This mid–20th century photograph shows an aerial view of Terminal Station. The Virginian Railway used the station's top three floors as its headquarters until it merged with Norfolk & Western in 1959. The station also housed Norfolk Southern's general offices until the early 1960s when the railroad moved its headquarters to Raleigh, North Carolina. (Courtesy of Kurt Reisweber.)

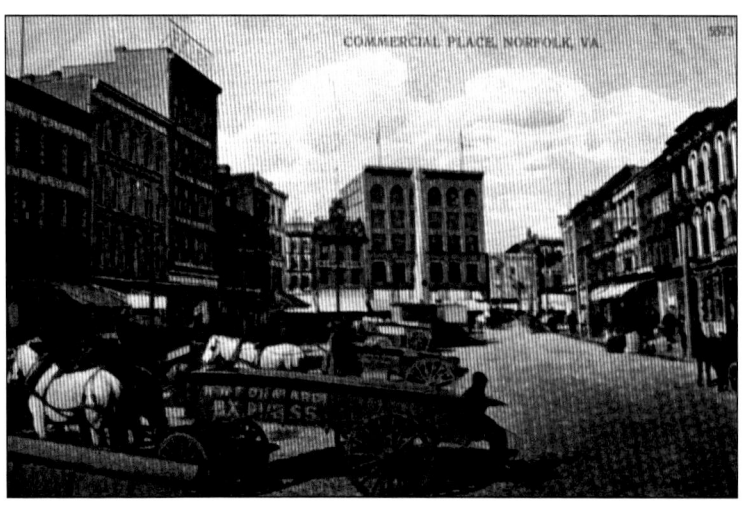

Norfolk's Commercial Place, site of the future Norfolk Southern headquarters, was a bustling scene in 1909. Nearly 80 years later, Norfolk Southern's building would be constructed on the right. (Author's collection.)

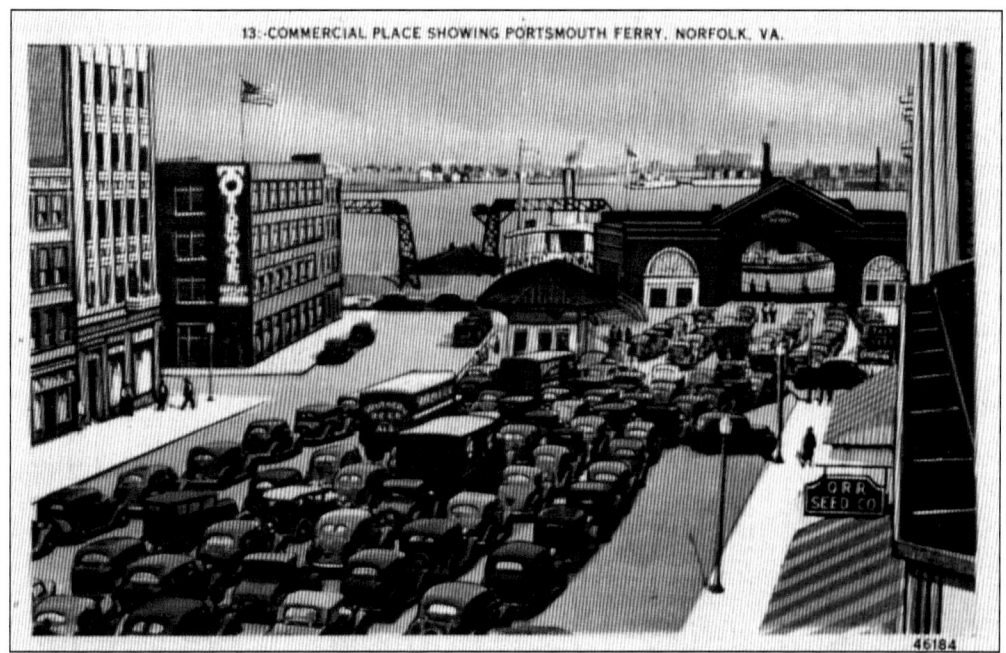

Another postcard from the early 1900s shows cars lining up on Commercial Place for the Portsmouth ferry. At the time, Norfolk Southern predecessor Norfolk & Western had several piers and warehouses along the waterfront. (Author's collection.)

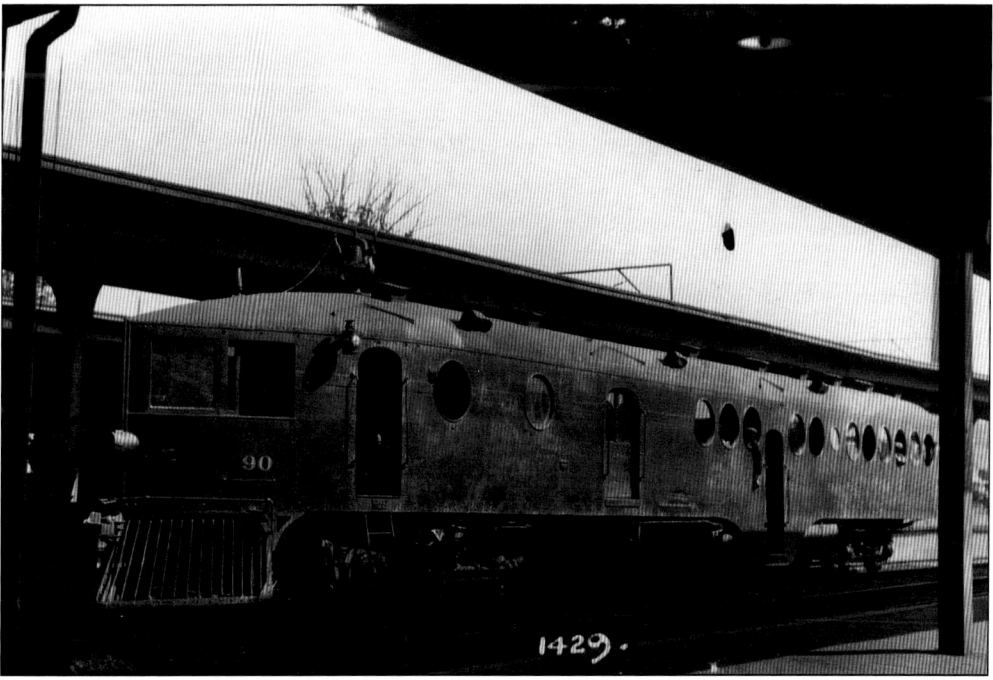

One of Norfolk Southern's early gasoline motor cars is pictured at Terminal Station during World War I. The railroad purchased the 70-foot car in 1909. The cars were the world's first all-steel, self-propelled train car design. (Courtesy of Kurt Reisweber.)

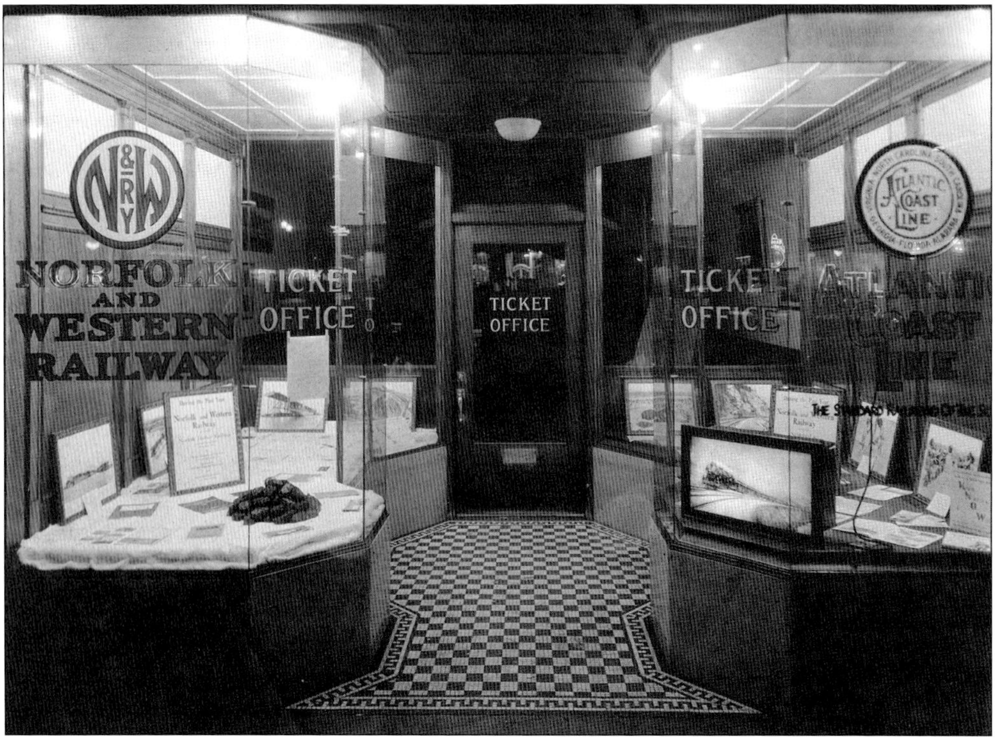

Norfolk & Western's ticket office in downtown Norfolk also housed ticket functions for the Atlantic Coast Line, as shown in this 1933 photograph of the office's window display. The Atlantic Coast Line existed from 1900 until 1967 when it merged with rival Seaboard Air Line Railroad to form the Seaboard Coast Line Railroad. (Courtesy of Norfolk Southern.)

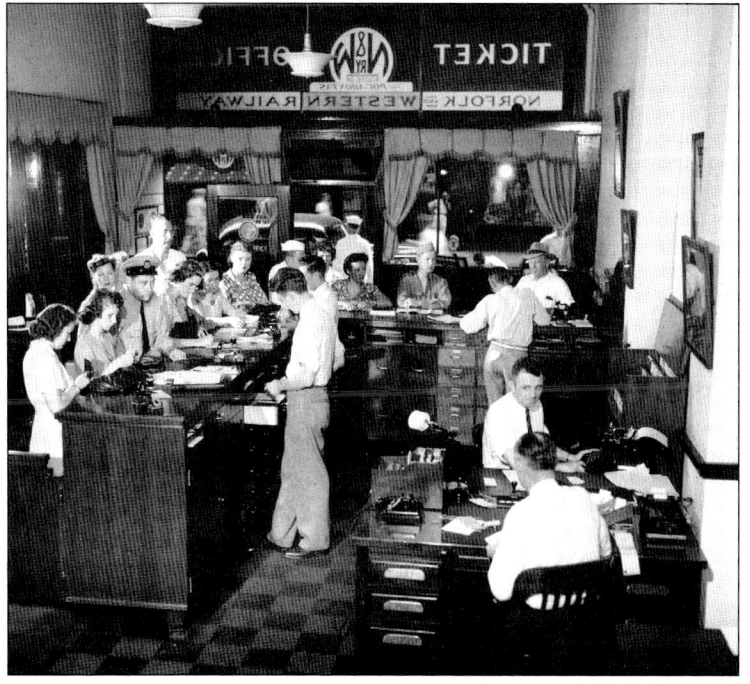

In this 1940s-era photograph, agents assist travelers at Norfolk & Western's busy downtown Norfolk ticket office. Despite the office's bustling appearance, passenger service never provided a substantial portion of Norfolk & Western's revenue. (Courtesy of Norfolk Southern.)

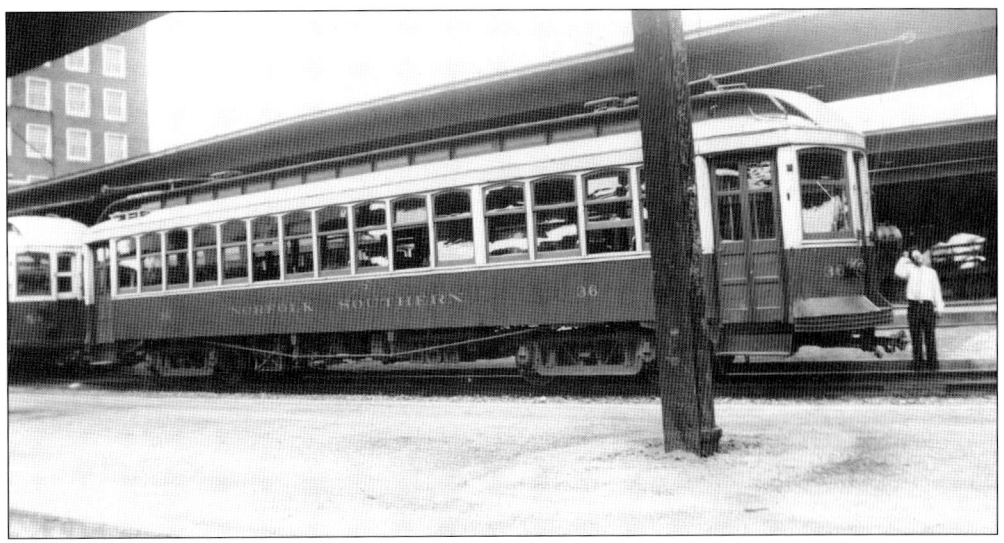

One of Norfolk Southern's electrified cars sits at Terminal Station before heading to Virginia Beach in the late 1930s. Rail lines to Virginia Beach were electrified for many years. (Courtesy of Kurt Reisweber.)

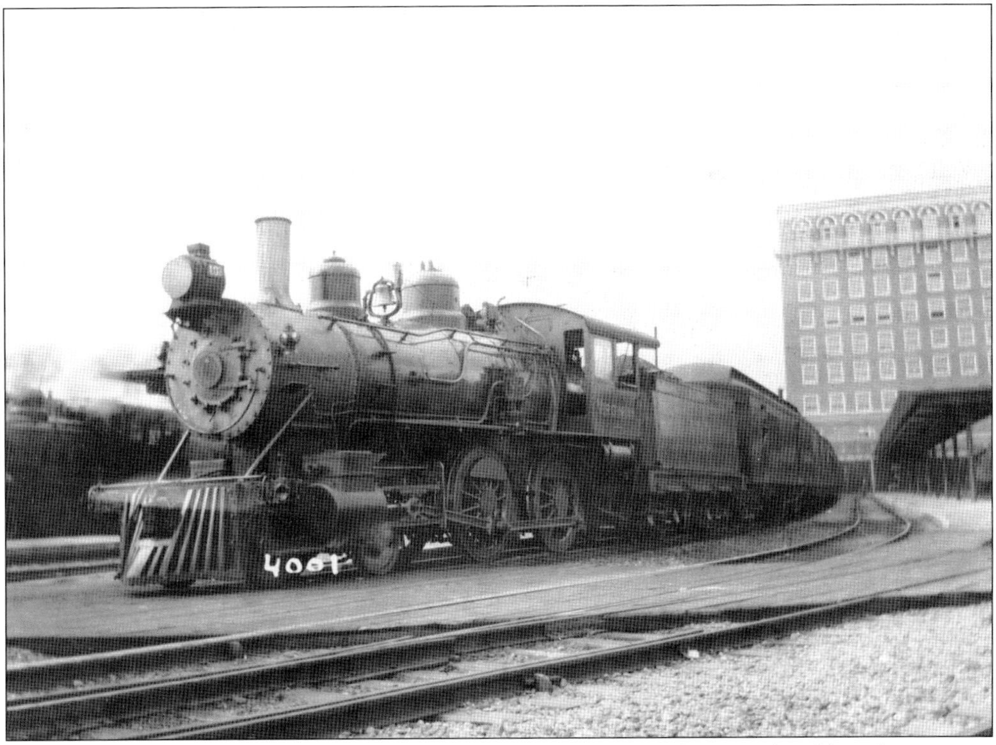

A Virginian Railway train leaves Terminal Station in this c. 1930s photograph. Although passenger service was available on all of the Virginian's lines during its early years, by 1941 it was only offered on the main line. (Photograph by Railroad Museum of Pennsylvania; courtesy of Kurt Reisweber.)

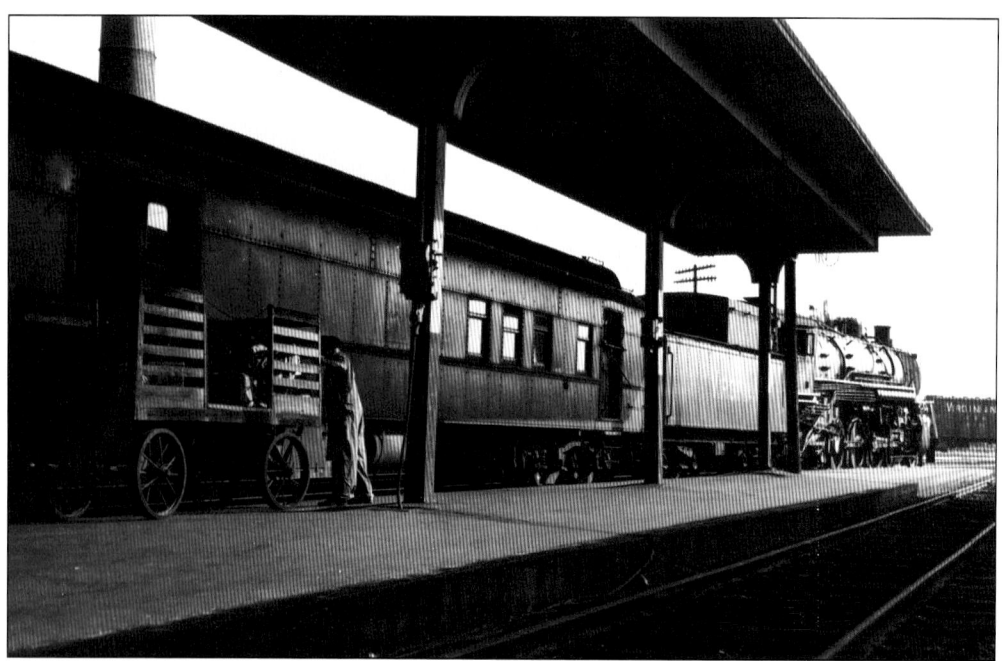

Luggage is loaded onto a Virginian Railway passenger train in this undated photograph The Virginian continued to provide passenger service to Norfolk from Roanoke until 1956. (Courtesy of Kurt Reisweber.)

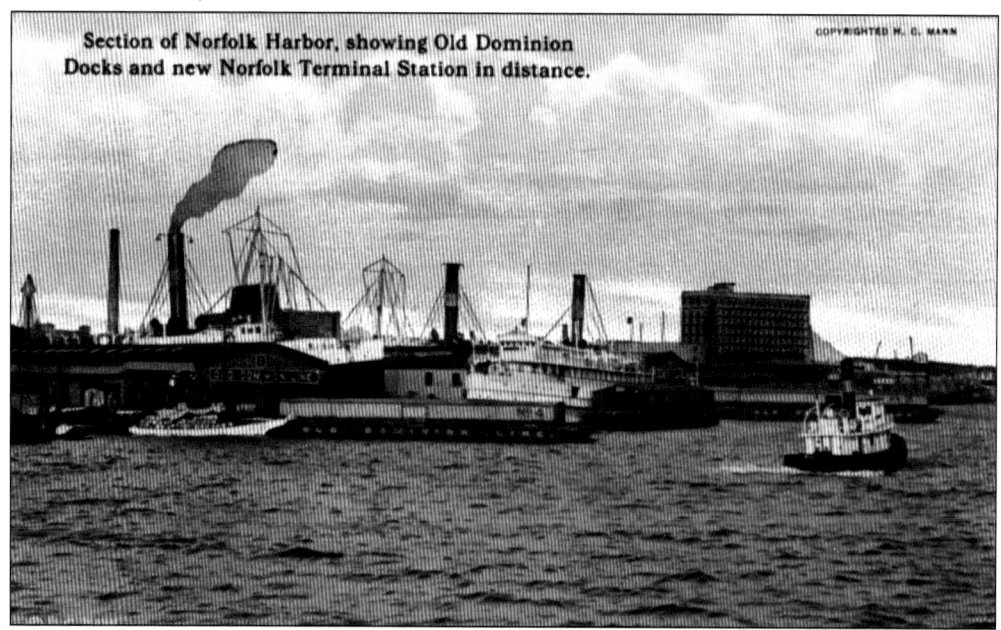

In the background, the new Norfolk Terminal Station towers above the Old Dominion Docks and other Norfolk harbor warehouses in this c. 1915 postcard. During the 1970s and 1980s, some of these waterfront warehouses were used as a farmers' market and concert venue before being demolished. In 1993, Harbor Park, home of the minor league baseball Norfolk Tides, opened in the area that once housed Terminal Station and Norfolk & Western's rail yard. (Courtesy of Kurt Reisweber.)

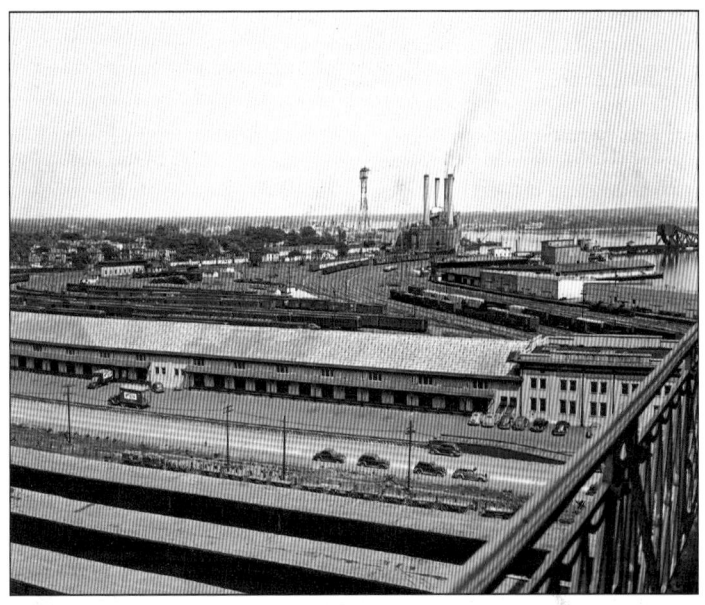

The railway yard behind the Norfolk Terminal Station was uncharacteristically empty as a nationwide railroad strike began in May 1946, idling trains and crippling transportation. Pres. Harry S. Truman threatened to seize control of the railroads and use the US Army as strikebreakers. The strike was settled before Truman could carry out the threat. (Courtesy of Sargeant Memorial Collection, Norfolk Public Library.)

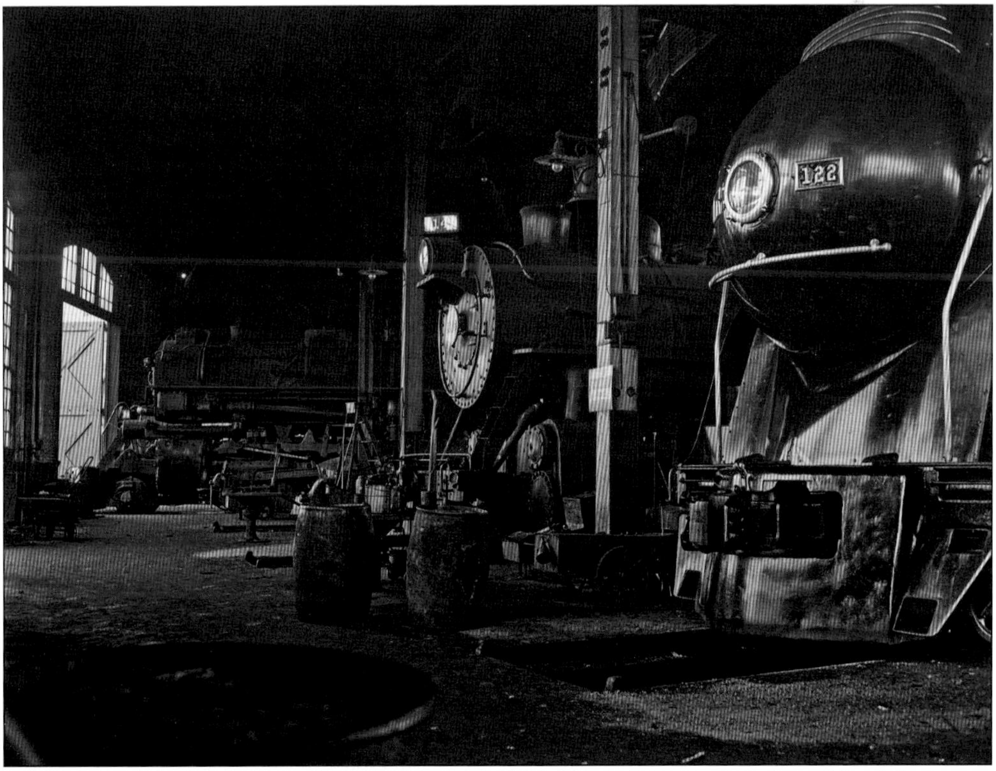

Idled train engines were parked in the Norfolk & Western roundhouse in Norfolk during the railroad strike. According to the caption to this photograph in the *Virginian-Pilot*, "The Cannonball wasn't fired last night: her crew let her boiler stay cold. Instead of making her normal run at 7:40 p.m., the streamlined locomotive at extreme right rested in the Norfolk & Western roundhouse with a couple of dozen other engines." (Courtesy of Sargeant Memorial Collection, Norfolk Public Library.)

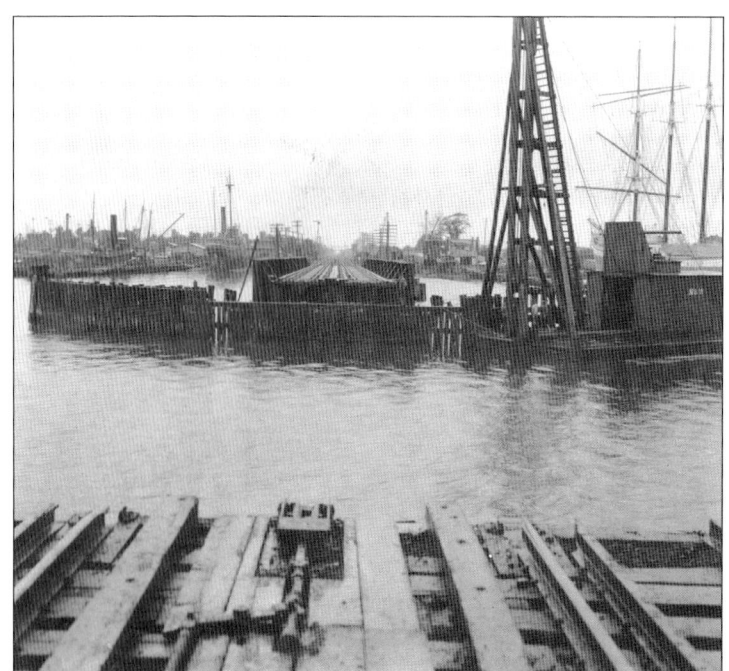

This undated photograph shows Norfolk & Western's Bridge 5 over the Eastern Branch of the Elizabeth River just south of downtown Norfolk looking toward Berkley. The truss bridge was built in 1947. Norfolk & Western's Norfolk Yard and Terminal Station were across the tracks to the right of and behind the photographer. The bridge was operated from a tower seen at right and was manned 24 hours a day, seven days a week. (Courtesy of Norfolk Southern.)

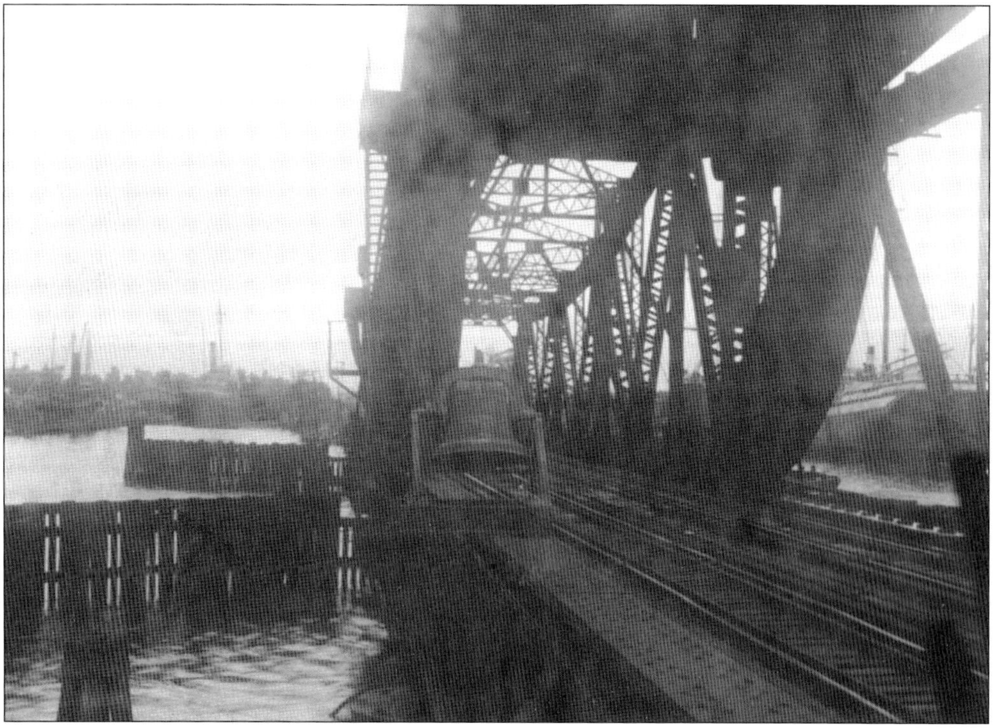

This view of Norfolk & Western's Bridge 5 is looking south from the Norfolk side across the Eastern Branch of the Elizabeth River toward Norfolk. The bell was a signaling device used to warn when the bridge would be raised and lowered. Bridge 5 was located where the Lamberts Point branch joined the original main line. (Courtesy of Norfolk Southern.)

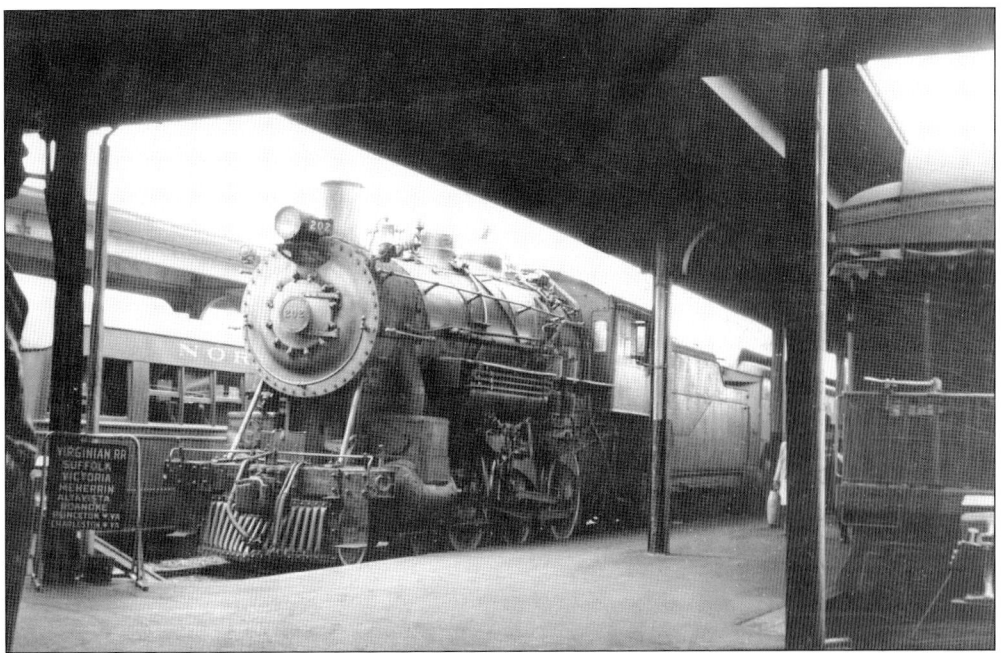

Virginian Railway's No. 202 Class TA steam locomotive, pulling a passenger train, is shown at the Norfolk Terminal Station in 1948. The railroad ran both daytime and overnight trains between Roanoke and Norfolk until 1937. (Photograph by H. Reid; courtesy of Kurt Reisweber.)

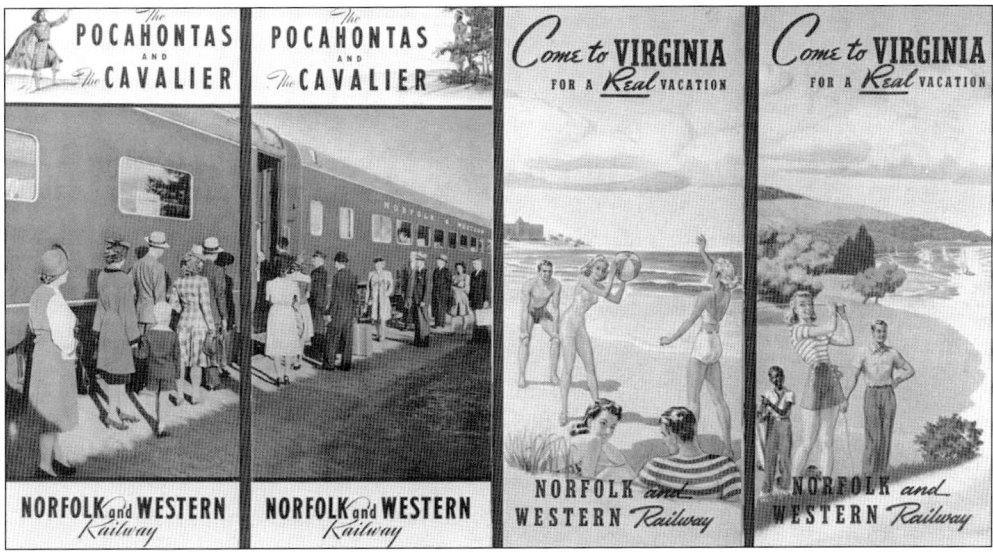

After World War II ended and the economy was once again booming, Americans were ready to get out and explore their country. Norfolk & Western was eager to welcome passengers aboard its passenger trains, the Pocahontas and the Cavalier, for travel to a relaxing vacation in Virginia. (Courtesy of Norfolk Southern.)

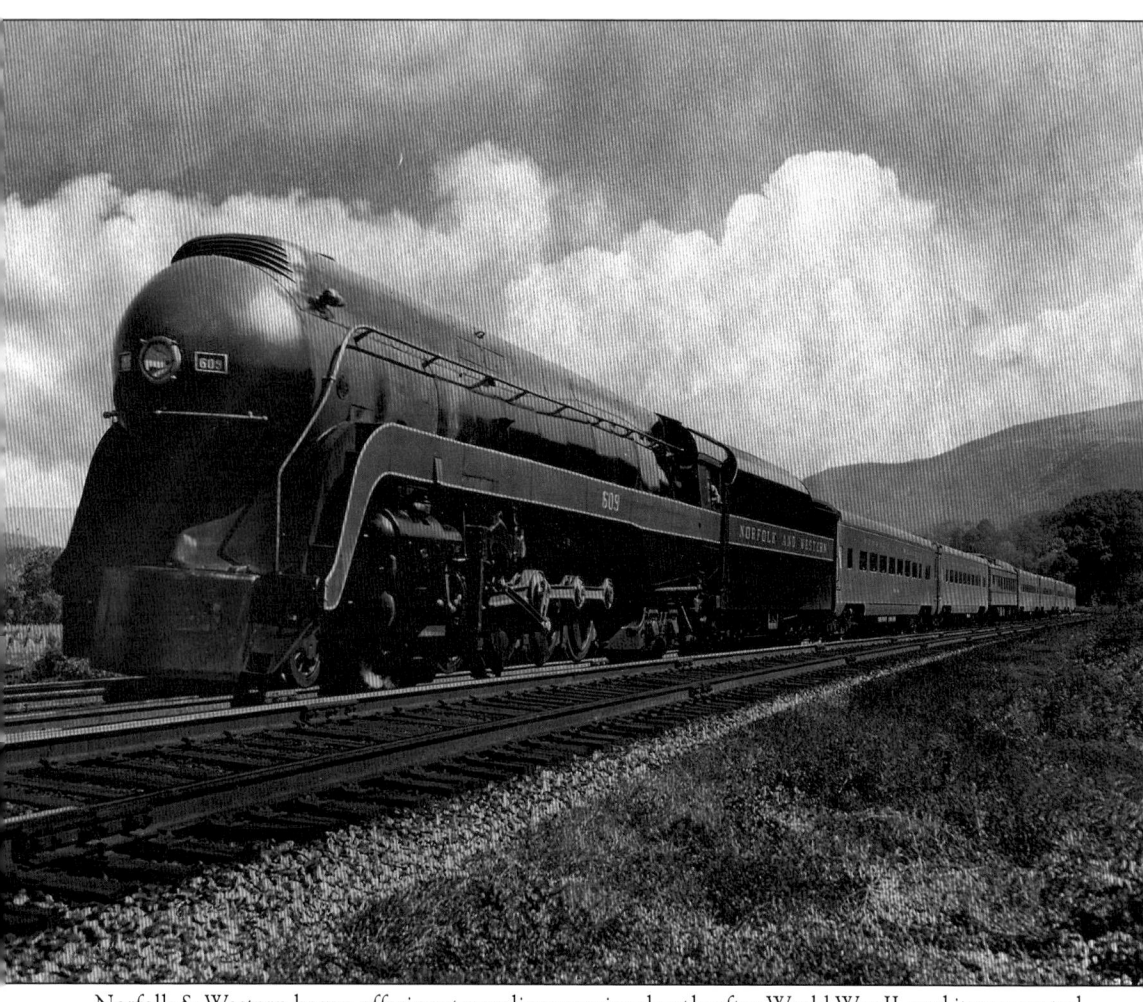

Norfolk & Western began offering streamliner service shortly after World War II, and its renovated prewar equipment was launched as the Powhatan Arrow on April 28, 1946. The railroad's Class J 4-8-4 steam locomotive pulled the train on its 676-mile trip from Norfolk to Cincinnati, Ohio. The trip took 15 hours and 45 minutes, including 13 stops. In 1949, new Pullman-Standard lightweight coaches and dinner and tavern-lounge cars replaced the renovated equipment, with Class J locomotives continuing to provide power. The Powhatan Arrow ran until 1969. (Courtesy of Norfolk Southern.)

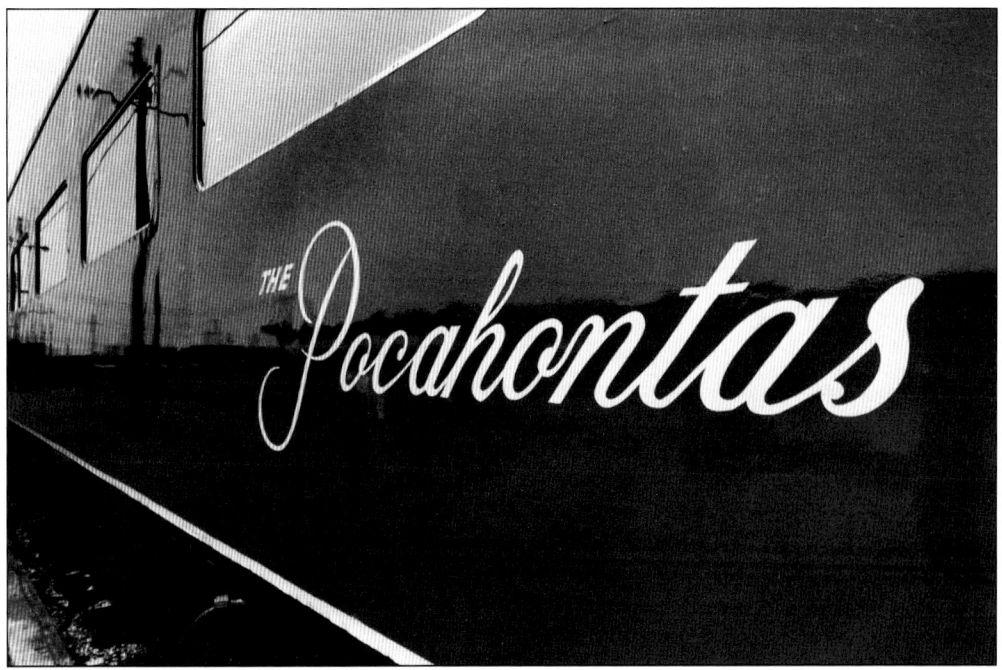

When Norfolk & Western added a passenger train to its fleet in 1926, the railroad held a contest to decide its name. The Pocahontas was also known as "Pokey," although it was advertised as "a new fast train connecting the Midwest with the Carolinas and the Atlantic Coast." (Courtesy of Norfolk Southern.)

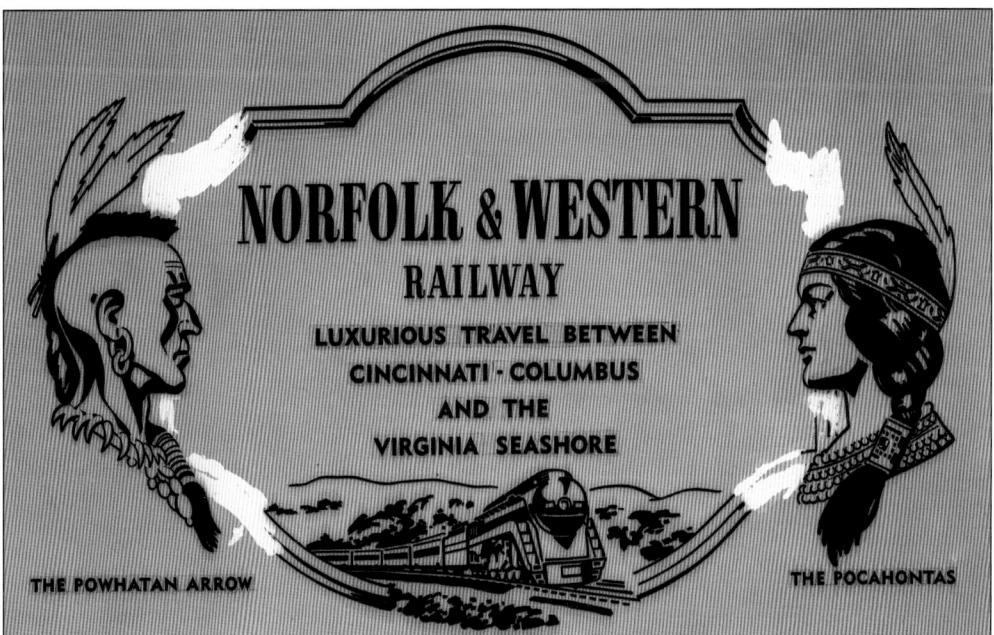

This 1950s advertisement promoted luxurious travel between Ohio and the Virginia coast aboard two of Norfolk & Western's passenger trains—the Powhatan Arrow and the Pocahontas. Passenger service was never a substantial part of Norfolk & Western's business, and demand waned throughout the 1960s. The railroad ended passenger service in May 1971. (Courtesy of Norfolk Southern.)

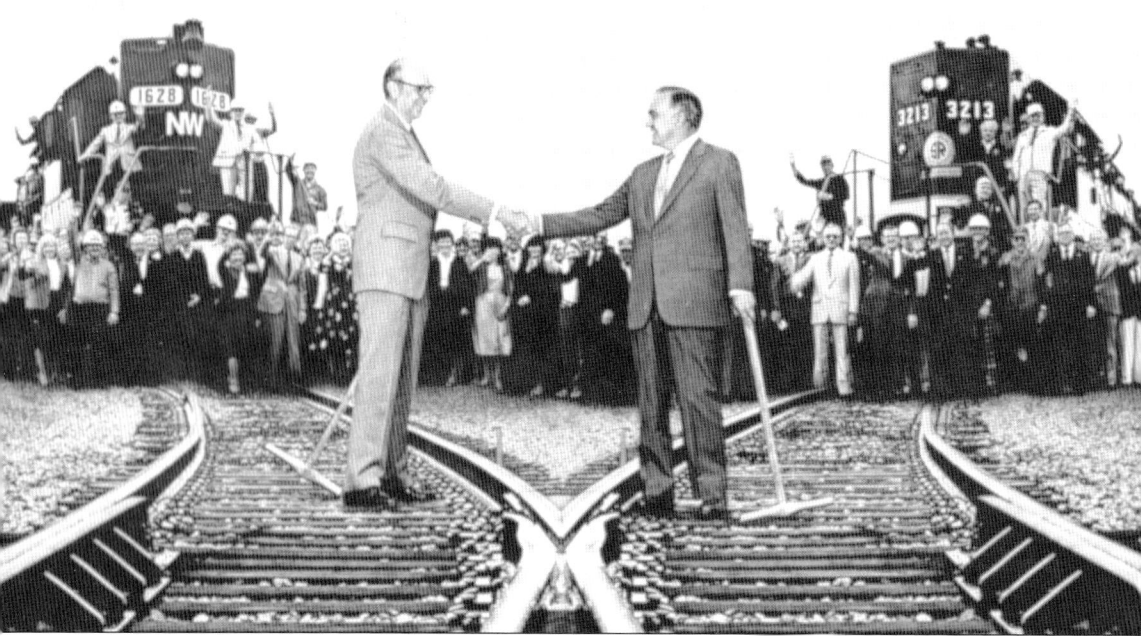

In this 1982 publicity photograph, Robert B. Claytor (left), president of Norfolk & Western, and Harold H. Hall, president of Southern Railway, pose with Norfolk & Western and Southern employees and locomotives as the two railroads merged to form Norfolk Southern. Claytor became Norfolk Southern's first chairman and CEO, while Hall was named president and chief operating officer. In a joint statement, Claytor and Hall said that Norfolk was an ideal location for the new company's headquarters. "It is an attractive and progressive city with excellent transportation, communications and residential facilities. And, of course, both railroads serve Norfolk, hauling substantial traffic in and out of that city." (Courtesy of Norfolk Southern.)

Norfolk Southern's downtown office tower opened in 1988 with 188 employees. It took the equivalent of 92 tractor trailer loads to move the railroad's supplies, equipment, and furniture into the new facility. The building was named in honor of retired president and CEO Arnold B. McKinnon in 2007. (Courtesy of Norfolk Southern.)

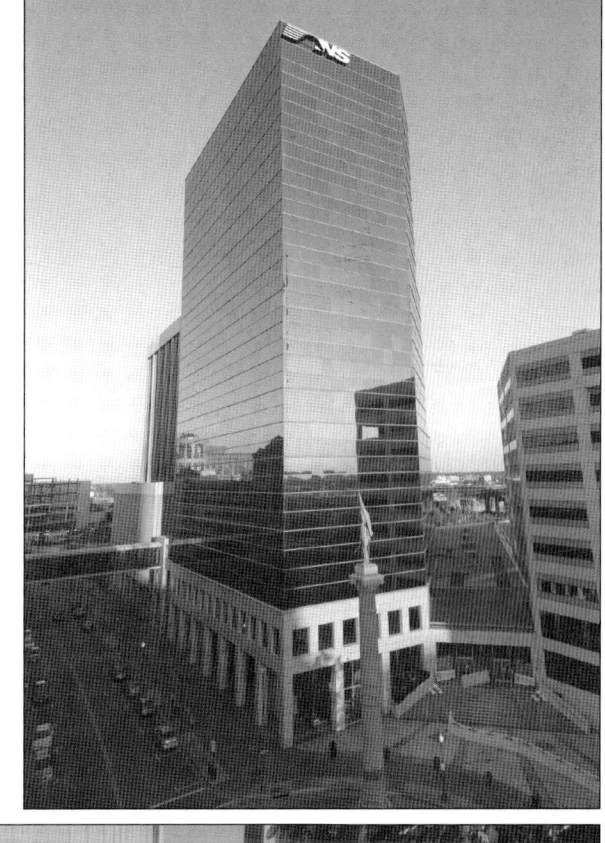

North Carolina native Arnold B. McKinnon succeeded Robert Claytor as Norfolk Southern president and CEO in 1987, serving until 1992. He placed a renewed emphasis on enhancing safety as well as focusing on customers and marketing to a global economy. McKinnon died in 2009. (Courtesy of Norfolk Southern.)

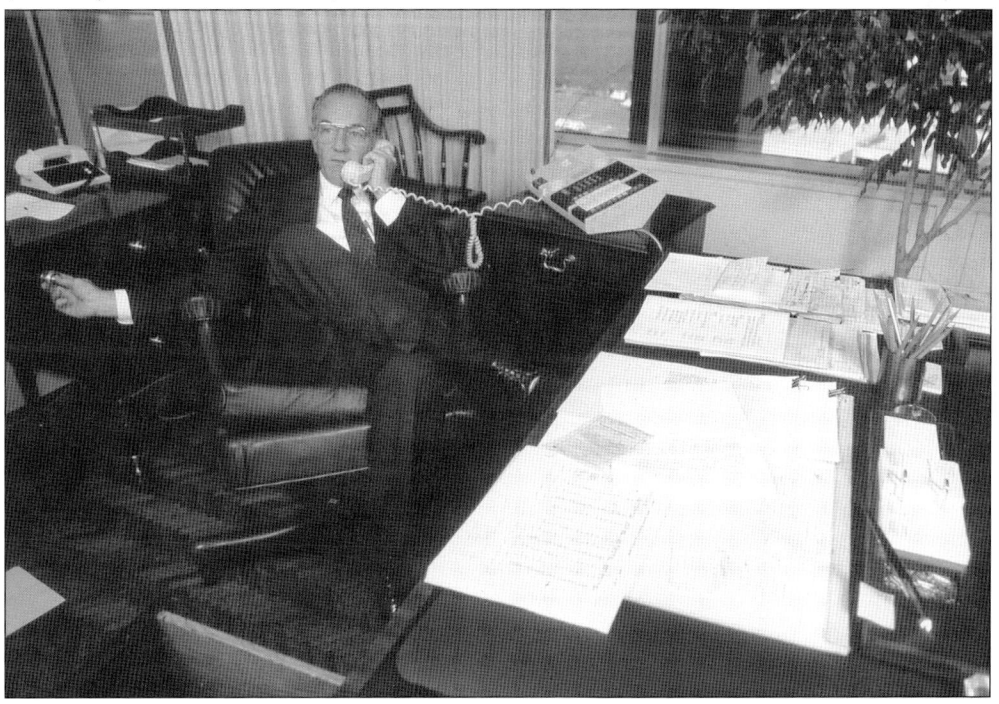

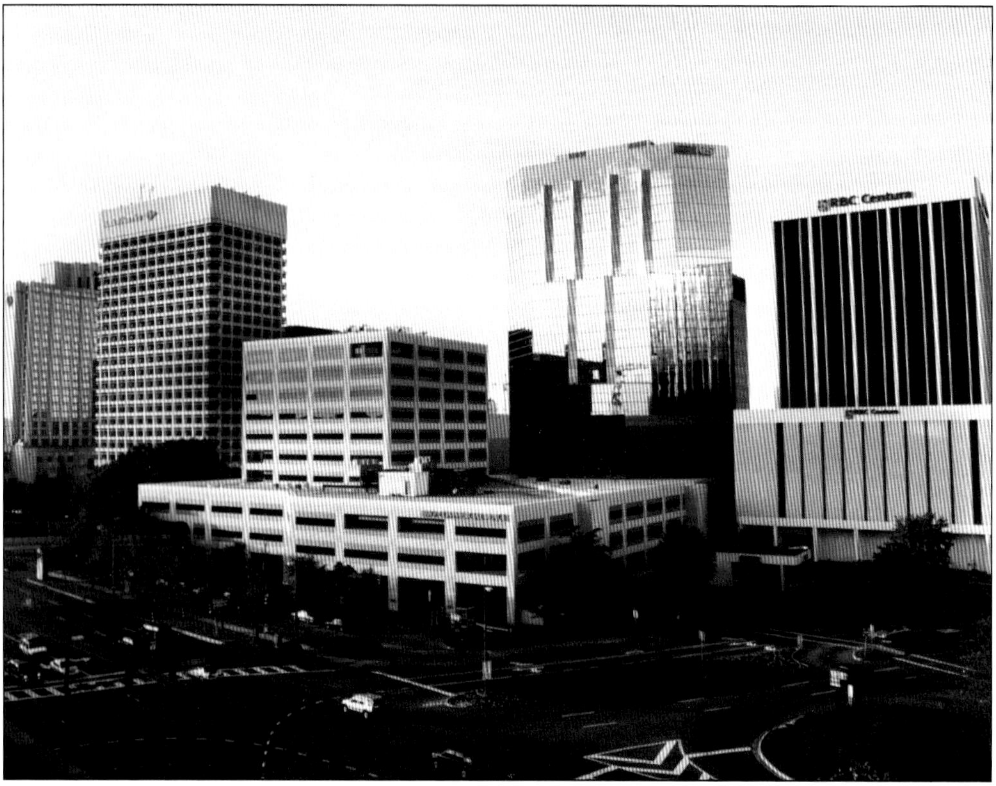

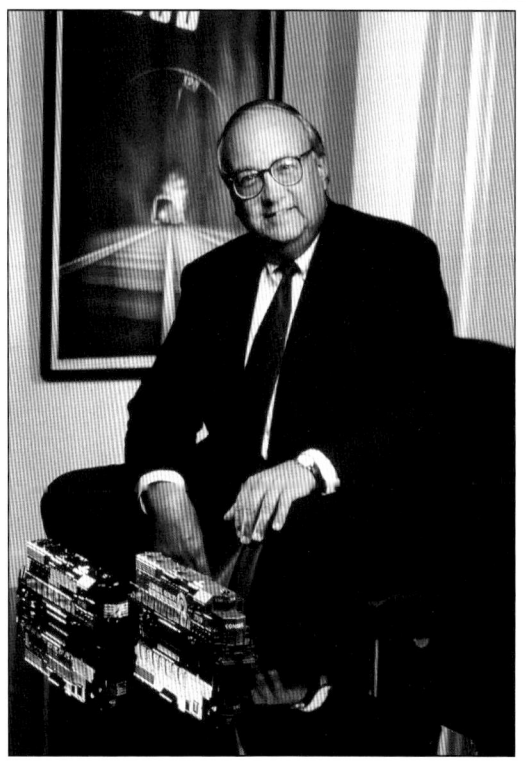

Located at 3 Commercial Place, Norfolk Southern's 22-story, emerald-green office tower became a prominent part of the city's financial district. The Norfolk Southern Museum, tracing the company's heritage, opened in 2005 on the building's ground floor at the initiative of David R. Goode, president and CEO. Museum visitors could operate a locomotive simulator and view various artifacts from the railroad's past, including a Norfolk & Western passenger ticket from the 1890s, Civil War–era rail, and a 900-pound railroad coupler. (Courtesy of Norfolk Southern.)

Bedford County, Virginia, native David R. Goode joined Norfolk & Western in 1965 as a tax attorney. He served as chairman, president, and CEO of Norfolk Southern from 1992 to 2004. While leading Norfolk Southern, Goode negotiated a bidding war for northeastern US railroad Conrail against CSX with Conrail's assets split 58 to 42 percent between Norfolk Southern and CSX in 1999. (Courtesy of Norfolk Southern.)

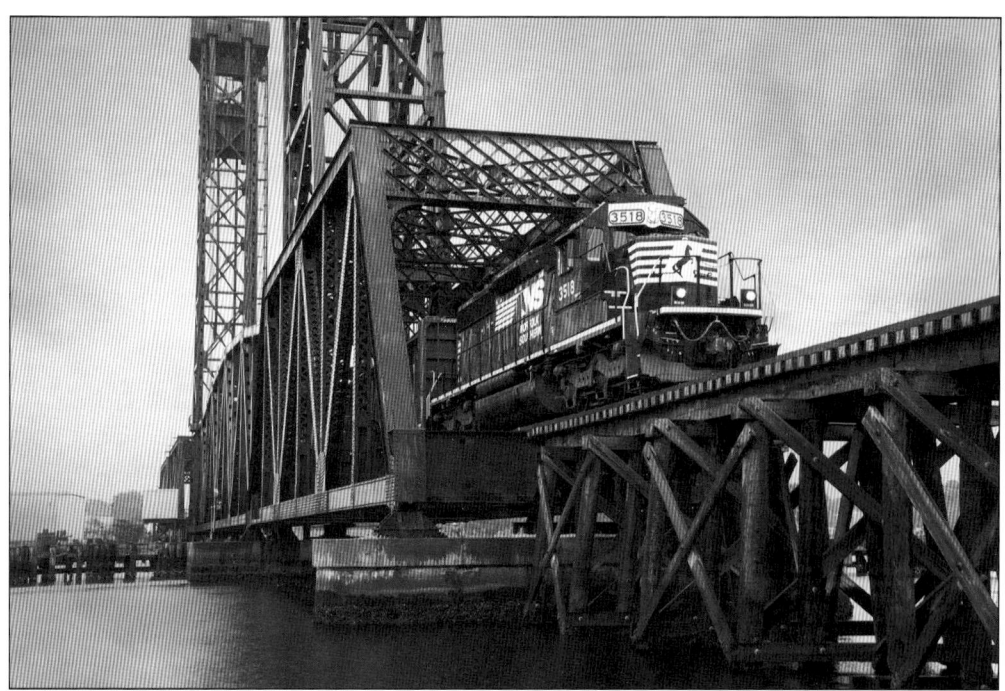

Powered by locomotive No. 3518, a Norfolk Southern train crosses the bridge over the Southern Branch of the Elizabeth River. The truss bridge was built in 1908. (Courtesy of Norfolk Southern.)

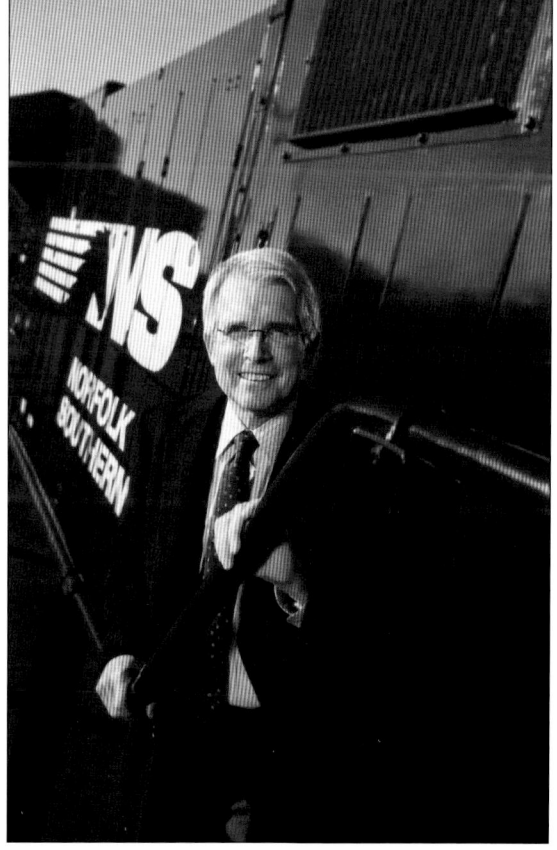

Charles W. "Wick" Moorman served as Norfolk Southern's CEO from 2005 until 2015. The Mississippi native joined Southern Railway in 1970 as a co-op student while attending Georgia Tech. Under Moorman's leadership, Norfolk Southern focused on technological innovations and public-private partnerships, including the $290 million Heartland Corridor collaboration with the Federal Highway Administration and three US states to enhance the railroad's capacity on lines between Norfolk and the Midwest. The project included raising clearances in 29 tunnels for double-stacked intermodal trains. After retiring from Norfolk Southern, Moorman served as president and CEO of Amtrak. (Courtesy of Norfolk Southern.)

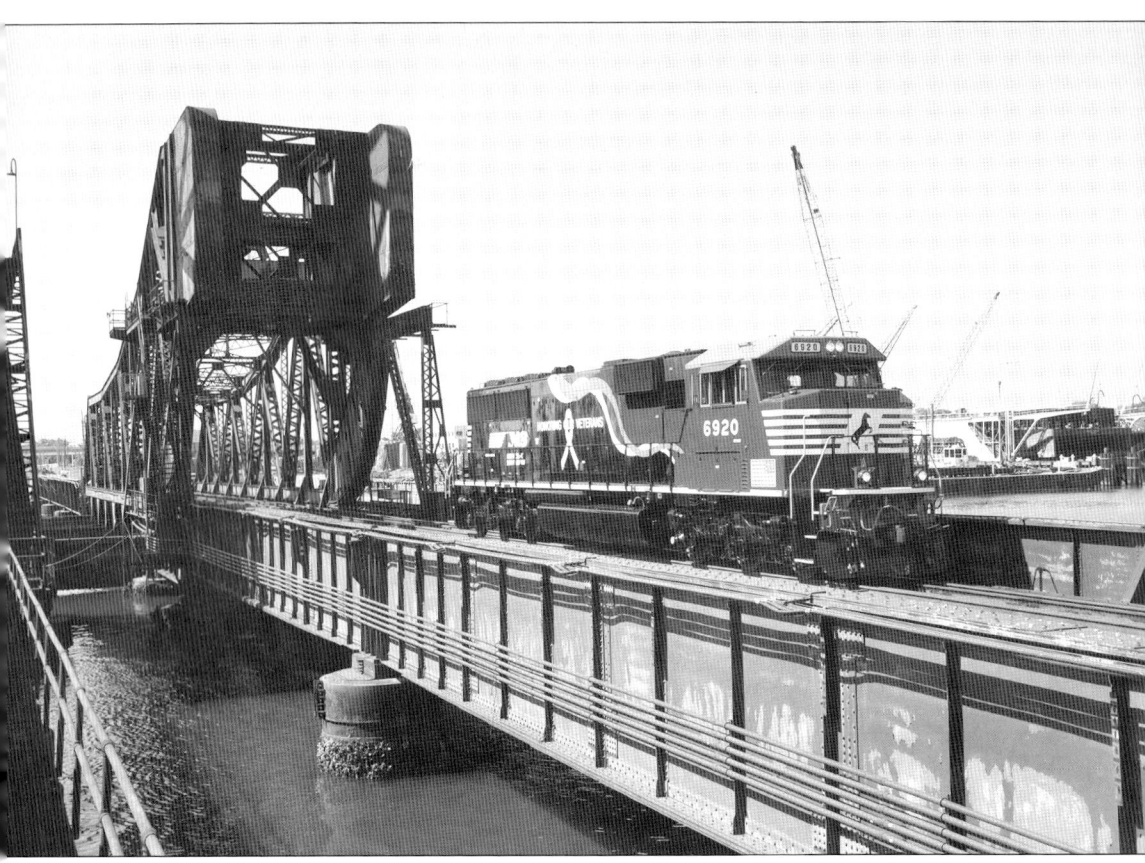

Norfolk Southern's Veterans Locomotive crosses the Elizabeth River headed to Harbor Park for the 2013 Ride 2 Recovery, a rehabilitation program for wounded veterans that features cycling as its core activity. The railroad added the locomotive to its fleet in 2012 to honor those who have served in the military and reserves. The locomotive's red, white, and blue paint scheme and yellow ribbon with the message "Honoring our Veterans" was chosen by a group of railroad employees representing all branches of the armed forces. (Courtesy of Norfolk Southern.)

Seven
BERKLEY AND PORTLOCK

Across the Eastern Branch of the Elizabeth River from downtown Norfolk, Berkley played a significant role in the railroading industry through its busy port and shipyard facilities and textile industries of the late 19th and early 20th centuries.

In the 1880s, Berkley was the northern terminus of the original Norfolk Southern, which ran trains over a 600-mile route from Norfolk to Charlotte, North Carolina. Passengers disembarked at Norfolk Southern's terminal in Berkley and traveled by ferry across the Elizabeth River to downtown Norfolk. The terminal also included storehouses; an oil house; car, paint, machine, and blacksmith shops; and an enginehouse with a 55-foot turntable. In 1911, the railroad opened new shops at Carolina Junction Yard, a mile southeast of Berkley.

After Southern Railway merged with Norfolk & Western, most of Carolina Junction Yard's remaining functions were moved to Norfolk & Western's Portlock Yard, named for the small community within the Chesapeake borough of South Norfolk. Located off Atlantic Avenue, the yard is more than a century old and is an interchange for short line railroads in South Hampton Roads, except for the Commonwealth Railway.

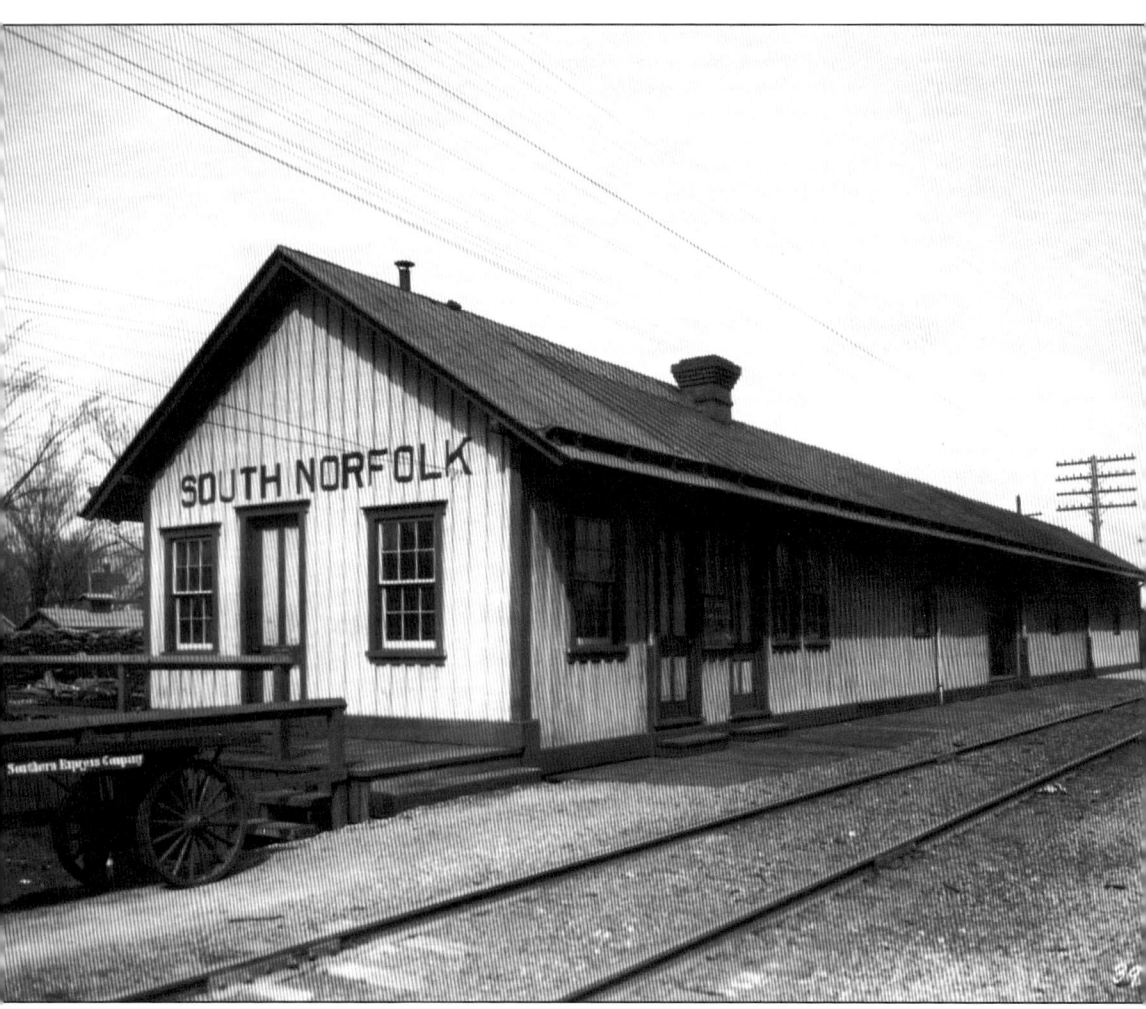

Norfolk & Western's South Norfolk station was off Seaboard Avenue at the end of Guerriere Street. Beginning in the 1880s, trains stopped at the station to pick up passengers and freight, much of which originated from the Elizabeth Knitting Mill in South Norfolk and the Chesapeake Knitting Mill in Berkley. The station was torn down in 1962. (Courtesy of Norfolk Southern.)

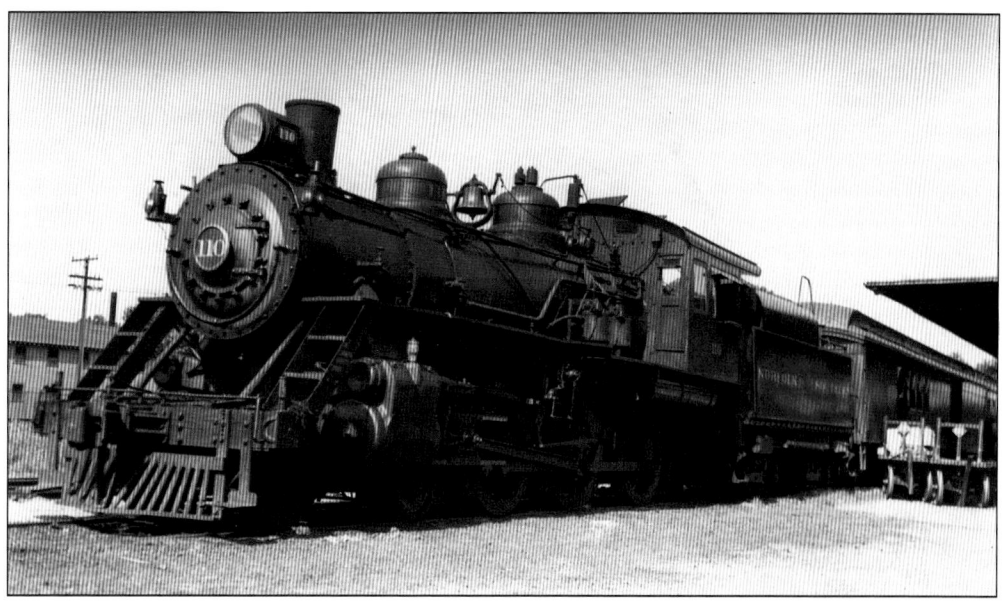

A Norfolk Southern passenger train had just arrived at the Berkley station when this photograph was taken in 1949. Norfolk Southern trains stopped at Berkley after leaving Terminal Station in downtown Norfolk. (Courtesy of Kurt Reisweber.)

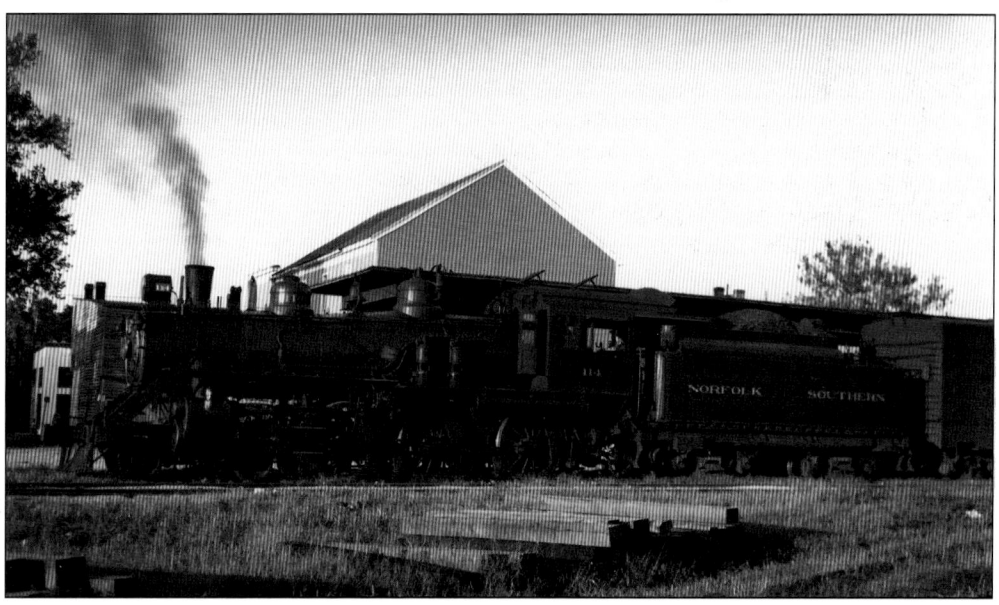

Powered by a steam engine, a Norfolk Southern Railway train arrives at the Berkley passenger station in 1949. The railroad carried passengers and freight. (Courtesy of Kurt Reisweber.)

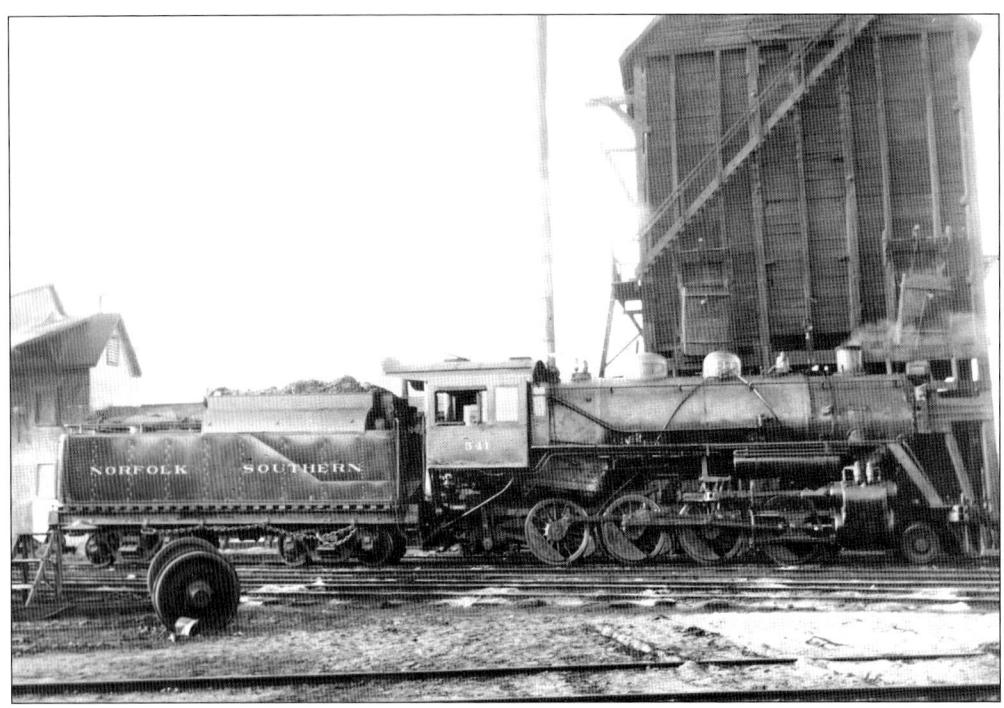

In its heyday, Carolina Junction Yard was the largest yard on the Norfolk Southern system and the railroad's main yard in Hampton Roads. The yard was largely dismantled after Norfolk Southern merged with Southern Railway. By 1999, it was only used to store freight cars and as an interchange between Norfolk Southern and the Chesapeake & Albemarle Railroad. (Both, courtesy of Kurt Reisweber.)

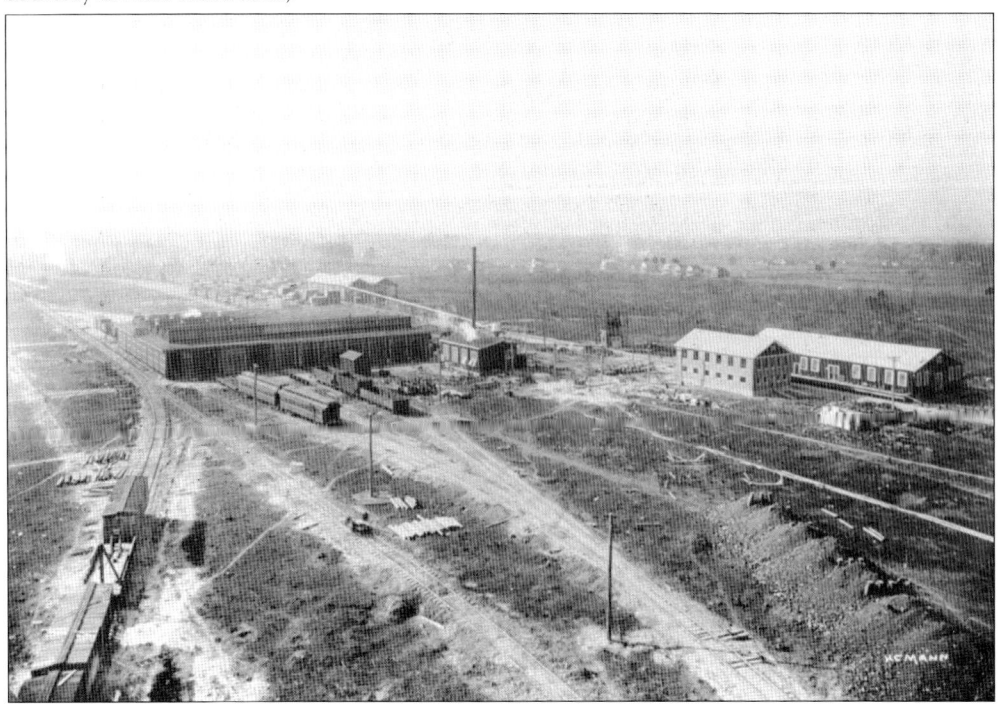

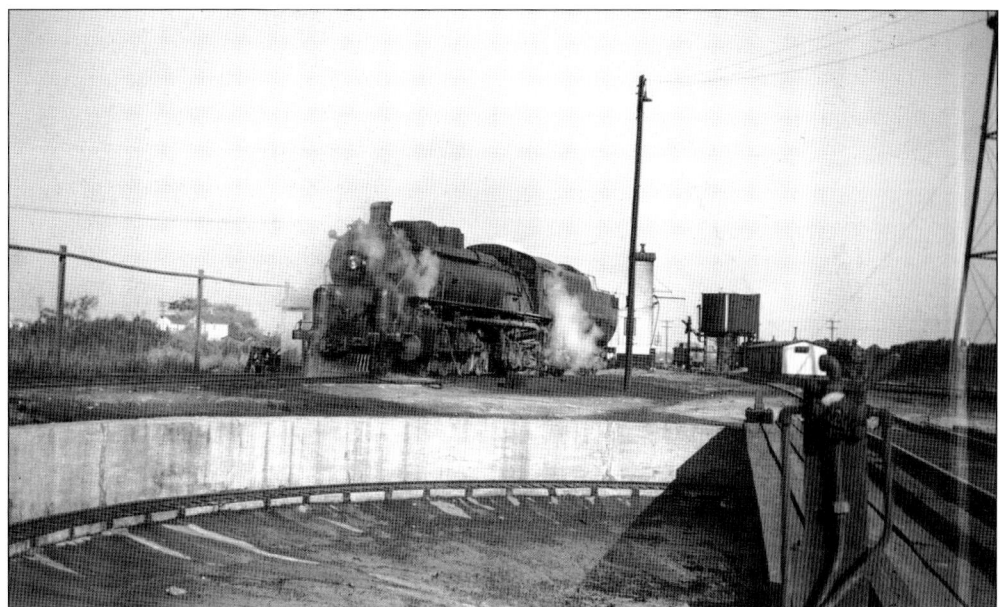

Led by steam engine No. 602, a Norfolk Southern train approaches the turntable at Carolina Junction Yard in 1949. Rapidly outgrowing its Berkley yard and shops, Norfolk Southern opened Carolina Junction Yard in 1911. (Courtesy of Kurt Reisweber.)

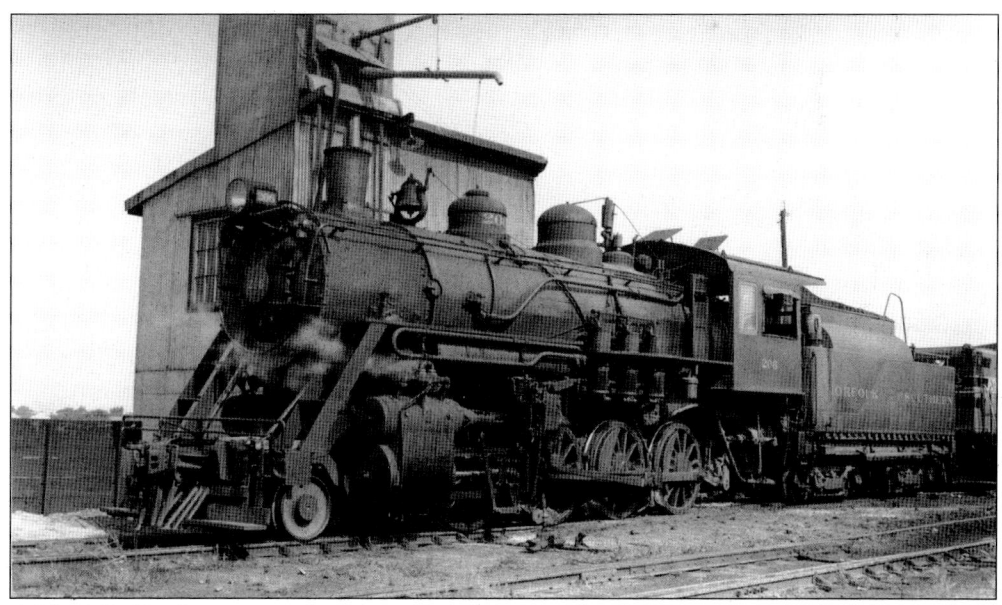

A Norfolk Southern steam locomotive is shown at Carolina Junction Yard in this c. 1940s photograph. Norfolk Southern's main line extended from Berkley to North Carolina and crossed the Virginian Railway's track at Carolina Junction Yard. (Courtesy of Kurt Reisweber.)

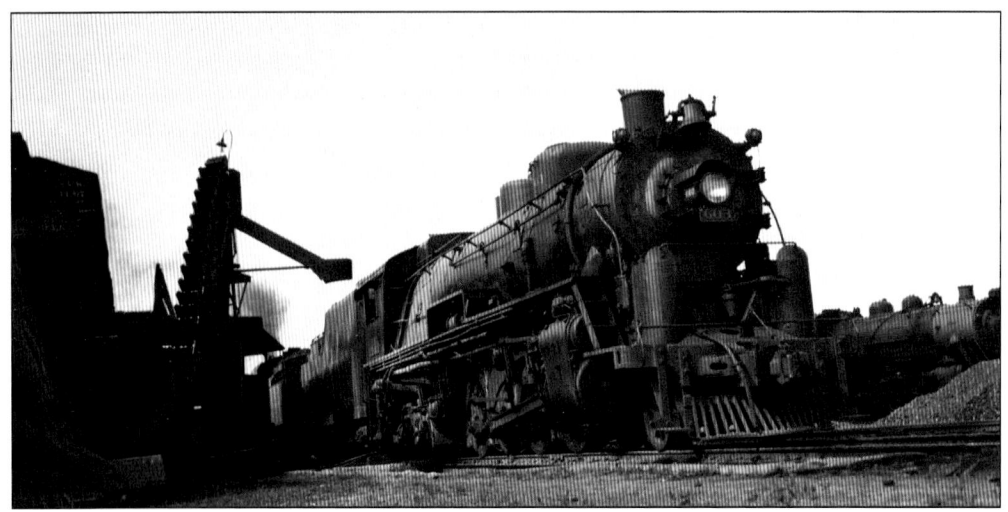

In its early days, Carolina Junction Yard included a shop for locomotive service. After Norfolk Southern merged with Southern Railway in 1974, the locomotive shop was demolished, and locomotive repair functions were transferred to other Southern shops. (Courtesy of Kurt Reisweber.)

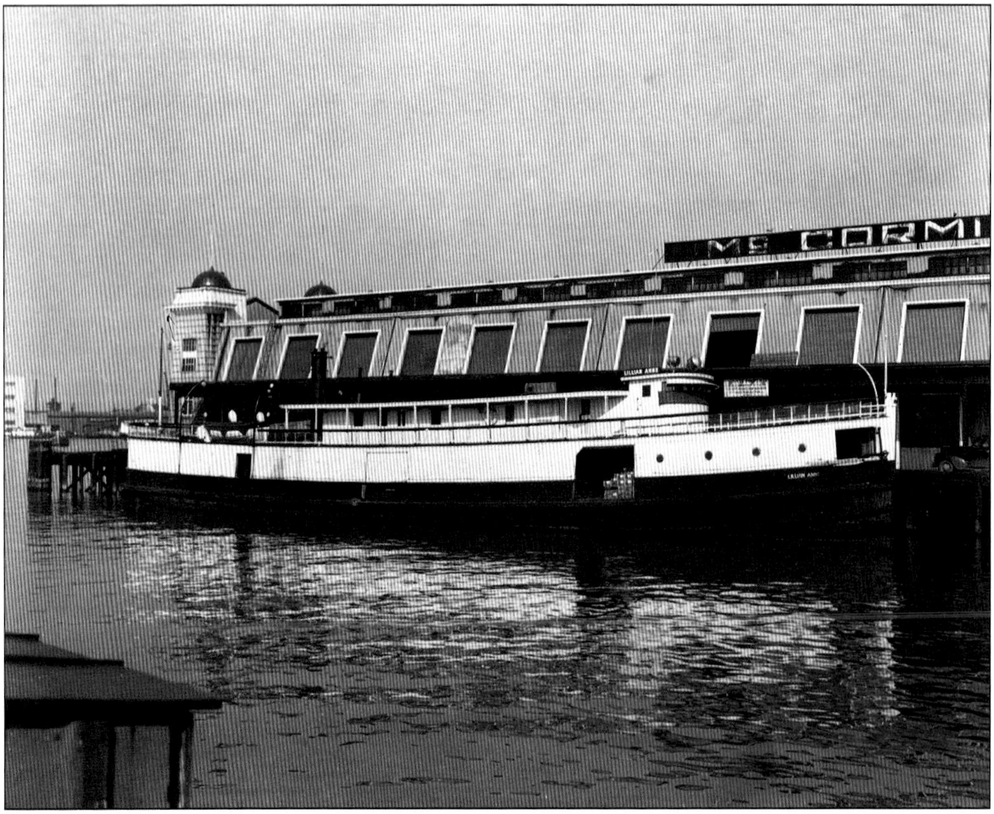

The *Lillian Anne* ferry is shown alongside Southern Railway's pier in Berkley. Constructed in 1895, the ferry was acquired by the US Navy in 1942 and served the Fifth Naval District, including Norfolk, until July 1943. (Courtesy of Sargeant Memorial Collection, Norfolk Public Library.)

A Norfolk & Western freight train arrives at Portlock in this 1949 photograph. After Southern Railway merged with Norfolk & Western, Southern moved its repair and service functions from Carolina Junction Yard to the nearby Portlock Yard. (Courtesy of Kurt Reisweber.)

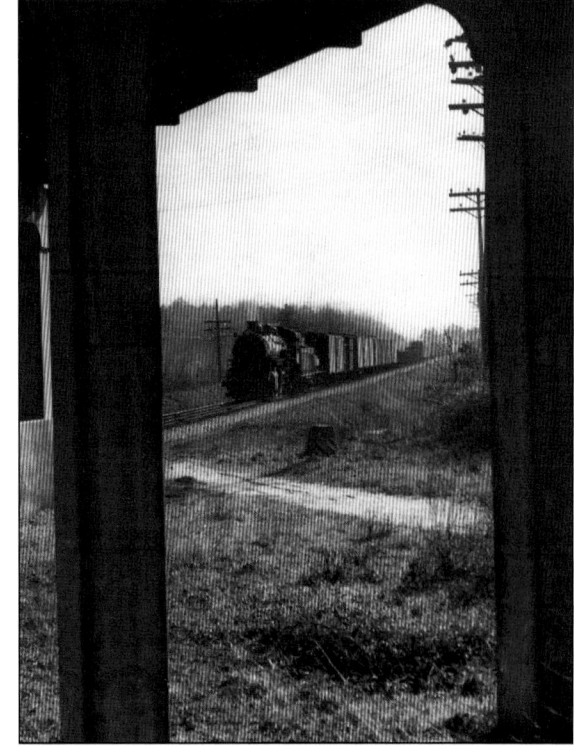

The west end of Norfolk & Western's Portlock Yard is shown in this c. 1960 photograph. The yard was originally named the South Norfolk Yard but was changed to reflect the community's ties to the Portlock family who settled there in the 1600s. (Courtesy of Norfolk Southern.)

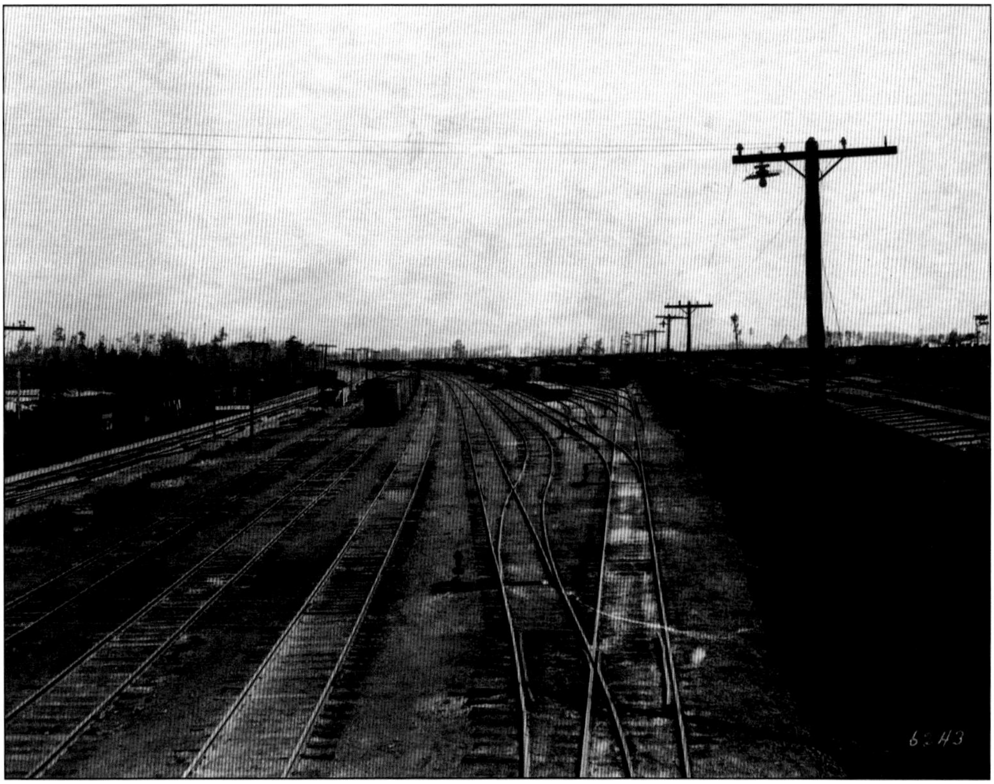

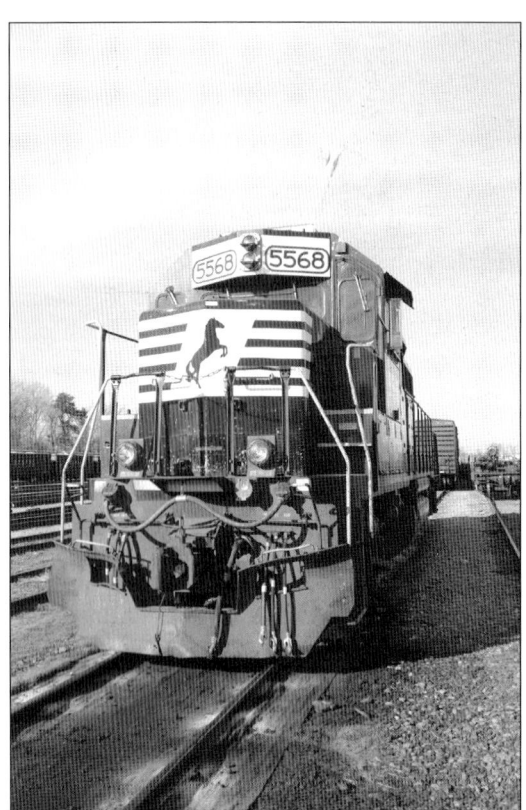

Norfolk Southern locomotive No. 5568 is pictured at the Portlock Yard in 2011. Portlock includes a yard for intermodal traffic as well as a marshalling area for freight traffic. (Courtesy of Norfolk Southern.)

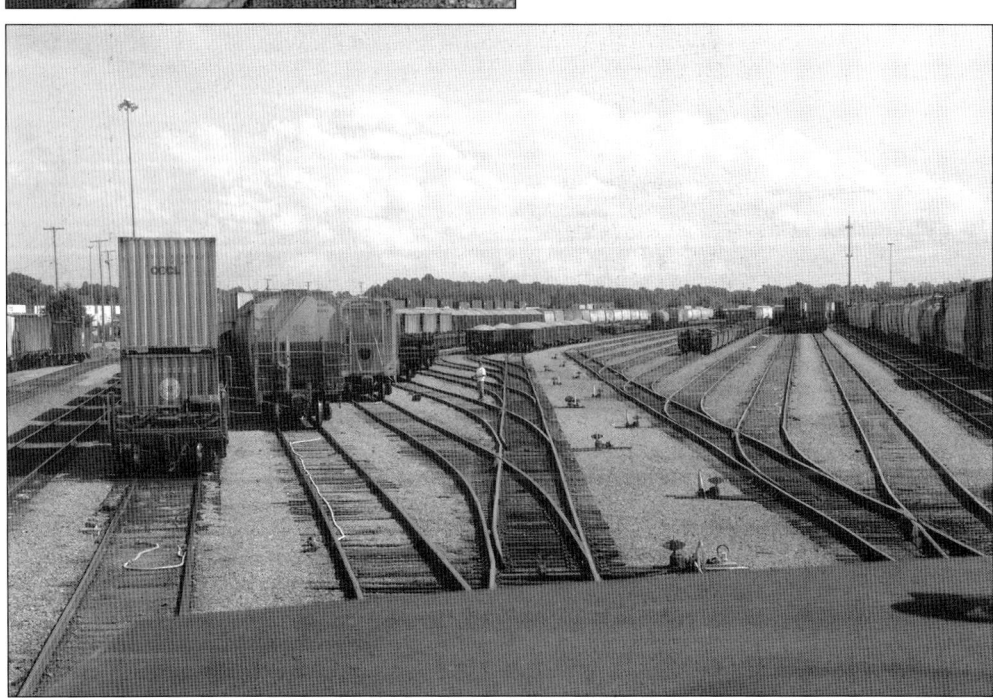

This 2017 photograph shows the switching yard at Portlock. The yard was expanded in 2013 to accommodate Amtrak service to Norfolk. (Courtesy of Norfolk Southern.)

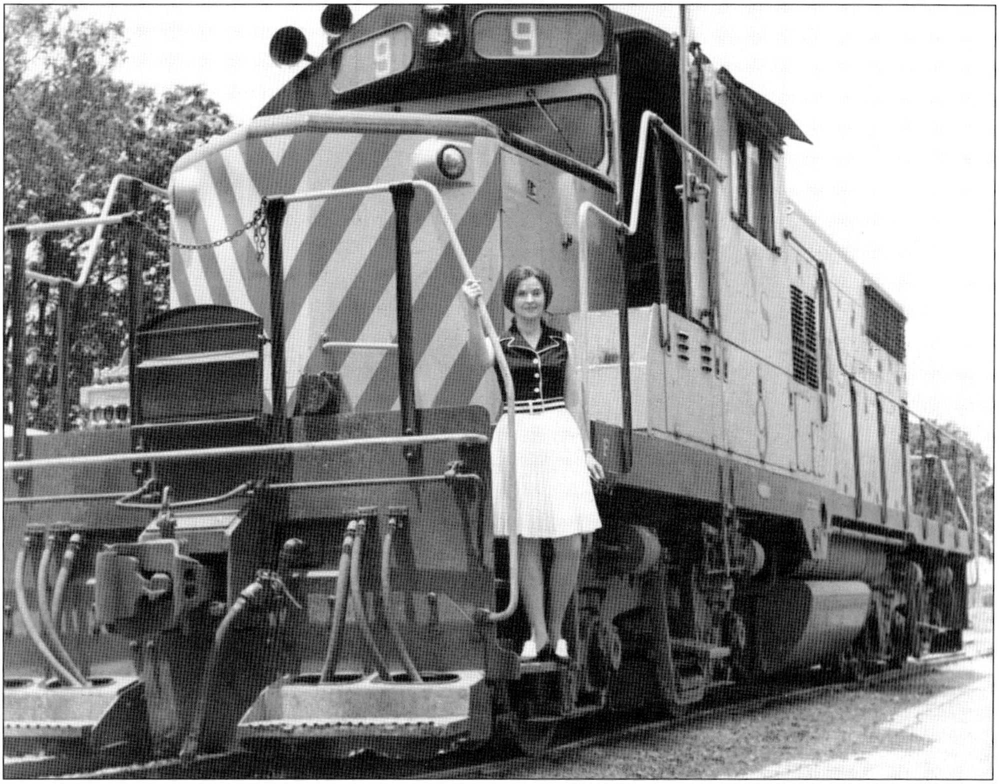

Norfolk Southern sales secretary Hazel Cutler stands atop Norfolk Southern No. 9 at Carolina Junction Yard in South Norfolk in this c. 1970 photograph. A native of Chesapeake, Cutler retired from Norfolk Southern in 1987. Her obituary in 2011 described Norfolk Southern as her "second love." (Courtesy of Norfolk Southern.)

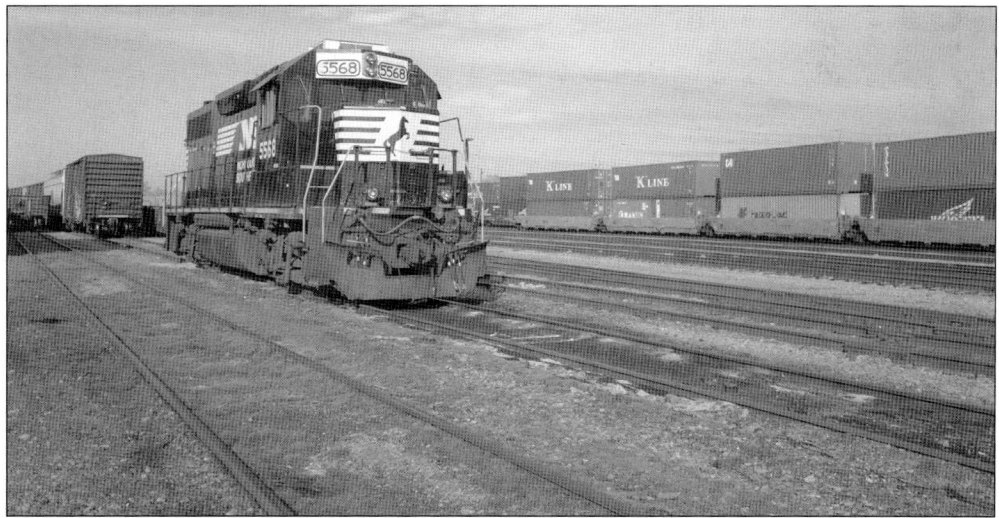

Double-stack containers placed on flat cars bound for Norfolk International Terminals are seen in this 2011 photograph of Portlock Yard. Norfolk Southern has access to more than 40 ports and provides comprehensive on-dock and near-dock intermodal services at all major East Coast container ports. (Courtesy of Norfolk Southern.)

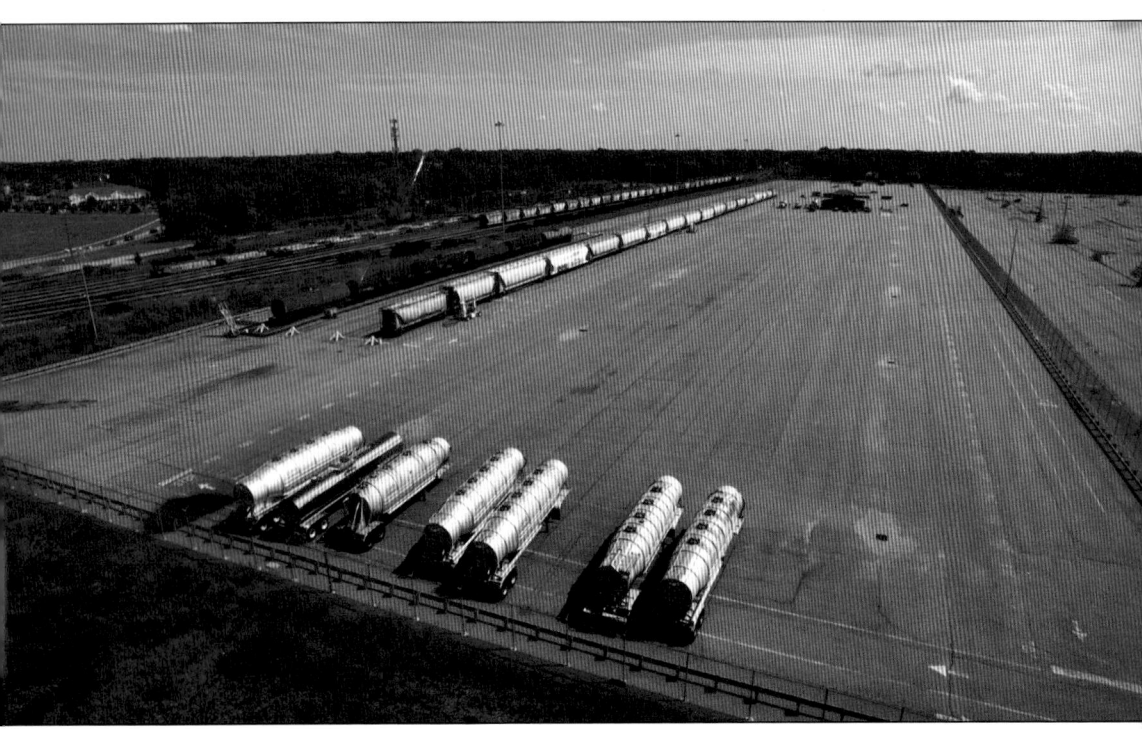

This aerial photograph shows Norfolk Southern's Chesapeake Thoroughbred Bulk Transfer (TBT) terminal, set on 40 acres at the former Carolina Junction Yard. The railroad opened the terminal in 2014 to serve shippers of dry and liquid bulk cargo, such as flour, sugar, and grains. The TBT terminals, which are owned by Norfolk Southern and operated by independent contractors, allow customers to transfer a large variety of goods between railcars and trucks. (Courtesy of Norfolk Southern.)

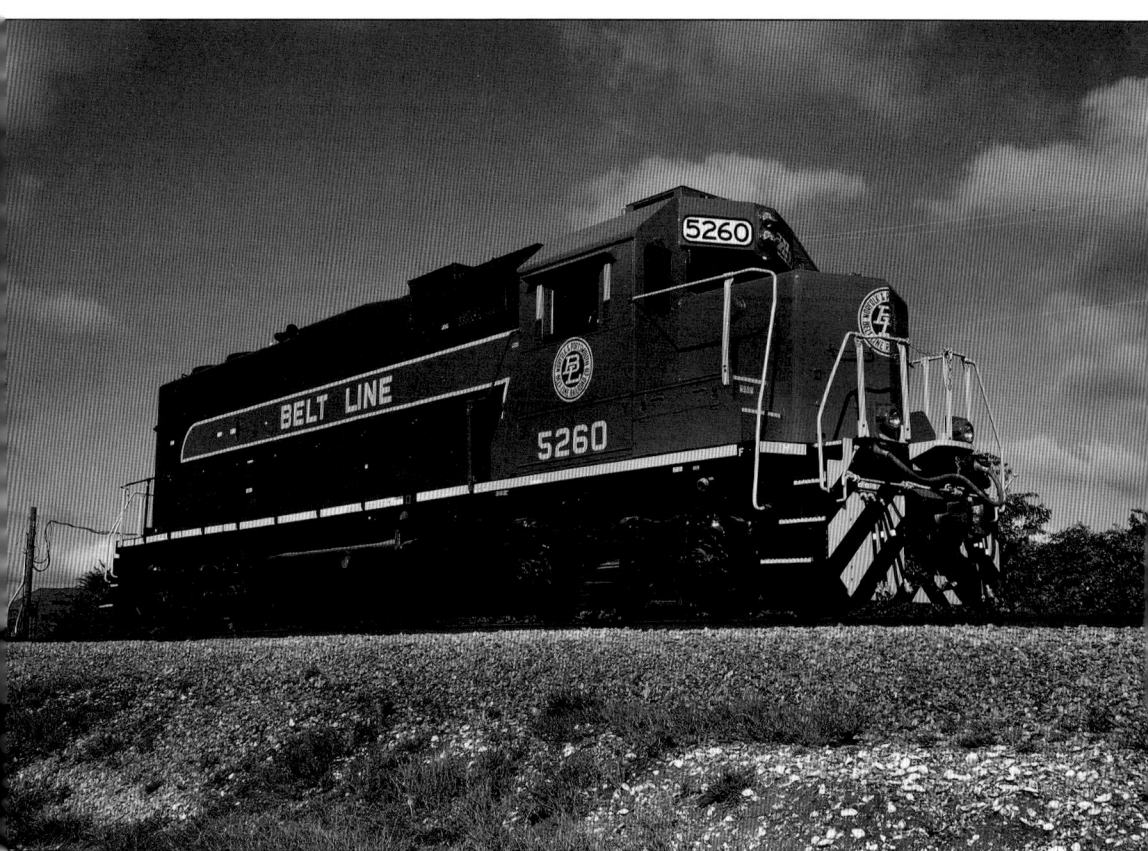

The Norfolk and Portsmouth Belt Line Railroad Company was established in 1896 as the Southeastern and Atlantic Railroad Company. The Class III terminal switching railroad was initially owned by eight railroads, including the New York, Philadelphia & Norfolk Railroad; Norfolk & Western; the Chesapeake & Ohio Railroad; Southern Railway; Atlantic & Danville Railroad; Atlantic Coast Line; Norfolk & Southern Railroad; and Seaboard Air Line Railroad. Norfolk Southern and CSX Transportation are now the company's sole shareholders. The Norfolk and Portsmouth Belt Line Railroad Company operates over 26 miles of railroad. (Courtesy of Norfolk Southern.)

Discover Thousands of Local History Books Featuring Millions of Vintage Images

Arcadia Publishing, the leading local history publisher in the United States, is committed to making history accessible and meaningful through publishing books that celebrate and preserve the heritage of America's people and places.

Find more books like this at
www.arcadiapublishing.com

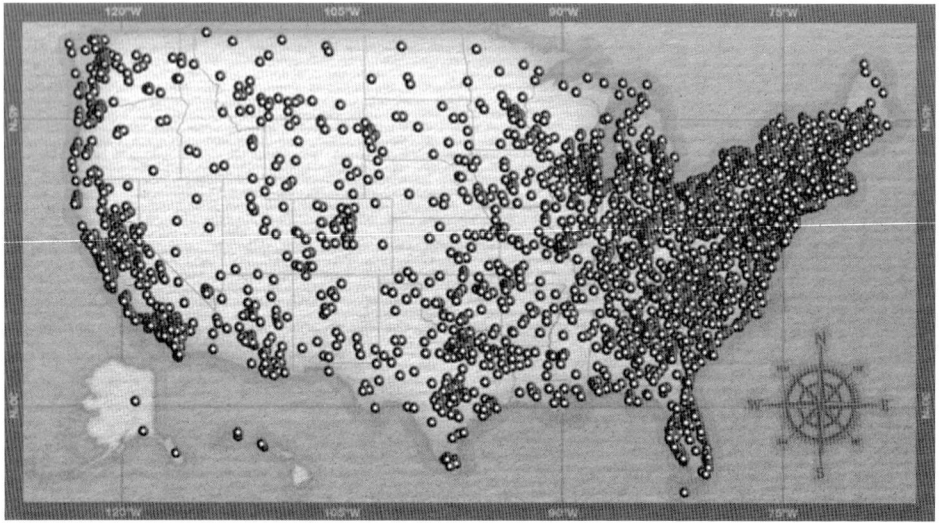

Search for your hometown history, your old stomping grounds, and even your favorite sports team.

Consistent with our mission to preserve history on a local level, this book was printed in South Carolina on American-made paper and manufactured entirely in the United States. Products carrying the accredited Forest Stewardship Council (FSC) label are printed on 100 percent FSC-certified paper.

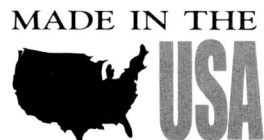